Aileen Irvine

Computer Learner Corpora, Second Language Acquisition and Foreign Language Teaching

Language Learning and Language Teaching

The *LL&LT* monograph series publishes monographs as well as edited volumes on applied and methodological issues in the field of language pedagogy. The focus of the series is on subjects such as classroom discourse and interaction; language diversity in educational settings; bilingual education; language testing and language assessment; teaching methods and teaching performance; learning trajectories in second language acquisition; and written language learning in educational settings.

Series editors

Birgit Harley
Ontario Institute for Studies in Education, University of Toronto

Jan H. Hulstijn
Department of Second Language Acquisition, University of Amsterdam

Volume 6

Computer Learner Corpora, Second Language Acquisition and
Foreign Language Teaching
Edited by Sylviane Granger, Joseph Hung and Stephanie Petch-Tyson

Computer Learner Corpora, Second Language Acquisition and Foreign Language Teaching

Edited by

Sylviane Granger
Université catholique de Louvain

Joseph Hung
Chinese University of Hong Kong

Stephanie Petch-Tyson
Université catholique de Louvain

John Benjamins Publishing Company
Amsterdam / Philadelphia

™ The paper used in this publication meets the minimum requirements of American National Standard for Information Sciences – Permanence of Paper for Printed Library Materials, ANSI z39.48-1984.

Library of Congress Cataloging-in-Publication Data

Computer learner corpora, second language acquisition and foreign language teaching / edited by Sylviane Granger, Joseph Hung and Stephanie Petch-Tyson.
    p. cm. (Language Learning and Language Teaching, ISSN 1569-9471 ; v. 6)
Includes bibliographical references and index.
    1. Language and languages--Computer-assisted instruction. 2. Second language acquisition--Computer-assisted instruction. I. Granger, Sylviane, 1951- II. Hung, Joseph. III. Petch-Tyson, Stephanie. IV. Series.

P53.28.C6644   2002
418'.00285-dc21   2002027701
ISBN 90 272 1701 7 (Eur.) / 1 58811 293 4 (US) (Hb; alk. paper)
ISBN 90 272 1702 5 (Eur.) / 1 58811 294 2 (US) (Pb; alk. paper)

John Benjamins Publishing Co. · P.O. Box 36224 · 1020 ME Amsterdam · The Netherlands
John Benjamins North America · P.O. Box 27519 · Philadelphia PA 19118-0519 · USA

Table of contents

Preface

Computer learner corpora are electronic collections of spoken or written texts produced by foreign or second language learners in a variety of language settings. Once computerised, these data can be analysed with linguistic software tools, from simple ones, which search, count and display, to the most advanced ones, which provide sophisticated analyses of the data.

Interest in computer learner corpora is growing fast, amidst increasing recognition of their theoretical and practical value, and a number of these corpora, representing a range of mediums and genres and of varying sizes, either have been or are currently being compiled. This volume takes stock of current research into computer learner corpora conducted both by ELT and SLA specialists and should be of particular interest to researchers looking to assess its relevance to SLA theory and ELT practice. Throughout the volume, emphasis is also placed on practical, methodological aspects of computer learner corpus research, in particular the contribution of technology to the research process. The advantages and disadvantages of automated and semi-automated approaches are analysed, the capabilities of linguistic software tools investigated, the corpora (and compilation processes) described in detail. In this way, an important function of the volume is to give practical insight to researchers who may be considering compiling a corpus of learner data or embarking on learner corpus research.

Impetus for the book came from the *International Symposium on Computer Learner Corpora, Second Language Acquisition and Foreign Language Teaching* organised by Joseph Hung and Sylviane Granger at the Chinese University of Hong Kong in 1998. The volume is not a proceedings volume however, but a collection of articles which focus specifically on the interrelationships between computer learner corpora, second language acquisition and foreign language teaching.

The volume is divided into three sections:

The **first section** by Granger provides a general overview of learner corpus research and situates learner corpora within Second Language Acquisition studies and Foreign Language Teaching.

The three chapters in the **second section** illustrate a range of corpus-based approaches to interlanguage analysis. The first chapter by Altenberg illustrates how *contrastive analysis*, an approach to learner language whose validity has very much been challenged over the years, has now been reinterpreted within a learner corpus perspective and can offer valuable insights into transfer-related language phenomena. The following two studies, one cross-sectional by Aijmer and the other longitudinal by Housen, demonstrate the power of learner corpus data to uncover features of interlanguage grammar.

The chapters in the **third section** demonstrate the direct pedagogical relevance of learner corpus work. In the first chapter, Meunier analyses the current and potential contribution of native and learner corpora to the field of grammar teaching. In the following chapter, Hasselgren's analysis of a corpus of spoken learner language is an attempt to put measurable parameters on the notoriously difficult to define notion of 'fluency', with the ultimate aim of introducing increased objectivity into evaluating fluency within testing procedures. In their study of job applications, Connor, Precht and Upton argue for the value of genre-specific corpora in understanding more about learner language use, and demonstrate how a learner-corpus based approach to the ESP field can be used to refine current approaches to ESP pedagogy. The last two chapters show how the use of learner corpus data can lead to the development of new teaching and learning tools (Allan) and classroom methodologies (Seidlhofer).

Finally, we would like to express our gratitude to the acquisition editor, Kees Vaes, for his continuing support and encouragement and the two series editors, Jan Hulstijn and Birgit Harley, for their insightful comments on preliminary versions of the volume. We would also like to express our gratitude to all the authors who have contributed to the volume for their patient wait for the volume to appear and their ever-willingness to effect the changes asked of them.

Sylviane Granger, Joseph Hung and Stephanie Petch-Tyson
Louvain-la-Neuve and Hong Kong
January 2002

List of contributors

Quentin Grant Allan
University of Hong Kong, China

Karin Aijmer
Göteborg University, Sweden

Bengt Altenberg
Lund University, Sweden

Ulla Connor
Indiana University – Purdue University Indianapolis, USA

Sylviane Granger
Université catholique de Louvain, Belgium

Angela Hasselgren
University of Bergen, Norway

Alex Housen
Vrije Universiteit Brussel, Belgium

Kristen Precht
Northern Arizona University, USA

Fanny Meunier
Université catholique de Louvain, Belgium

Barbara Seidlhofer
University of Vienna, Austria

Thomas Upton
Indiana University – Purdue University Indianapolis, USA

I. The role of computer learner corpora in SLA research and FLT

A Bird's-eye view of learner corpus research

Sylviane Granger

Université catholique de Louvain, Belgium

Chapter overview

This chapter is intended to provide a practical, comprehensive overview of learner corpus research. Granger first situates learner corpus research in relation to SLA and ELT research then goes on to discuss corpus compilation, highlighting the importance of establishing clear design criteria, which she argues should always bear a close relation to a particular research objective. Then follows a detailed discussion of methodologies commonly associated with computer learner corpus (CLC) research: comparisons between native and L2 learners of a language and between different types of L2 learners of a language. She also introduces the different types of linguistic analyses which can be used to effect these comparisons. In particular she demonstrates the power of text retrieval software in accessing new descriptions of L2 language. Section 6 provides an overview of the most useful types of corpus annotation, including entirely automatic (such as part-of-speech tagging) and computer-aided (such as error tagging) techniques and gives examples of the types of results that can be obtained. Section 7 is given over to a discussion of the use of CLC in pedagogical research, curriculum and materials design and classroom methodology. Here Granger highlights the great benefits that are to be had from incorporating information from CLC into, inter alia, learners' dictionaries, CALL programs and web-based teaching. In the concluding section of her article, Granger calls for a greater degree of interdisciplinarity in CLC research, arguing that the greatest research benefits are to be gained by creating interdisciplinary research teams of SLA, FLT and NLP researchers, each of whom brings particular expertise.

1. Corpus linguistics

The area of linguistic enquiry known as learner corpus research, which has only existed since the late 1980s, has created an important link between the two previously disparate fields of corpus linguistics and foreign/second language research. Using the main principles, tools and methods from corpus linguistics, it aims to provide improved descriptions of learner language which can be used for a wide range of purposes in foreign/second language acquisition research and also to improve foreign language teaching.

Corpus linguistics can best be defined as a linguistic methodology which is founded on the use of electronic collections of naturally occurring texts, viz. corpora. It is neither a new branch of linguistics nor a new theory of language, but the very nature of the evidence it uses makes it a particularly powerful methodology, one which has the potential to change perspectives on language. For Leech (1992: 106) it is a "new research enterprise, [...] a new philosophical approach to the subject, [...] an 'open sesame' to a new way of thinking about language". The power of computer software tools combined with the impressive amount and diversity of the language data used as evidence has revealed and will continue to reveal previously unsuspected linguistic phenomena. For Stubbs (1996: 232) "the heuristic power of corpus methods is no longer in doubt". Corpus linguistics has contributed to the discovery of new facts which "have led to far-reaching new hypotheses about language, for example about the co-selection of lexis and syntax".

Although corpora are but one source of evidence among many, complementing rather than replacing other data sources such as introspection and elicitation, there is general agreement today that they are "the only reliable source of evidence for such features as frequency" (McEnery & Wilson 1996: 12). Frequency is an aspect of language of which we have very little intuitive awareness but one that plays a major part in many linguistic applications which require a knowledge not only of what is possible in language but what is likely to occur. The major obvious strength of the computer corpus methodology lies in its suitability for conducting quantitative analyses. The type of insights this approach can bring are highlighted in the work of researchers such as Biber (1988), who demonstrates how using corpus-based techniques in the study of language variation can help bring out the distinctive patterns of distribution of each variety. Conducting quantitative comparisons of a wide range of linguistic features in corpora representing different varieties of language, he shows how different features cluster together in distinctive distributional patterns, effectively creating different text types.

Corpus-based studies conducted over the last twenty or so years have led to much better descriptions of many of the different registers[1] (informal conversation, formal speech, journalese, academic writing, sports reporting, etc.) and dialects of native English (British English vs American English; male vs female language, etc.). However, investigations of non-native varieties have been a relatively recent departure: it was not until the late 1980s and early 1990s that academics and publishers started collecting corpora of non-native English, which have come to be referred to as learner corpora.

2. Learner data in SLA and FLT research

Learner corpora provide a new type of data which can inform thinking both in SLA (Second Language Acquisition) research, which tries to understand the mechanisms of foreign/second language acquisition, and in FLT (Foreign Language Teaching) research, the aim of which is to improve the learning and teaching of foreign/second languages.

SLA research has traditionally drawn on a variety of data types, among which Ellis (1994: 670) distinguishes three major categories: language use data, metalingual judgements and self-report data (see Figure 1). Much current SLA research favours experimental and introspective data and tends to be dismissive of natural language use data. There are several reasons for this, prime among

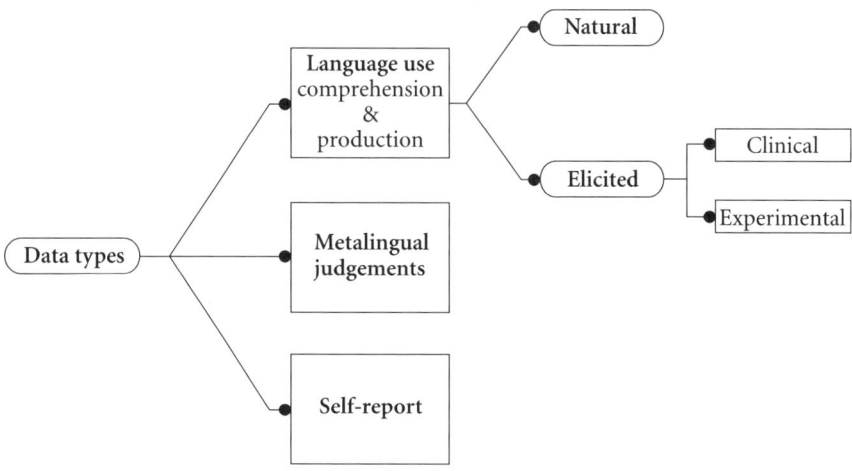

Figure 1. Data types used in SLA research (Ellis 1994)

which is the difficulty of controlling the variables that affect learner output in a non-experimental context. As it is difficult to subject a large number of informants to experimentation, SLA research tends to be based on a relatively narrow empirical base, focusing on the language of a very limited number of subjects, which consequently raises questions about the generalizability of the results.

Looking at the situation from a more pedagogical perspective, Mark (1998:78ff) makes the same observation, pointing out that some of the factors that play a part in language learning and teaching have received more attention than others. Mainstream language teaching approaches have dealt mainly with the three components represented in Figure 2. Great efforts have been made to improve the description of the target language. There has been an increased interest in learner variables, such as motivation, learning styles, needs, attitudes, etc., and our understanding of both the target language and the learner has contributed to the development of more efficient language learning tasks, syllabuses and curricula.

What is noticeably absent, however, is the learner output. Mark deplores the peripheral position of learner language. In Figure 3, which incorporates learner output, Mark shows how improved knowledge of actual learner output would illuminate the other three areas. For Mark (ibid:84), "it simply goes against common sense to base instruction on limited learner data and to ignore, in all aspects of pedagogy from task to curriculum level, knowledge of learner language".

It is encouraging, therefore, to note that gradually the attention of the SLA and FLT research communities is turning towards learner corpora and the types of descriptions and insights they have the potential to provide. It is to be hoped that learner corpora will contribute to rehabilitating learner output by providing researchers with substantial sources of tightly controlled com-

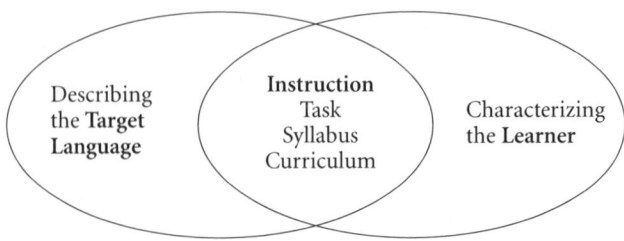

Figure 2. The concerns of mainstream language teaching (Mark 1998)

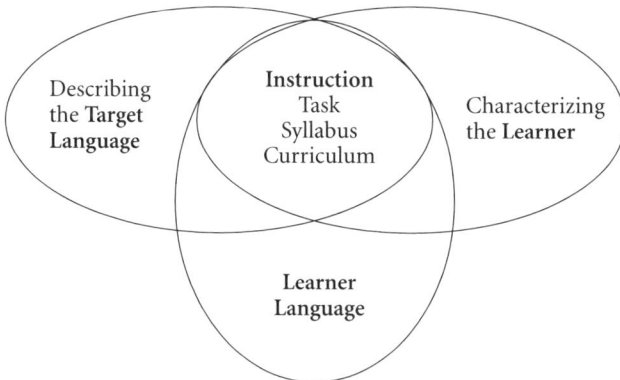

Figure 3. Focus on learner output (Mark 1998)

puterised data which can be analysed at a range of levels using increasingly powerful linguistic software tools.

3.   Computer learner corpora

One of the reasons why the samples of learner data used in SLA studies have traditionally been rather small is that until quite recently data collection and analysis required tremendous time and effort on the part of the researcher. Now, however, technological progress has made it perfectly possible to collect learner data in large quantities, store it on the computer and analyse it automatically or semi-automatically using currently available linguistic software.

Although computer learner corpora (CLC) can be roughly defined as electronic collections of learner data, this type of fuzzy definition should be avoided because it leads to the term being used for data types which are in effect not corpora at all. I suggest adopting the following definition, which is based on Sinclair's (1996) definition of corpora:[2]

> Computer learner corpora are electronic collections of authentic FL/SL textual data assembled according to explicit design criteria for a particular SLA/FLT purpose. They are encoded in a standardised and homogeneous way and documented as to their origin and provenance.

There are several key notions in this definition worthy of further comment.

AUTHENTICITY

Sinclair (1996) describes the default value for corpora for Quality as 'authentic': "All the material is gathered from the genuine communications of people going about their normal business" unlike data gathered "in experimental conditions or in artificial conditions of various kinds".

Applied to the foreign/second language field, this means that purely experimental data resulting from elicitation techniques does not qualify as learner corpus data. However, the notion of authenticity is somewhat problematic in the case of learner language. Even the most authentic data from non-native speakers is rarely as authentic as native speaker data, especially in the case of EFL learners, who learn English in the classroom. We all know that the foreign language teaching context usually involves some degree of 'artificiality' and that learner data is therefore rarely **fully** natural. A number of learner corpora involve some degree of control. Free compositions, for instance, are 'natural' in the sense that they represent 'free writing': learners are free to write what they like rather than having to produce items the investigator is interested in. But they are also to some extent elicited since some task variables, such as the topic or the time limit, are often imposed on the learner.

In relation to learner corpora the term 'authentic' therefore covers different degrees of authenticity, ranging from "gathered from the genuine communications of people going about their normal business" to "resulting from authentic classroom activity". In as far as essay writing is an authentic classroom activity, learner corpora of essay writing can be considered to be authentic written data, and similarly a text read aloud can be considered to be authentic spoken data.[3]

FL AND SL VARIETIES

Learner corpora are situated within the non-native varieties of English, which can be broken down into English as an Official Language (EOL), English as a Second Language (ESL) and English as a Foreign Language (EFL) (see Figure 4). EOL is a cover term for indigenised or nativised varieties of English, such as Nigerian English or Indian English. ESL is sometimes referred to as Immigrant ESL: it refers to English acquired in an English-speaking environment (such as Britain or the US). EFL covers English learned primarily in a classroom setting in a non-English-speaking country (Belgium, Germany, etc.). Learner corpora cover the last two non-native varieties: EFL and ESL.[4]

TEXTUAL DATA

To qualify as learner corpus data the language sample must consist of continuous stretches of discourse, not isolated sentences or words. It is therefore

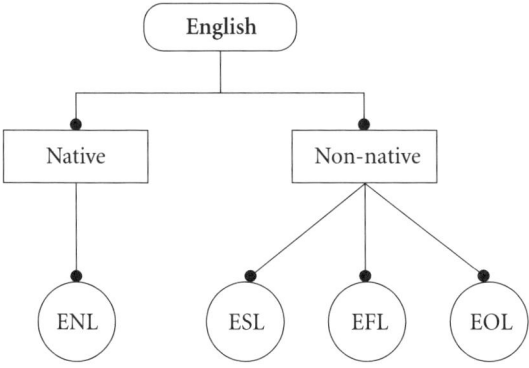

Figure 4. Varieties of English

misleading to speak of 'corpora of errors' (cf. James 1998: 124). One cannot use the term 'corpus' to refer to a collection of erroneous sentences extracted from learner texts. Learner corpora are made up of continuous stretches of discourse which contain both erroneous and correct use of the language.

EXPLICIT DESIGN CRITERIA

Design criteria are very important in the case of learner data because there is so much variation in EFL/ESL. A random collection of heterogeneous learner data does not qualify as a learner corpus. Learner corpora should be compiled according to strict design criteria, some of which are the same as for native corpora (as clearly described in Atkins & Clear 1992), while others, relating to both the learner and the task, are specific to learner corpora. Some of these CLC-specific criteria are represented in Figure 5.

The usefulness of a learner corpus is directly proportional to the care that has been exerted in controlling and encoding the variables.

LEARNER	TASK SETTINGS
• Learning context	• Time limit
• Mother tongue	• Use of reference tools
• Other foreign languages	• Exam
• Level of proficiency	• Audience/interlocutor
• […]	• […]

Figure 5. CLC – specific design criteria

SLA/FLT PURPOSE

A learner corpus is collected for a particular SLA or FLT purpose. Researchers may want to test or improve some aspect of SLA theory, for example by confirming or disconfirming theories about transfer from L1 or the order of acquisition of morphemes, or they may want to contribute to the production of better FLT tools and methods.

STANDARDIZATION AND DOCUMENTATION

A learner corpus can be produced in a variety of formats. It can take the form of a raw corpus, i.e. a corpus of plain texts with no extra features added, or of an annotated corpus, i.e. a corpus enriched with linguistic or textual information, such as grammatical categories or syntactic structures. An annotated learner corpus should ideally be based on standardised annotation software in order to ensure comparability of annotated learner corpora with native annotated corpora. However, the deviant nature of the learner data may make these tools less reliable or may call for the development of new software tools, such as error tagging software (see section 6 below).

A learner corpus should also be documented for learner and task variables. Full details about these variables must be recorded for each text and either made available to researchers in the form of SGML file headers or stored separately but linked to the text by a reference system. This documentation will enable researchers to compile subcorpora which match a set of predefined attributes and effect interesting comparisons, for example between spoken and written productions from the same learner population or between similar-type learners from different mother tongue backgrounds.

4. Learner corpus typology

Corpus typology is often described in terms of dichotomies, four of which are particularly relevant to learner corpora (see Figure 6). An examination of current CLC publications shows that in each case it is the feature on the left that is prominent in current research.

In the first place, learner corpora are usually **monolingual**, although in fact a small number of learner translation corpora have been compiled. Spence (1998), for instance, has collected an EFL translation corpus from German undergraduate students of translation, and demonstrates the usefulness of this kind of corpus in throwing light on the complex relations between the notions of 'non-nativeness', 'translationese' and 'un-Englishness'.

Monolingual ⇔	Bilingual
General ⇔	Technical
Synchronic ⇔	Diachronic
Written ⇔	Spoken

Figure 6. Learner corpus typology

In addition, existing learner corpora tend to contain samples of **non-specialist language**. ESP learner corpora such as the *Indiana Business Learner Corpus*, compiled by Connor et al. (this volume), are the exception rather than the rule.

Current learner corpora tend, furthermore, to be **synchronic**, i.e. describe learner use at a particular point in time. There are very few longitudinal corpora, i.e. corpora which cover the evolution of learner use. The reason is simple: such corpora are very difficult to compile as they require a learner population to be followed for months or, preferably, years. Housen (this volume) is an exception from that point of view: his *Corpus of Young Learner Interlanguage* consists of EFL data from European School pupils at different stages of development and from different L1 backgrounds. Generally, however, researchers who are interested in the development of learners' proficiency collect 'quasi-longitudinal' data, i.e. they collect data from a homogeneous group of learners at different levels of proficiency. Examples are Dagneaux et al. (1998) and Granger (1999), which report on a comparison of data from a group of first- and third-year students and analyse the data in terms of progress or lack of it.

The difficulties inherent in corpus compilation are all the more marked when it comes to collecting oral data, which undoubtedly explains why there are many more **written** than spoken learner corpora. Nevertheless, some spoken corpora are being compiled. Housen's corpus, described in this volume, is a spoken corpus. The *LINDSEI*[5] corpus is also a spoken corpus and, when complete, will contain EFL and ESL spoken data from a variety of mother tongue backgrounds.

5.   Linguistic analysis

Linguistic exploitation of learner corpora usually involves one of the following two methodological approaches: Contrastive Interlanguage Analysis and

Computer-aided Error Analysis. The first method is contrastive, and consists in carrying out quantitative and qualitative comparisons between native (NS) and non-native (NNS) data or between different varieties of non-native data. The second focuses on errors in interlanguage and uses computer tools to tag, retrieve and analyse them.

5.1 Contrastive interlanguage analysis

Contrastive Interlanguage Analysis (CIA) involves two types of comparison (see Figure 7).

NS/NNS comparisons are intended to shed light on non-native features of learner writing and speech through detailed comparisons of linguistic features in native and non-native corpora. A crucial issue in this type of comparison is the choice of control corpus of native English, a particularly difficult choice as it involves selecting a dialectal variant (British English, American English, Canadian English, Australian English, etc.) and a diatypic variant (medium, level of formality, field, etc.). Another thing to consider is the level of proficiency of the native speakers. Lorenz (1999) has demonstrated the value of comparing learner texts with both native professional writers and native students (and hence the importance of a fully documented corpus with a search interface to select appropriate texts which are comparable to learner data). Fortunately for the CLC researcher, there is now a wide range of native corpora available and hence a wide range of 'norms' to choose from.[6]

NS/NNS comparisons can highlight a range of features of non-nativeness in learner writing and speech, i.e. not only errors, but also instances of under- and overrepresentation of words, phrases and structures. Several examples of this methodology can be found in this volume and in Granger (1998). Some linguists have fundamental objections to this type of comparison because they consider that interlanguage should be studied in its own right and not as somehow deficient as compared to the native 'norm'. It is important to stress that the

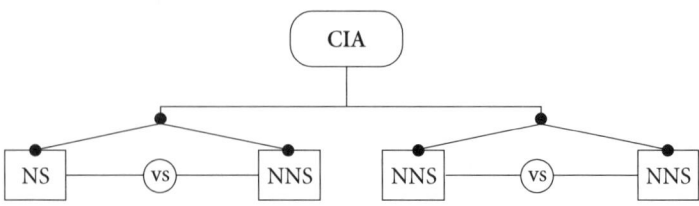

Figure 7. Contrastive Interlanguage Analysis

two positions are not irreconcilable. One can engage in close investigation of interlanguage in order to understand the system underlying it and concurrently or subsequently compare the interlanguage with one or more native speaker norms in order to assess the extent of the deviation. If learner corpus research has some applied aim, the comparison with native data is essential since the aim of all foreign language teaching is to improve the learners' proficiency, which in essence means bringing it closer to some NS norm(s).[7]

CIA also involves NNS/NNS comparisons. By comparing different learner populations, researchers improve their knowledge of interlanguage. In particular, comparisons of learner data from different mother tongue backgrounds help researchers to differentiate between features which are shared by several learner populations and are therefore more likely to be developmental and those which are peculiar to one national group and therefore possibly L1-dependent. Granger & Tyson's (1996) study of connectors suggests that overuse of sentence-initial connectors may well be developmental as it is found to be characteristic of three learner populations (French, Dutch and Chinese), while the use of individual connectors, which displays wide variation between the national learner groups, provides evidence of interlingual influence.

In order to interpret results or formulate hypotheses, it is useful to have access to bilingual corpora containing both the learner's mother tongue and English. CIA and classical CA (Contrastive Analysis) are highly complementary when it comes to interpreting findings. The overuse of sentence-initial connectors by three learner groups may well be due to a high frequency of connectors in that position in the L1s of the three learner groups. Only a close comparison between the learners' L1s and English can help solve this question. In the case of French-speaking learners, Anthone's (1996) bilingual study of connectors in English and French journalese rules out the interlingual interpretation as French proves to have far fewer sentence-initial connectors than English in this particular variety.[8] The developmental interpretation is therefore reinforced. Altenberg's study of causative constructions in this volume highlights the value of a combined CIA/CA perspective.

5.2 Computer-aided error analysis

Error-oriented approaches to learner corpora are quite different from previous EA studies because they are computer-aided and involve a higher degree of standardization and, even more importantly perhaps, because errors are presented in the full context of the text, alongside non-erroneous forms.

Computer-aided error analysis usually involves one of the following two methods. The first simply consists in selecting an error-prone linguistic item (word, phrase, word category, syntactic structure) and scanning the corpus to retrieve all instances of misuse of the item with the help of standard text retrieval software tools (see section 6.1.). The advantage of this method is that it is extremely fast; the disadvantage is that the analyst has to preempt the issue: the search is limited to those items which he considers to be problematic. The second method is more time-consuming but also much more powerful in that it may lead the analyst to discover learner difficulties of which he was not aware. The method consists in devising a standardised system of error tags and tagging all the errors in a learner corpus or, at least, all errors in a particular category (for instance, verb complementation or modals). This process is admittedly very labour-intensive, but the error tagging process can be greatly helped by the use of an error editor and, more importantly, once the work has been done and researchers are in possession of a fully error-tagged corpus, the range of possible applications that can be derived from it is absolutely huge.

Error analysis (EA) often arouses negative reactions: it is felt to be retrograde, a return to the old days when errors were considered to be an entirely negative aspect of learner language. However, analysing learner errors is not a negative enterprise: on the contrary, it is a key aspect of the process which takes us towards understanding interlanguage development and one which must be considered essential within a pedagogical framework. Teachers and materials designers need to have much more information about what learners can be expected to have acquired by what stage if they are to provide the most useful input to the learners, and analysing errors is a valuable source of information. Of course, this does not mean that classroom activities need to be focused on errors, but more learner-aware teaching can only be profitable. It is also worth noting that current EA practice is quite different from that of the 1970s. Whereas former EA was characterized by decontextualization of errors, disregard for learners' correct use of the language and non-standardised error typologies, today's EA investigates contextualised errors: both the context of use and the linguistic context (co-text) is permanently available to the analyst. Erroneous occurrences of a linguistic item can be visualised in one or more sentences, a paragraph or the whole text, alongside correct instances. And finally, in line with current corpus linguistics procedures, error tagging is standardised: error categories are well defined and fully documented (see section 6.2.2.).

6.   Software tools

As learner corpora contain data in electronic form, they can in principle be analysed with software tools developed by corpus linguists for the analysis of native corpora.

Computerised learner data have two major advantages for researchers: they are more manageable, and therefore easier to analyse, and they make it easier to supplement the raw data with extra linguistic information, using either automatic or semi-automatic techniques.

6.1 Text retrieval

The type of software which has achieved the most startling results has been text retrieval software. As Rundell & Stock (1992: 14) point out, text retrieval software liberates linguists from drudgery and empowers them to "focus their creative energies to doing what machines cannot do". It would be wrong to believe, however, that such software is just a dumb slave: it enables researchers to effect quite sophisticated searches which they would never be able to do manually. Text retrieval software such as *WordSmith Tools*[9] can count not only words but also word partials and sequences of words, which it can sort into alphabetical and frequency order. The 'concord' option is also extremely valuable since it throws light on the collocates or patterns that learners use, correctly or incorrectly. In addition, an option called 'compare lists' enables researchers to carry out comparisons of items in two corpora and bring out the statistically significant differences. If the two corpora represent native and learner language, such a comparison will give the analyst immediate access to those items which are either under- or overused by learners.

However, researchers should be aware that when using non-native language data, some degree of caution should be exercised with these tools, whether they are used to analyse lexis or grammar. In a lexical frequency study, Granger & Wynne (1999) applied a series of lexical variation measures to both native and learner corpora. The most commonly used measure, the type/token (T/t) ratio, counts the number of different words in a text. It is computed by means of the following formula:

$$\text{T/t ratio} = \frac{\text{Number of word types} \times 100}{\text{Number of word tokens} \times 1}$$

A text retrieval program such as *WordSmith Tools* computes this measure automatically and it is tempting for researchers simply to feed in their learner data and use the type/token results to draw conclusions on lexical richness in learner texts. Granger & Wynne's study shows that this would be very unwise because a learner corpus may contain a very high rate of non-standard forms – both spelling and morphological errors – and these forms may significantly boost the type/token ratios. This is exactly what happened with the Spanish learner corpus: it proved to have one of the highest type/token ratios in the learner sample but closer examination of the data showed that this high ratio was due mainly to a very high rate of non-standard forms.

6.2 Annotation

The second major advantage of computerised learner data is that it is possible to enrich the data with all kinds of linguistic annotation automatically or semi-automatically. Leech (1993: 275) defines corpus annotation as 'the practice of adding interpretative (especially linguistic) information to an existing corpus of spoken and/or written language by some kind of coding attached to, or interspersed with, the electronic representation of the language material itself'. How the annotation is inserted depends on the type of information being added. In some cases the process can be fully automated, in others semi-automated, and in yet others it has to be almost entirely manual.

Part-of-speech (POS) tagging is a good example of fully automatic annotation. A POS tagger assigns to each word in a corpus a tag indicating its word-class membership. This sort of annotation is of obvious interest to SLA/FLT researchers, making it possible for them to conduct selective searches of particular parts of speech in learner language, especially error-prone categories like prepositions or modals.

Semi-automatic annotation tools enable researchers to introduce linguistic annotation interactively. For instance, using the *Tree Editor* developed at the University of Nijmegen, it is possible to build or edit syntactic structures, using the categories and templates provided or loading one's own categories.[10] Meunier (2000) has used the software to compare the complexity of the noun phrase in native and non-native texts. Another example of a semi-automatic annotation tool is an error editor, which allows researchers to mark errors in a text (see 6.2.2.).

Even if the researcher is interested in linguistic features not catered for by currently available software tools, working with computerised data still has advantages. Any linguistic feature can be annotated with tags developed for a particular research purpose and introduced manually (often this process can be supported by the use of macros) into the corpus. Once the tags have been inserted in the text files, they can be searched for and sorted using standard text retrieval software.

In general terms, then, the computerised learner corpus presents the researcher with a range of options for analysis. In the following sections I will focus more particularly on two types of annotation which are particularly relevant to learner corpus research: POS tagging and error tagging

6.2.1 *Part-of-speech tagging*

Part-of-speech taggers have many advantages: they are fully automatic, widely available and inexpensive, and claim a high overall success rate. They have differing degrees of granularity: some have a very reduced tagset of circa 50 tags while others have over 250 tags (for a survey of taggers and other software tools, see Meunier 1998 & 2000). The value of using POS-tagged learner corpora is shown clearly by Table 1, which lists the top 15 word forms extracted from a raw learner corpus of French learner writing and the top 15 word + tag combinations extracted from the same corpus tagged with the CLAWS tagger.[11]

The plus and minus signs indicate significant over- or underuse in comparison with frequencies in a control corpus of similar writing by native students of English. For a word like *the*, which is relatively unambiguous, occurrences of *the* as an adverb (as in *the more, the merrier*) being infrequent, there is little advantage in using a POS-tagged corpus. Likewise in the case of *a* or *and*. However, where *to* is concerned, the advantage of annotation is obvious. *To*

Table 1. Top 15 word forms and word + tag combinations in French learner corpus

	word forms	word + tag combinations
1.	the −	the – AT
2.	of	of – IO
3.	to	and + CC
4.	a +	a + AT1
5.	and +	to TO
6.	is +	is + VBZ
7.	in −	in – II
8.	that −	it + PPH1
9.	it +	that – CST
10.	be +	be + VBI
11.	are +	are + VBR
12.	not +	not + XX
13.	this	to – II
14.	as −	this DD1
15.	they +	they + PPHS2

occupies the third position in the frequency list and has more or less the same frequency as in the control NS corpus (as indicated by the absence of a plus or minus sign). But this frequency information is not particularly useful since it fails to distinguish between the particle *to* and the preposition *to*. The second column is much more informative. Here we see that the particle *to* (TO) is more frequent than the preposition *to* (II) and is used with similar frequency in the NNS and NS corpora, while the preposition *to* proves to be underused by learners. The same is true of *that*, where overall underuse of the word form proves to be due to an underuse of its function as a conjunction (CST).

The use of annotated and in particular POS-tagged learner corpora should be encouraged as they allow for more refined linguistic analysis. However, POS-taggers ought to be used with a full awareness of their limitations. For one thing, researchers should be aware of the fact that automatic tagging is never 100% error-free. Typical claims of success rates in the region of 95% or more refer to overall rates. For problematic categories like that of adverbial particles, the success rate can drop to 70% (Massart 1998). In fact, any analysis of a tagged corpus, whether native or non-native, should be preceded by a pilot study in which the results of the automatic search are compared with those of a purely manual search (for a full description of this methodology, see Granger 1997). This is all the more necessary when the tagged corpus is a learner corpus, as POS-taggers are trained on NS data and can be expected to have a lower success rate when applied to NNS data. Experiments have shown that if the learner output is quite advanced, with a low proportion of spelling and morphological errors, the success rate of the tagger is similar to that obtained when tagging NS data. But the more deviant the data, the less accurate the tagging will be, to the point of making the use of the tagger impracticable .

Probably because of these difficulties, few studies have been based on POS-tagged learner corpora. However, those that exist demonstrate their tremendous potential in highlighting flaws in the syntactic and stylistic behaviour of EFL learners (see Aarts & Granger 1998; de Haan 1998 and Granger & Rayson 1998).

6.2.2   *Error tagging*
Being 'special corpora' (Sinclair 1995: 24), computer learner corpora quite naturally call for their own techniques of analysis. The traditional types of annotation (part-of-speech tagging, parsing, semantic tagging) are extremely useful but they need to be supplemented with new types of annotation, such as error tagging, which are specially designed to cater for the anomalous nature of learner language.

There are many ways of analysing learner errors and hence many possible error tagging systems. One major decision to make is whether to tag errors in terms of their nature (grammatical, lexical, etc.) or their source (interlingual, intralingual, etc.). The former is arguably preferable in that it involves less subjective interpretation and is therefore likely to be applied with greater consistency and reliability by different analysts. The error tagging system developed at Louvain[12] is hierarchical: it attaches to each error a series of codes which go from the general to the more specific. The first letter of the code refers to the error domain: G for grammatical, L for lexical, X for lexico-grammatical, F for formal, R for register, W for syntax and S for style. The following letters give more precision on the nature of the error. For instance, all the grammatical errors affecting verbs are given the GV code, which itself is subdivided into GVAUX (auxiliary errors), GVM (morphological errors), GVN (number errors), GVNF (finite/non-finite errors), GVT (tense errors) and GVV (voice errors). The system is flexible and allows the analyst to add or delete codes to suit his particular research interests.

To support this system, two additional tools have been developed. The first is an error tagging manual which defines and illustrates all the categories and records the coding practices created in order to ensure that researchers working independently assign the error codes in the same way. The second is an editing tool, designed to facilitate error tagging. Figure 8 shows the interface of the Louvain error editor, *UCLEE*, which allows researchers to insert error tags and corrections in the text files.[13] By clicking on the relevant tag from the error tag menu, the analyst can insert it at the appropriate point in the text. Using the correction box, he can also insert the corrected form with the appropriate formatting symbols.

The codes are enclosed in round brackets and placed just in front of the erroneous form while the correction, which is enclosed by two dollar signs, follows the error. Once files have been error-tagged, it is possible to search for any error category and sort them in various ways. Figure 9 contains a sample from the output of the search for the category XVPR, a lexico-grammatical error category containing erroneous dependent prepositions following verbs, and the category XNUC, containing lexico-grammatical errors relating to the count/uncount status of nouns.

There is obvious potential for integrating information derived from error-tagged corpora into most types of ELT tools – grammars, vocabulary textbooks, monolingual learners' dictionaries and bilingual dictionaries, grammar and style checkers, CALL programs. Concrete examples of how this can be done will be given in the following section.

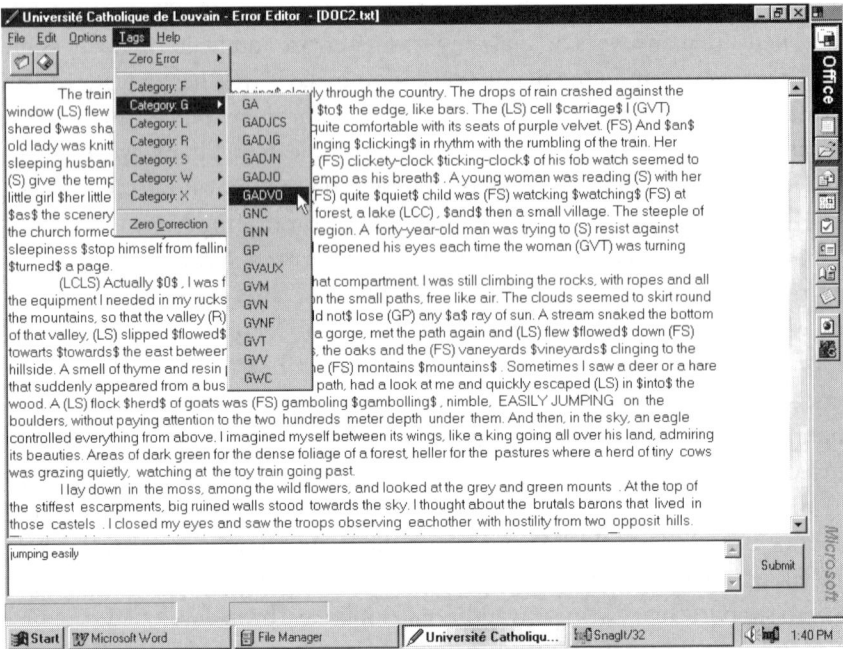

Figure 8. Error editor screen dump

the fact that we could	(XVPR) argue on $argue about$ the definition of
want to be parents, do not	(XVPR) care of $care about$ the sex
is rising. These people who	(XVPR) come in $come to$ Belgium
Family planning	(XVPR) consists on $consists of$
have the possibility to	(XVPR) discuss about $discuss$ their problems
which the purchaser cannot	(XVPR) dispense of $dispense with$
the health. Nobody	(XVPR) doubts about $doubts$ that.
harvest they get is often	(XVPR) exported in $exported to$ countries
of advice on	(XNUC) a 0 better health care
for years. Undoubtedly	(XNUC) a 0 big progress has been made
characteristic	(XNUC) behaviours $behaviour$
It provides	(XNUC) employments $employment$
combining study life and	(XNUC) entertainments $entertainment$
are many other	(XNUC) leisures $leisure facilities$
a balance between work and	(XNUC) spare times $spare time$
need to do some	(XNUC) works $work$ or simply for your personal

Figure 9. Error tag search: verb dependent prepositions and count/uncount nouns

7. CLC-based pedagogical research

7.1 Native corpora and ELT

Although the concept of using learner corpora in ELT research is a new one, native corpora have been used in ELT research for quite a number of years and nobody today would deny that they have had a profound and positive impact on the field. While there is certainly no general agreement on what Murison-Bowie (1996: 182) calls the 'strong case' which maintains that without a corpus there is no meaningful work to be done, there is general consensus today that corpus data opens up interesting descriptive and pedagogic perspectives.

The two areas which appear to have benefited most from corpus-based work are materials design and classroom methodology. In materials design by far the most noteworthy change has taken place in the field of EFL dictionaries. The use of mega-corpora has made for richer and altogether more useful dictionaries, which provide detailed information on the ranking of meanings, collocations, grammatical patterns, style and frequency. EFL grammars have also benefited from corpus data, notably through the inclusion of lexico-grammatical information, but while I would not hesitate to use the word 'revolution' in talking about the dictionary field, I do not think we can speak of a revolution in the grammar field, as there has been no radical change yet in the selection, sequencing and respective weighting of grammatical phenomena.[14] As for EFL textbooks, the main gain seems to me to be lexical. Corpus data has provided a much more objective basis for vocabulary selection, has led to greater attention to word combinations of all types (collocations, prefabs or semi-prefabs) and has also greatly improved the description of genre differences. In the field of classroom methodology, concordance-based exercises constitute a useful addition to the battery of teaching techniques. They fit marvellously well in the new Observe – Hypothesise – Experiment paradigm which is gaining ground over the traditional Present – Practise – Produce paradigm. Tim Johns (1991 & 1994) has been one the leading pioneers of this new teaching practice, which is now commonly known as data-driven learning or DDL.

It is quite clear therefore that the enriched description of the target language provided by native corpora is a plus for foreign language teaching. However, the view I would like to put forward is that it is not sufficient. Native corpora provide valuable information on the frequency and use of words, phrases and structures but give no indication whatsoever of the difficulty they present for learners in general or for a specific category of learners. They will therefore always be of limited value and may even lead to ill-judged pedagogical deci-

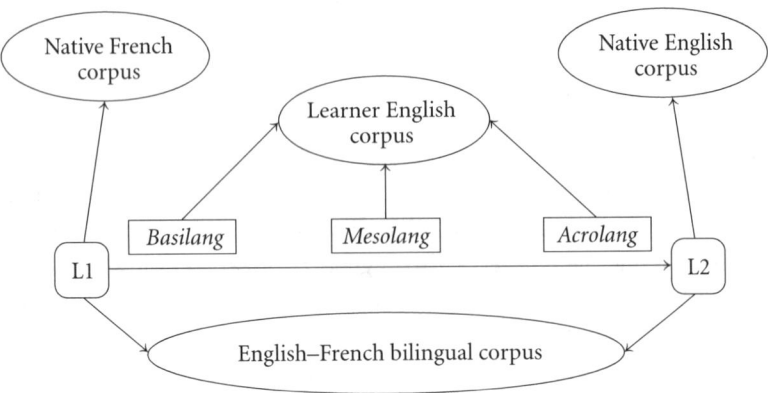

Figure 10. Learner corpus environment

sions unless they are complemented with the equally rich and pedagogically more relevant type of data provided by learner corpora. In addition, data derived from bilingual corpora representing the target language and the learner's mother tongue also provide interesting insights. Figure 10 represents the ideal corpus environment for the analysis of French-speaking learners' interlanguage and design of FLT materials for them.

Although the field of learner corpus research is still very young, it opens up exciting prospects for ELT pedagogy, especially as regards curriculum design, materials design, classroom methodology and language testing. In the following lines I will focus on the first three fields. For interesting possibilities in the area of language testing, see Hasselgren this volume.

7.2 Curriculum design

Learner corpus data has an important role to play in the selection and structuring of teaching content. The frequency information provided by native corpora is undoubtedly useful but, as rightly pointed out by Widdowson (1991:20–21), frequency profiles "do not of themselves carry any guarantee of pedagogic relevance".

In the field of vocabulary teaching, for instance, specialists are in agreement that both frequency and difficulty have to be taken into account. This comes out clearly in Sökmen's (1997:239–240) survey of current trends in vocabulary teaching: "Difficult words need attention as well. Because students will avoid words which are difficult in meaning, in pronunciation, or in use, preferring words which can be generalized (...), lessons must be designed to tackle the tricky, less-frequent words along with the highly-frequent. Focusing on words which will cause confusion, e.g. false cognates, and presenting them with an eye to clearing up confusion is also time well-spent". Teachers and researchers often have useful intuitions about what does or does not constitute an area of difficulty for learners, but this intuition needs to be borne out by empirical data from learner corpora.

Grammar teaching would also benefit greatly from this combined native/non-native corpus perspective, but here I feel that we are much less advanced than in the field of vocabulary teaching. Very little progress has been made in the selection and sequencing of grammatical phenomena. Corpora give us the opportunity to do exactly this. In what follows I will show how insights gained from native and learner corpora can help materials designers decide what room to allocate to descriptions of the different types of postmodification in EFL grammars.

In an article published in 1994, Biber et al. demonstrate that there is a great discrepancy between the number of pages devoted to the different types of noun phrase postmodification in EFL grammars and their actual frequency in corpora. Table 2 (adapted from Biber et al. 1994) presents the frequency of prepositional phrases (*the man in the corner*), relative clauses (*the man who is standing in the corner*) and participial clauses (*the man standing in the corner*) in three registers of English: editorials, fiction and letters.

As the table shows, prepositional phrases are by far the most frequent type of postnominal modifiers in all three registers, followed by relative clauses and then participial clauses. Biber et al's investigation shows that this is not reflected in EFL grammars, where relative clauses, for instance, receive much more extensive discussion than prepositional phrases. The authors insist that frequency should play a greater part in syllabus design. They admit that other factors, such as difficulty and teachability, also play a part but regard "the actual patterns of use as an equally important consideration" (ibid: 174). I agree with the authors that both the native and the learner angle are important, but I would not put the two on the same footing and label them "equally important". When there is a clash between insights derived from native and learner corpora, it

Table 2. Frequency of postnominal modifiers (adapted from Biber et al. 1994)

Postnominal modifiers	Editorials	Fiction	Letters
Prepositional phrases	38.2	15.2	16.8
Relative clauses	9.2	5.1	2.1
Participial clauses	4.9	1.8	0.2

is always the learner angle which should be given priority. Recent research on postmodification in learner corpora will help me clarify my position.

A recent study of postnominal modifiers (Meunier 2000) in the written English of native speakers and French learners shows a clear deficit in prepositional phrases and participial clauses in the learner writing and a significant overuse of relative clauses. This may be partly teaching-induced but may also be partly due to cross-linguistic reasons: prepositional and participial postmodification is less common in French than in English.[15] In addition, there is also evidence from the Louvain error-tagged corpus of French learner writing that learners have persistent difficulty with relative pronoun selection. Here too crosslinguistic factors are probably at play as pronoun selection is governed by totally different principles in English and French. What lessons for syllabus design can one draw from these findings?

As far as prepositional postmodifiers are concerned, the situation is clear: the evidence from both native and learner data points to a need for more extensive treatment in EFL grammars and textbooks designed for French-speaking learners. On the other hand, the low frequency of relative modifiers in the native data would indicate that they should be given low priority, but it would nevertheless seem essential to give them extensive treatment in EFL grammars in view of the difficulty they have been shown to present for French-speaking learners and indeed for other categories of learners as well. In addition, the fact that underuse of prepositional modifiers goes hand in hand with underuse of participial modifiers and is coupled with overuse of relative clauses indicates that French-speaking learners need to have more practice in reducing full clauses to prepositional and participial clauses.

This example illustrates the value of combining native and non-native data and indeed bilingual data when selecting the topics to be focused on in teaching and deciding on the relative weighting that each should be assigned .

7.3 Materials design

Closely linked to curriculum design, the field of materials design also stands to gain from the findings of learner corpus research. Indeed, in the fields of ELT dictionaries, CALL programs and web-based teaching, learner corpus research is already bearing fruit.

Monolingual learners' dictionaries stand to benefit chiefly by using learner corpus data to enrich usage notes. The *Longman Essential Activator Dictionary* is the first dictionary to have integrated such data. It contains help boxes such

> ! Don't say 'informations'. Say **information**.
> ! Don't say 'an information'. Say **a piece of information** or **some information**.

> ! Don't say 'an important problem'. Say **a serious problem** or **a big problem**.

Figure 11. Help boxes in the *Essential Activator Dictionary*

as that represented in Figure 11 which draw learners' attention to common mistakes extracted from the Longman Learners' Corpus.

As for bilingual dictionaries, incorporating information from L1-specific error catalogues into the usage notes would represent a significant step forward in tailoring these dictionaries to the particular difficulties experienced by learners from different mother tongue backgrounds.

CALL programs constitute another promising field. On the basis of CLC data it is becoming possible to create tailor-made software tools for particular groups of learners. Milton's *WordPilot* program[16] is a case in point. It is a writing kit especially designed for Hong Kong EFL learners and contains error recognition exercises intended to sensitize learners to the most common errors made by Hong Kong learners. In addition, it contains user-friendly text retrieval techniques which enable learners to access native corpora of specific text types, thus nicely combining the native and learner angle. There is also some very active related work going on in the NLP field, with researchers such as Menzel et al. (2000) using spoken learner corpora to train voice recognition and pronunciation training tools capable of coping with learner output. Learner corpus-based NLP applications are particularly promising. On the basis of learner corpus data, it is becoming possible to create tailor-made software tools for particular groups of non-native users, for instance voice recognition and pronunciation training tools for speech and spelling and grammar checkers for writing.

Finally, another extremely exciting project is the web-based *TeleNex* project,[17] described in detail by Allan (this volume). *TeleNex* is a computer network which is designed to provide support for secondary level English teachers in Hong Kong. Although quite a lot of the material is only accessible to registered Hong Kong teachers, there is enough accessible material to form an idea of the tremendous potential of this kind of environment. A large learner corpus, the *TELEC Student Corpus*, has been used to compile Students' problem files in *TeleGram*, a hypertext pedagogic grammar database. For a whole range of problematic areas (passive, uncountable nouns, etc.), there are a series of tools for teachers, including a tool called 'Students' problems', which highlight students' attested difficulties, and another tool called 'Teaching implications', which suggest teaching methods designed to help students avoid producing such mistakes.

7.4 Classroom methodology

The use of learner corpus data in the classroom is a highly controversial issue. While recognizing the danger of exposing learners to erroneous data, I would argue for the use of CLC data in the classroom in the following two contexts.

The first use is situated within the general field of **form-focused instruction** (cf. Granger & Tribble 1998). It is useful, especially in the case of fossilized language use, to get learners to notice the gap between their own and target language forms, and comparisons of native and non-native concordances of problematic words and patterns may be very useful here. For instance, to take the example of connectors again, a comparison of the frequency and use of the connector 'indeed' in native and non-native data may be very effective in making French learners aware of their overuse and misuse of this word. Obviously, for items such as connectors, it is necessary to present the words in more than one line of context. Hands-on exercises are interesting here because learners can manipulate the context, visualizing the word in one line, three or five lines of context or indeed in the whole text.

Seidlhofer (this volume) suggests using learner data not in the context of data-driven learning but rather of **learning-driven data**. In a very interesting teaching experiment, she had learners write a summary of a text and a short personal reaction to it and then made these texts the primary objects of analysis, in effect getting the learners to work with and on their own output. Seidlhofer points out that the experiment was particularly successful because learners played much more active and responsible roles in their learning.

Experiments using learner data in the classroom are thin on the ground and those that have been attempted have been with more advanced learners. Although this remains to be tested, it seems likely that the approach is likely to be more successful with advanced learners.

8. The way forward

Although the field of learner corpus research is still in its infancy, the sheer number of publications bears witness to the vitality in this field.[18] But as Leech

(1998:xx) rightly points out "Like any healthily active and developing field of inquiry, learner corpus research has to continue to face challenges both material and intellectual before it wins a secure and accepted place in the discipline of applied linguistics". Among the challenges that lie ahead, the following three seem to me to be the most pressing: corpus compilation, corpus analysis and interdisciplinarity.

8.1 Corpus compilation

Although many learner corpora have been compiled or are in the process of being compiled, few are available. Those collected by publishers such as the Longman Learners' Corpus or the Cambridge Learners' Corpus are in-house tools, designed to improve reference tools, such as grammars and dictionaries. Those collected by academics have also often been produced for internal use and have required so much time and effort to collect that their authors tend to keep them for themselves. Academics who are ready to share their data find that the lack of standardization and documentation of the data makes its distribution difficult. It is hoped that the *International Corpus of Learner English (ICLE),* due to be published on CD-ROM in 2002 and described briefly below, will be the first of many.

   ICLE is a corpus of writing by higher intermediate to advanced learners. The corpus is the result of a collaborative project in which several academic teams internationally participated. It contains over 2 million words of EFL writing from 11 categories of learners: Bulgarian, Czech, Dutch, Finnish, French, German, Italian, Polish, Russian, Spanish and Swedish.[19] In the CD-ROM, each subcorpus is also fully documented. There is also a search interface allowing researchers to compile their own tailor-made corpora on the basis of a set of predefined attributes relating to the learner or the task. The accompanying handbook contains a full description of the corpora as well as an overview of the ELT situation in the countries of origin of the learners[20] (Granger et al., in press).

   Apart from large learner corpora such as *ICLE,* there is also great value in collecting smaller in-house corpora. It is now becoming progressively easier for teachers to collect their own pupils' work on diskette or via email. This material can either be used for form-focused instruction or for the type of work suggested by Seidlhofer (this volume).

8.2 Corpus analysis

Computer learner corpora are a very rich type of resource which lends itself to a wide range of analyses. In what follows, I discuss three avenues for future research which seem particularly promising. First, we need more research based on linguistically annotated learner corpora and more studies like de Haan (2000), de Mönnink (2000) and de Mönnink & Meunier (2001) which check the success rate of linguistic annotation software when applied to learner corpora. Insertion of linguistic annotation will allow researchers to depart from the essentially word-based type of research that dominates the CLC field today and to reach the neglected domains of syntax and discourse. Secondly, there is a need for more longitudinal studies. The fact that students are increasingly submitting their written work in electronic form and are making increased use of email should make the compilation of such corpora much easier than in the past. Thirdly, quantitative product-oriented studies should be supplemented with more qualitative process-oriented studies such as Flowerdew's (2000) computer-assisted analysis of learner diaries which aims to identify students' attitudes towards language learning.

8.3 Interdisciplinarity

There is a need for diversification in the type of people doing CLC research. As noted by Hasselgard (1999), learner corpus research has so far mainly been conducted by corpus linguists rather than by SLA specialists: "A question that remains unanswered is whether corpus linguistics and SLA have really met in learner corpus research. While learner language corpus research does not seem to be very controversial in relation to traditional corpus linguistics, some potential conflicts are not resolved, nor commented on by anyone from 'the other side'". For learner corpus research to realise its enormous potential, cooperative involvement on the part of SLA, ELT and NLP researchers would seem to be essential. Only in this way will it be possible to ensure that the research, and especially its applications, are in keeping with current SLA theory and ELT practice and that useful electronic tools geared to learner input are developed.

   With more and better learner corpora and truly interdisciplinary research teams, there is no doubt that learner corpus research has the potential radically to improve knowledge about learner language and language learning.

Notes

1. "Registers should be distinguished from 'dialects'. Registers are defined according to their situations of use (taking into consideration their purpose, topic, setting, interactiveness, mode, etc.). In contrast, dialects are defined by their association with different speaker groups (e.g. speakers living in a particular region or speakers belonging to a particular social group) (Biber et al. 1998: 135).

2. "A corpus is a collection of pieces of language that are selected and ordered according to explicit linguistic criteria in order to be used as a sample of the language. [...] A computer corpus is a corpus which is encoded in a standardised and homogeneous way for open-ended retrieval tasks. Its constituent pieces of language are documented as to their origin and provenance" (Sinclair 1996)

3. Sinclair (1996) was aware of the difficulty of drawing the line between what is authentic and what is experimental. His suggestion was that major intervention by the linguist, or the creation of special scenarios, be recorded in the name of the corpus by giving it the label of 'experimental corpus'. Speech corpora, for instance, are often experimental: they may be "very small and be the product of asking subjects to read out strange messages in anechoic chambers".

4. The demarcation line with EOL is sometimes very fuzzy and comparisons between EOL and ESL/EFL are potentially very interesting. Indeed, linguists such as Sridhar & Sridhar (1986) have argued for a rapprochement between the two fields but to my knowledge this has not yet led to any concrete studies.

5. *LINDSEI* stands for *Louvain International Database of Spoken English Interlanguage*. Further information on the corpus can be found on the following website: http://www.fltr.ucl.ac .be/fltr/germ/etan/cecl/Cecl-Projects/Lindsei/lindsei.htm

6. For a comprehensive survey of currently available English corpora, see Kennedy (1998).

7. As English is increasingly being used as an international language by non-native speakers to communicate with other non-native speakers, Widdowson (1997) and others have argued against modelling learner language on native speaker norms. Although there is certainly validity in this argument, it is currently impossible to use this international variety of English as a norm since it has not been described yet. This situation may change in future, as corpora of English as an International Language (EIL) or English as a Lingua Franca (ELF) are being compiled (see Seidlhofer 2000).

8. The proportion of sentence-initial connectors is 80.5% in English and 56.5% in French. For medial position the proportions are 17.5% and 42% respectively.

9. For more information on WordSmith Tools, consult Mike Scott's website:http://www.liv .ac.uk/~ms2928/index.htm

10. For more information on the *Tree Editor,* contact tosca@let.kun.nl

11. *CLAWS* is available from http:// www.comp.lancs.ac.uk/computing/research/ucrel/claws/

12. For a description of the Louvain error tagging system, see Dagneaux et al. (1998). A different error tagging system for English has been developed by Milton & Chowdury (1994). The Louvain error tagging system has also been adapted for French (see Granger et al. 2001).

13. To get a copy of *UCLEE (Université Catholique de Louvain Error Editor)*, contact granger@lige.ucl.ac.be.

14. This situation may soon change. The wealth of frequency information contained in the *Longman Grammar of Spoken and Written English* (Biber et al. 1999) could result in more importance being attached to the frequency of grammatical phenomena in EFL grammars.

15. Indeed, in English-to-French translation it is quite usual to expand an English prepositional modifier, for instance, into a full relative clause, as illustrated by the following examples borrowed from Chuquet & Paillard (1987:15): I picked up a magazine from the stack on the table > Je pris un magazine dans la pile qui se trouvait sur la table.

16. More information on WordPilot can be found in Milton 1998 and on the following website: http://home.ust.hk/~autolang/download_WP.htm

17. For more information, consult the following website: http://www.telenex.hku.hk/telec/

18. A comprehensive learner corpus bibliography is available from the following website: http://www.fltr.ucl.ac.be/FLTR/GERM/ETAN/CECL/cecl.htm

19. Other learner corpora (Brazilian, Chinese, Japanese, Norwegian) are being compiled and will be made available in subsequent versions of the CD-ROM.

20. More information on ICLE can be found on the following website: http://www.fltr.ucl.ac .be/fltr/germ/etan/cecl/Cecl-Projects/Icle/icle.htm

References

Aarts J., & Granger, S. (1998). Tag sequences in learner corpora: a key to interlanguage grammar and discourse. In S. Granger (Ed.), *Learner English on Computer* (pp. 132–141).

Anthone, A. (1996). *Patterns of French/English Conjunct Use in Original and Translated Journalese*. Université Catholique de Louvain: unpublished MA dissertation.

Atkins, S., & Clear, J. (1992). Corpus design criteria. *Literary and Linguistic Computing, 7*(1), 1–16.

Biber, D. (1988). *Variation Across Speech and Writing*. Cambridge: Cambridge University Press.

Biber, D., Conrad, S., & Reppen, R. (1998). *Corpus Linguistics. Investigating Language and Structure and Use*. Cambridge: Cambridge University Press.

Biber, D., Conrad, S., & Reppen, R. (1994). Corpus-based approaches to issues in applied linguistics. *Applied Linguistics, 15*(2), 169–189.

Biber, D., Johansson, S., Leech, G., Conrad, S., & Finegan, E. (1999). *Longman Grammar of Spoken and Written English*. Harlow: Longman.

Chuquet, H., & Paillard, M. (1987). *Approches linguistiques des problèmes de traduction anglais><français*. Paris: Ophrys.

Dagneaux, E., Denness, S., & Granger, S. (1998). Computer-aided error analysis. *System. An International Journal of Educational Technology and Applied Linguistics, 26*(2), 163–174.

Ellis, R. (1994). *The Study of Second Language Acquisition*. Oxford: Oxford University Press.

Flowerdew, J. (2000). Computer-assisted analysis of language learner diaries: a qualitative application of word frequency and concordancing software. Proceedings of the *4th International Conference on Teaching and Language Corpora- TALC 2000*, Graz, 19–23, July 2000, 27.

Granger, S. (1994). The learner corpus: a revolution in applied linguistics. *English Today, 39*(10/3), 25–29.

Granger, S. (1997). Automated retrieval of passives from native and learner corpora: precision and recall. *Journal of English Linguistics, 25*(4), 365–374.

Granger, S. (Ed.). (1998). *Learner English on Computer*. London and New York: Addison Wesley Longman.

Granger, S. (1999). Use of tenses by advanced EFL learners: evidence from an error-tagged computer corpus. In H. Hasselgard & S. Oksefjell (Eds.), *Out of Corpora. Studies in Honour of Stig Johansson* (pp. 191–202). Amsterdam & Atlanta: Rodopi.

Granger, S., Dagneaux, E., & Meunier, F. (in press). International Corpus of Learner English. CD-ROM & Handbook. Louvain-la-Neuve: Presses universitaires de Louvain.

Granger, S., & Rayson, P. (1998). Automatic profiling of learner texts. In S. Granger (Ed.), *Learner English on Computer* (pp. 119–131).

Granger, S., & Tribble, C. (1998). Learner corpus data in the foreign language classroom: form-focused instruction and data-driven learning. In S. Granger (Ed.), *Learner English on Computer* (pp. 119–131).

Granger, S., & Tyson, S. (1996). Connector usage in the English essay writing of native and non-native EFL speakers of English. *World Englishes, 15*, 19–29.

Granger, S., Vandeventer, A., & Hamel, M.-J. (2001). Analyse de corpus d'apprenants pour l'ELAO basé sur le TAL. *Linguistique de Corpus*. Special issue of *Traitement automatique des langues, 42*(2), 609–621.

Granger, S., & Wynne, M. (1999). Optimising measures of lexical variation in EFL learner corpora. In J. Kirk (Ed.), *Corpora Galore* (pp. 249–257). Amsterdam & Atlanta: Rodopi.

de Haan, P. (1998). English writing by Dutch-speaking students. In H. Hasselgard & S. Oksefjell (Eds.), *Out of Corpora*, (pp. 203–212). Amsterdam & Atlanta: Rodopi.

de Haan, P. (2000). Tagging non-native English with the TOSCA-ICLE tagger. In C. Mair & M. Hundt (Eds.), *Corpus Linguistics and Linguistic Theory* (pp. 69–79). Amsterdam & Atlanta: Rodopi.

Hasselgard, H. (1999). Review of S. Granger (Ed.) Learner English on Computer. *ICAME Journal, 23*, 148–152.

James, C. (1998). *Errors in Language Learning and Use. Exploring Error Analysis*. London & New York: Longman.

Johns, T. (1991). Should you be persuaded – two examples of data-driven learning materials. *English Language Research Journal, 4*, 1–16.

Johns, T. (1994). From printout to handout: grammar and vocabulary teaching in the context of data-driven learning. In T. Odlin (Ed.), *Perspectives on Pedagogical Grammar* (pp. 293–317). Cambridge: Cambridge University Press.

Kennedy, G. (1998). *An Introduction to Corpus Linguistics*. London & New York: Addison Wesley Longman.

Leech, G. (1992). Corpora and theories of linguistic performance. In J. Svartvik (Ed.), *Directions in Corpus Linguistics* (pp. 105–122). Berlin: Mouton de Gruyter.

Leech, G. (1993). Corpus annotation schemes. *Literary and Linguistic Computing, 8*(4), 275–281.

Leech, G. (1998). Learner corpora: what they are and what can be done with them. In S. Granger (Ed.), *Learner English on Computer* (pp. xiv–xx).

Longman Essential Activator. (1997). Addison Wesley Longman.

Lorenz, G. (1999). *Adjective Intensification – Learners vs Native Speakers. A Corpus Study of Argumentative Writing.* Amsterdam & Atlanta: Rodopi.

Mark, K. L. (1998). The significance of learner corpus data in relation to the problems of language teaching. *Bulletin of General Education, 312,* 77–90.

Massart, D. (1998). The Use of Phrasal Verbs by EFL Learners. A Cross-linguistic Approach. Université Catholique de Louvain. Unpublished MA dissertation.

McEnery, T., & Wilson, A. (1996). *Corpus Linguistics.* Edinburgh: Edinburgh University Press.

Menzel, W., Atwell, E., Bonaventura, P., Herron, D., Howarth, P., Morton, R. & Souter, C. (2000). The ISLE corpus of non-native spoken English. *Proceedings of the Second International Conference on Language Resources and Evaluation,* 31 May-2 June 2000, Athens.

Meunier, F. (1998). Computer tools for interlanguage analysis: a critical approach. In S. Granger (Ed.), *Learner English on Computer* (pp. 19–37).

Meunier, F. (2000). *A computer corpus linguistics approach to interlanguage grammar: noun phrase complexity in advanced learner writing.* Unpublished PhD thesis. Université Catholique de Louvain, Louvain-la-Neuve. Centre for English Corpus Linguistics.

Milton, J. (1998a). Exploiting L1 and interlanguage corpora in the design of an electronic language learning and production environment. In S. Granger (Ed.), *Learner English on Computer* (pp. 186–198).

Milton, J. (1998b). WORDPILOT: enabling learners to navigate lexical universes. In S. Granger & J. Hung (Eds.), *Proceedings of the International Symposium on Computer Learner Corpora, Second Language Acquisition and Foreign Language Teaching* (pp. 97–98). The Chinese University of Hong Kong.

Milton, J., & Chowdury, N. (1994). Tagging the interlanguage of Chinese learners of English. In L. Flowerdew & K. K. Tong (Eds.), *Entering Text* (pp. 127–143). Hong Kong: The Hong Kong University of Science and Technology.

de Mönnink, I. (2000). Parsing a learner corpus? In C. Mair & M. Hundt (Eds.), *Corpus Linguistics and Linguistic Theory* (pp. 81–90). Amsterdam & Atlanta: Rodopi.

de Mönnink, I., & Meunier, F. (2001). Assessing the success rate of EFL learner corpus tagging. In S. De Cock, G. Gilquin, S. Granger & S. Petch-Tyson (Eds.), *Proceedings of the 22nd International Computer Archive of Modern and Medieval English Conference, ICAME 2001: Future Challenges for Corpus Linguistics* (pp. 59–60). Centre for English Corpus Linguistics, Université catholique de Louvain.

Murison-Bowie, S. (1996). Linguistic corpora and language teaching. *Annual Review of Applied Linguistics, 16,* 182–199.

Rundell, M., & Stock, P. (1992). The corpus revolution. *English Today, 30,* 9–14.

Scott, M. (1996). *WordSmith Tools.* Oxford: Oxford University Press: http://oup.com/elt/global/isbn/6890

Seidlhofer, B. (2000). Towards the teaching of lingua franca English: The Vienna ELF Corpus. Paper presented at the 4th International Conference on Teaching and Language Corpora (TALC 2000), Graz, 19–23 July, 2000.

Sinclair, J. (1996). *EAGLES. Preliminary recommendations on Corpus Typology.* http://www.ilc.pi.it/EAGLES96/corpustyp/corpustyp.html

Sökmen, A. J. (1997). Current trends in teaching second language vocabulary. In N. Schmidt & M. McCarthy (Eds.), *Vocabulary. Description, Acquisition and Pedagogy* (pp. 237–257). Cambridge: Cambridge University Press.

Spence, R. (1998). A corpus of student L1–L2 translations. In S. Granger & J. Hung (Eds.), *Proceedings of the International Symposium on Computer Learner Corpora, Second Language Acquisition and Foreign Language Teaching* (pp. 110–112). Hong-Kong: The Chinese University of Hong Kong.

Sridhar, K. K., & Sridhar, S. N. (1986). Bridging the Gap: Second Language Acquisition Theory and Indigenized Varieties of English. *World Englishes, 5*(1), 3–14.

Stubbs, M. (1996). *Text and Corpus Analysis.* Oxford: Blackwell.

Widdowson, H. G. (1991). The description and prescription of language. In J. E. Alatis (Ed.), *Georgetown University Round Table on Language and Linguistics. Language, Communication and Social Meaning.* Washington DC: Georgetown University Press.

Widdowson, H. G. (1997). EIL, ESL, EFL: global issues and local interests. *World Englishes, 16*(1), 135–146.

II. Corpus-based approaches to interlanguage

Using bilingual corpus evidence in learner corpus research

Bengt Altenberg
University of Lund, Sweden

Chapter overview

In this chapter, Altenberg sets out to demonstrate the value of combining bilingual and learner corpus analysis techniques in providing empirical evidence of L1 transfer in advanced L2 writing. This study is a follow-up to a comparative study of the use of *make* in native English and advanced French and Swedish L2 writing which identified differences in the use of *make* in the native and learner groups and also in the two different learner groups. Using an aligned Swedish-English bilingual corpus, Altenberg carries out comparisons of original-version and translated written Swedish and English to test the hypothesis that overuse of causative *make* with adjective complements by Swedish L2 writers is due to L1 transfer. The data provides support for this hypothesis: Altenberg finds that the overuse is brought about by an overgeneralisation of the cross-linguistic similarity between *make* and *göra*, the most common unmarked equivalent of *make* in Swedish.

1. Learner and bilingual corpora

This chapter aims to show the relationship between bilingual and interlanguage corpus research and in particular to highlight the explanatory power of bilingual corpora in assessing the role of transfer in interlanguage (IL) data.

Opinions as to the role of transfer in second language acquisition have fluctuated wildly over the years: from being initially considered as the single most important factor influencing learner output, it was then for a time considered to play a negligible role and today transfer is again widely acknowledged as one of a number of key factors in interlanguage. The phenomenon itself is now better understood. Kellerman (1978), for instance, has shown that transfer is affected by the learner's perception of the similarity between L1 and L2 structures and the degree of markedness of the L1 structures. These useful general principles are, however, not sufficient when it comes to interpreting a given interlanguage feature. In order to decide whether a feature of the learner's L2 is due to intralingual or interlingual factors, the analyst needs to have a precise idea of how the feature functions – if indeed it exists at all – in the learner's L1. As demonstrated by Kamimoto et al (1992), vague or faulty knowledge of the learners' L1 may lead the analyst to make invalid interpretations. More particularly, the authors show that contrastive data can lead to a reinterpretation of Schachter's influential 1974 paper, in which she attributes underuse of relative clause structures by Chinese learners to avoidance strategies. But given the much lower frequency of relative clauses in Chinese than in English, Kamimoto et al demonstrate that the underuse of these structures is more likely to be due to transfer of the frequency of relative clauses in the learners' L1. In fact, reliable interpretations of interlanguage features require thorough knowledge of the three 'languages' involved: the learner's interlanguage, his/her mother tongue and the target language. The means to carry out three-pronged investigations of this nature now exist, with the availability of large electronic corpora. For interlanguage investigations, there are learner corpora, containing learners' written or spoken output data. For mother tongue and target language descriptions there are monolingual corpora and bilingual corpora, which can be subdivided into comparable corpora containing similar texts in the native and target language and translation corpora, which contain texts in the original and translated versions.

Bilingual corpora can be used by the SLA specialist to interpret or predict interlanguage features. Kamimoto et al's article highlights the interpretative role of contrastive analysis (CA) data: the interlanguage analysis comes first; the contrastive analysis is used at a second stage to help interpret the IL data. It is also possible to start from CA, i.e. investigate a given language feature in a bilingual corpus and check the results against a learner corpus to see whether the learners' output shows evidence of transfer from their L1.

There is another interesting link between bilingual and learner corpus research. The two types of data can both be seen as involving an 'interlingua'. Both translated language and interlanguage can be considered as 'languages in between', situated somewhere between L1 (source language/mother tongue) and L2 (target language). Interestingly, the two interlinguae often turn out to have similar features, even when the translated texts have been translated by a native speaker of the target language, a claim supported by Schmied (1996: 48), who comments: "It is important to note that these processes occur not only in translations *from* the mother tongue but even *into* the mother tongue, so that native speakers (not only language learners) do not hit the 'natural' proportion of features. (...) Since translations into the mother tongue can obviously be influenced by L2 source texts, particularly at the level of the norm, we can see an obvious connection with interlanguage studies in general." In studies investigating particular features of translated and learner language which reveal similarities, the transfer interpretation of the IL features is reinforced, as demonstrated by the research into causative structures reported on in this chapter.

2. Background

In a recent study of the lexical and grammatical patterning of high-frequency verbs in the *International Corpus of Learner English*, Altenberg and Granger (2001) found that advanced French-speaking and Swedish EFL learners used the verb *make* differently from native American students.[1] While both learner groups underused (and misused) 'delexical' *make* (e.g. *make a decision, make a point*), clear differences emerged in their treatment of causative *make* (e.g. *make sb happy, make sb believe sth*). As shown in Table 1, the French-speaking learners significantly underused causative *make* with adjective and noun complements (e.g. *make sth possible, make sb a star*), whereas the Swedish learners revealed an equally significant overuse of causative *make* with adjective and verb complements (e.g. *make sth easier, make sb understand*).[2]

Another interesting finding was that the learners' treatment of causative *make* seldom resulted in clear errors but in a number of rather clumsy constructions, suggesting that the learners tended to opt for a semantically and grammatically 'decomposed' *make* + Object + Complement pattern in cases

Table 1. Causative uses of *make* by EFL and native American students

Complement	FR	SW	US
Adjective	98*	179*	130
Verb	67	125*	80
Noun	10*	23	26
Total	174*	327*	236

where a native writer might prefer a 'synthetic' causative verb alternative (e.g. *make the air polluted* instead of *pollute the air*):

1. The use of the plastic wrap not only increases the garbage mountain, it also <u>makes</u> the air <u>polluted</u> ... (*pollutes the air*)
2. Technology will never <u>make</u> imagination and dreams <u>unnecessary</u> ... (*replace*)
3. I love the way the differences between men and women are blurred, or even <u>made</u> <u>non-existing</u>. (*eliminated*)

The question that will be explored here is: how can the Swedish learners' overuse of causative *make* be explained? Two possible reasons suggest themselves: overgeneralization of the main English target pattern (intralingual influence) and transfer from Swedish (interlingual influence) (see Ellis 1994: 305). The intralingual explanation does not seem highly plausible, however, given that the Swedish and French-speaking learners display fundamentally different tendencies. If intralingual influence was the main conditioning factor, both learner groups could be expected to behave in the same way. This leaves interlingual influence, i.e. transfer from L1, as a potentially more fruitful hypothesis to explore.

3.   Causatives in English and Swedish

The suspicion that the Swedish learners' overuse of causative *make* may be the result of transfer from Swedish is intuitively supported by the similarity between the basic causative constructions in the two languages. As shown in Table 2, English causatives with *make* can be divided into three main 'analytical' types – as I will call them – depending on whether the complement following the object is an adjective phrase (Type A), an infinitive clause (Type B) or a noun phrase (Type C). Swedish has corresponding constructions with the verbs *göra* (Types A and C) and *få* (Type B).

Semantically and syntactically the constructions are very similar in the two languages. They are all 'complex-transitive' structures (cf. Quirk et al. 1985: 1195) in which the 'raised' object and the complement are notionally equivalent to the subject and predication of an underlying clause which expresses the result of the causative event (cf. also Juffs 1996 and Song 1996). The differences are relatively superficial: English has one prototypical causative verb, Swedish has two; the English B construction has a bare infinitive, the

Table 2. Main causative constructions in English and Swedish

	English	Swedish
Type A	*make* + Object + Adjective phrase: *She made him happy*	*göra* + Object + Adjective phrase: *Hon gjorde honom lycklig*
Type B	*make* + Object + Infinitive: *He made her laugh*	*få* + Object + Infinitive: *Han fick henne att skratta*
Type C	*make* + Object + Noun phrase: *They made it their home*	*göra* + Object + Prep. phrase: *De gjorde det till sitt hem*

Swedish infinitive is preceded by the marker *att* 'to'; the complement of the C construction is a noun phrase in English but a prepositional phrase in Swedish.

Apart from these analytical constructions, both languages have various other ways of expressing causative relations. For example, in English there are many synthetic causative verbs in which the resulting state or event is fused with the causative meaning of *make* into a single verb form: *make sth simple = simplify sth, make sth modern = modernise sth*. In addition, analytical causative relations can be expressed by verbs other than *make*, such as *cause, force, get, have* and *let*. Moreover, cause-effect relations can be expressed by conjunctions (e.g. *because*), by adverbial expressions (e.g. *because of* NP), by verbs (e.g. *result in*) and in a number of other ways. The same applies to Swedish.

Although both languages have various resources to express causative relations, it is reasonable to describe the analytical patterns as the basic or prototypical causative constructions in the two languages. Since there is a striking cross-linguistic parallelism between these constructions, it is natural to assume that the Swedish learners might be tempted to use the semantically and grammatically 'decomposed' *make* + NP + Complement pattern even in cases where a native writer would prefer a synthetic alternative (cf. such pairs as *make sb afraid – frighten sb, make sth bigger – increase sth, make sth easy/easier – facilitate sth*).

However, in the absence of a good contrastive description of causative constructions in English and Swedish this can only be a hypothesis. Our knowledge of the relative frequency of the various alternatives and of the 'prototypicality' of the analytical constructions in the two languages is very limited, and almost nothing is known about the degree of correspondence of the different alternatives across the two languages. The purpose of this study, therefore, is to find out something about this and thereby confirm or disconfirm the intuitive interlingual hypothesis relating to the Swedish learners' overuse of causative *make*-constructions. What follows is a contrastive examination of the main causative options available in English and Swedish and their distribution in a parallel corpus of English and Swedish texts, intended to complement the initial learner study.

4. Aim and material

For reasons of space, I will concentrate entirely on the A construction, the most frequent of the causative types in the learner corpus. The following questions will be explored:

- How 'central' are the analytical A constructions in the two languages?
- To what extent are the A constructions retained in translations between the two languages?
- Which are the main causative alternatives and how often are they used?
- How can contrastive data help to explain the Swedish learners' overuse of English A constructions?

The material used for the study consists of texts from the English-Swedish Parallel Corpus (see Aijmer et al. 1996). The corpus contains English text samples and their translations into Swedish and Swedish text samples and their translations into English. Each sample contains between 10,000–15,000 words of writing, and both fiction and non-fiction texts are represented. The original texts from the two languages have been matched as far as possible in terms of text type, purpose and register and the material therefore combines the advantages of a comparable corpus and a translation corpus. The original texts and the translations have been aligned at sentence level by means of the *Translation Corpus Aligner* (see Hofland & Johansson 1998). The aligned texts are stored in a database which can be searched by the *Translation Corpus Explorer* (see Ebeling 1998).

When the study was carried out, the corpus comprised 37 English text samples and their translations into Swedish and 31 Swedish text samples and their translations into English, as shown in Table 3. Since the text samples from the

Table 3. Material from the English-Swedish Parallel Corpus

Direction	Text samples			No. of
	Fiction	Non-fiction	Total	words
Eng. original → Swe. translation	20	17	37	992,000
Swe. original → Eng. translation	17	14	31	763,000

two languages are unevenly distributed, only relative frequencies will be used in the following comparison.

5. Method

The composition of the corpus makes it possible to compare the languages in several ways (cf. Aijmer et al. 1996):

a. *Source texts ↔ source texts.* By comparing the use of the A constructions in the original English and Swedish texts we can get an indication of their frequency and relative importance in each language.

b. *Source texts → translations.* Using the original texts as a starting-point and comparing them with the corresponding translations into the other language, we can find out how causative English *make* is translated into Swedish and how causative Swedish *göra* is translated into English. This will give us an indication of the main translation equivalents used to render the A constructions in each language and the relative importance of these equivalents.

c. *Translations → source texts.* Using the translations as a starting-point and comparing them with the corresponding source texts in the other language, we can find out which Swedish source constructions have ended up as causative *make*-constructions in the English translations and which English source constructions have ended up as causative *göra*-constructions in the Swedish translations. This 're-verse' approach will give an indication of the range of source constructions that have been used as a point of departure for the A constructions in the target language. Studying the translations in this direction will be a useful supplement to approach (b) and serve as a check on possible translation effects (cf. M. Johansson 1996:132 and S. Johansson 1998).

All three types of comparison will be used in the following cross-linguistic analysis, but the emphasis will be on approaches (b) and (c).

6. Analytical constructions in source texts and translations

The relative frequencies of English *make* and Swedish *göra* used in causative A constructions in the English and Swedish source texts and translations

Table 4. Relative frequency of causative English *make* and Swedish *göra* (type A)

	make	*göra*
Source texts	31.4	36.8
Translations	37.2	48.8

are shown in Table 4. The frequencies have been normalised to tokens per 100,000 words.

A comparison of the English and Swedish source texts shows that *göra* and *make* have similar frequencies. *Göra* is slightly more frequent than *make* but the difference is not statistically significant ($\chi^2 = 1.86$). However, there is a striking difference between English and Swedish when the source and translated texts are compared in each language. In English, there are more instances of *make* in the translations but the difference is not significant ($\chi^2 = 2.24$). In Swedish, however, there is a significantly higher number of occurrences of *göra* in the translations ($\chi^2 = 6.8$). This indicates that the Swedish translators had a tendency to overuse the analytical target form when they translated an English text. Using a term from Hasselgren (1994), we can say that the analytical target forms seem to act as lexico-grammatical 'teddy bears' both in the Swedish translations and in the Swedish learners' interlanguage. The difference is that while the Swedish learners overgeneralise the analytical form in their L2, the Swedish translators do so when they translate into in their own language. Both the learner and the bilingual data therefore suggest that the analytical causative structure may be more dominant in Swedish than in English. A detailed contrastive analysis of the English and Swedish structures is necessary if we want to substantiate this impression.

7.   Swedish equivalents of *make*

Let us now examine the Swedish equivalents of the English A construction with *make* in the corpus. As mentioned, these can be established in two ways: by looking at how *make* has been translated into Swedish and by looking at the Swedish sources of *make* in the English translations. The main Swedish equivalents which emerge from this analysis are listed in Table 5.

The table shows that the most common Swedish equivalent of *make* is a congruent A construction with *göra* (48%). Hence, on the basis of its relative frequency alone, *göra* can be described as the prototypical Swedish equivalent of English *make*. *Göra* is also more common in the Swedish translations than as

Table 5. Swedish equivalents of causative *make* (type A)

Types of Swedish equivalents	Swedish translations		Swedish sources		Total	
	n	%	n	%	n	%
(a) Congruent construction with GÖRA	79	51	68	45	147	48
(b) Synthetic causative verb	26	17	33	22	59	19
(c) GÖRA + finite clause	6	4	3	2	9	3
(d) Other causative verb + NP + Adj/Vinf	3	2	4	3	7	2
(e) Various other constructions	41	26	44	29	85	28
Total	155	100	152	100	307	100

a source of English *make*. This indicates that the translators perceive *göra* as the main – or most readily retrievable – Swedish equivalent and tend to 'overuse' it as a result.

However, although a congruent construction with *göra* is the most common Swedish equivalent of *make*, it only accounts for about half of the examples in the corpus. In other words, despite the parallelism between the A constructions in the two languages, other types of Swedish equivalents are equally common. Let us look briefly at these.

The second most common Swedish equivalent (19%) is the use of a synthetic verb combining the causative notion of *make* and the meaning of the adjective in the analytical construction: *make* NP *better* = *förbättra* NP 'improve NP'. This alternative is slightly less common in the Swedish translations than as a Swedish source of *make*, which suggests that it is a less obvious equivalent and less easily 'transferred' from the source language. Some typical examples are (the number of occurrences are given in parentheses):

English version	Swedish equivalents
make clear (7)	*klargöra* (3), *visa (tydligt)* (2), *förkunna, medvetengöra*
make public (6)	*offentliggöra* (6)
make known (5)	*framföra, meddela* (2), *fastslå, förkunna*
make possible (5)	*möjliggöra* (5)
make easier (2)	*underlätta* (2)
make efficient (2)	*effektivisera* (2)
make good (2)	*uppfylla, avhjälpa*
make active	*aktivera*
make better	*förbättra*

Most of these synthetic Swedish verbs are compounds of the pattern Adjective + *göra* (e.g. *möjliggöra* 'enable', *klargöra* 'clarify') or derivations from adjectives by affixation (e.g. *förbättra* 'improve', *underlätta* 'facilitate') but some are morphologically unrelated to a Swedish adjective (e.g. *träna* 'train', *trimma* 'trim', *visa* 'show'). For most of them analytical alternatives are available in Swedish, generally with *göra* (e.g. *möjliggöra* NP = *göra* NP *möjlig*) but occasionally with some other verb (*välkomna* NP = *hälsa* NP *välkommen*, not **göra* NP *välkommen*), i.e. a synthetic causative can generally be 'decomposed' into an analytical construction in Swedish. However, the reverse process – conflating an analytical causative to a single synthetic verb – is not always possible (e.g. *göra* NP *besviken* 'make NP disappointed' →*besvika NP 'disappoint NP'). The factors determining the choice between these two variants will be considered briefly in Section 9.

Another, less common, Swedish alternative (3%) is to use *göra* followed by a finite object clause, i.e. a finite variant of the B construction, in which the 'causee' (the object of the A construction) acts as the subject of the subordinate clause and the adjective of the A construction is either preserved as a complement or changed into a verb: *make* NP *irritable* = *göra att* NP *är lättretad* 'make that NP is irritable'; *make* NP *better off* = *göra att* NP *får det bättre* 'make that NP is better off'. A congruent Swedish A equivalent is sometimes theoretically possible (e.g. *göra* NP *lättretad*), but the finite construction is necessary when a contextually appropriate adjective is lacking in Swedish (e.g. *make* NP *better off* →?*göra* NP *rikare/mera välmående*).

Yet another alternative, also relatively uncommon, is to use a causative verb other than *göra* (2%): *make* NP *sore* = *nöta* NP *sårig* 'wear NP sore'; *make* NP *welcome* = *hälsa* NP *välkommen* 'greet NP welcome'. In these cases the verb is either a lexically more specific causative allowing a syntactically congruent construction (e.g. *nöta* 'wear thin', *hälsa* 'greet') or the general causative verb *få* 'get', which is commonly used in type B causatives (see Table 2) but sometimes occurs with an adjective complement when the result (rather than the cause) is emphasised and some degree of effort is implied. Other verbs are *låta* 'let' and – where no corresponding Swedish adjective is available and the cause is inanimate – the general causative verb *komma*, both governing a non-finite clause (type B).

In addition to these types of Swedish constructions, which all make use of a causative verb of some kind, the corpus also reveals a wide range of other Swedish alternatives (28%) in which the causative construction is syntactically (and sometimes lexically) reorganised in some way.

8. English equivalents of Swedish *göra*

Reversing the perspective, let us now look at the English equivalents of the Swedish A construction with *göra*. The main types are shown in Table 6.

Table 6. English equivalents of causative Swedish *göra* (type A)

Types of English equivalents	English translations		English sources		Total	
	n	%	n	%	n	%
(a) Congruent construction with MAKE	68	51	77	32	145	39
(b) Synthetic causative verb	29	22	59	25	88	24
(c) Other causative verb + NP + Adj	3	2	11	5	14	4
(d) Causative verb + NP + Vinf (type B)	8	6	5	2	13	3
(e) Various other constructions	26	19	86	36	112	30
Total	134	100	238	100	372	100

The most common English equivalent is a congruent A construction with *make* (39%). Hence, *make* can indeed be described as the main equivalent of Swedish *göra*, which confirms the picture of *make* and *göra* as mutually corresponding causative verbs. However, the frequency of *make* as an equivalent of *göra* in the English texts is lower than that of *göra* as an equivalent of *make* in the Swedish texts (cf. Table 5). The proportion is especially low in the English source texts (32%). The fact that other variants account for no less than 78% of the sources of Swedish *göra* suggests that *make* has greater competition from other causative alternatives in English than *göra* has in Swedish and again that *make* is a less dominant type A causative in English than *göra* is in Swedish.

The second most common English alternative turns out to be the use of a synthetic verb (24%). In both the translations and the source texts this alternative is more frequent than the corresponding variant is in the Swedish texts, suggesting that it is a more viable alternative to *make* in English than to *göra* in Swedish. The frequency of synthetic verbs is also slightly higher as a source than as a translation of *göra*, which confirms this picture: the Swedish translators cannot always find a corresponding synthetic equivalent and have to resort to analytical alternatives, as in the examples below:

Swedish version	English equivalents
göra NP *illa* (9)	*hurt* NP (9)
göra möjlig (7)	*enable* (3), *allow, let, permit, liberate*
göra gällande (6)	*claim* (3), *argue, show up, imply*
göra ren (4)	*clean* (4)

göra upprörd (4)	*upset* (3), *stir up*
göra generad (3)	*embarrass* (3)
göra förvånad (2)	*surprise* (2)
göra orolig(are) (2)	*unsettle, alarm*
göra rik(are) (2)	*enrich* (2)

Other less common English alternatives involve either (a) using grammatically congruent constructions with another causative verb (4%), examples 1–3 below, (b) switching from the A construction to the B construction, i.e. the adjective complement of the Swedish A construction is represented by an infinitive clause in the English version (3%), examples 4–6 below, and (c) a wide range of other alternatives that together account for 30% of all cases.

1.	*göra* NP *galen* (2)	*drive* NP *crazy, mad*
2.	*göra sig hörd*	*have one's voice heard*
3.	*göra* NP *gul*	*turn* NP *yellow*
4.	*göra* NP *bättre till mods*	*make* NP *feel better*
5.	*göra klart för* NP *att*	*let* NP *know that*
6.	*göra* NP *löjlig*	*make* NP *look foolish*

9. Causative options and choices

As this contrastive survey has demonstrated, English and Swedish have a similar range of resources for expressing causative relations. In both the English and Swedish texts the dominant type is the analytical A construction, with *make* as a 'periphrastic' causative verb in English and *göra* in Swedish. On the whole, this construction accounts for a little less than 50% of the examples in the corpus, a proportion that is generally lower in the source texts than in the translations. Despite competition from a number of other causative options in both languages, these dominant types are often translated into each other: a calculation of their mutual 'translatability' in the corpus shows a cross-linguistic correspondence of 55% (on this concept, see Altenberg 1999). These values may seem moderate, but to judge from the consistently higher proportion of A constructions in the translations, they are obviously perceived as the prototypical or unmarked translation equivalents in both languages.

Both languages also offer a similar range of causative alternatives to the basic A construction, such as

- synthetic verbs
- other causative verbs
- miscellaneous other constructions

Generally, the 'miscellaneous' category is the most common of these alternatives in both languages, especially in the source texts. The use of synthetic verbs is slightly more frequent in the English texts than in the Swedish texts. Other causative verbs are comparatively rare. In addition, each language offers some language-specific variants, but they are not very common and their structural deviation from the main alternatives is rather superficial.

In both languages, the choice between the various causative alternatives is determined by a variety of factors – lexical, grammatical, stylistic and textual. Generally speaking, the A construction is the 'unmarked' variant in both languages: it is not only the most frequent alternative, it is also the lexically most general, semantically most transparent, grammatically most versatile, and stylistically most neutral. One of its grammatical advantages over synthetic verbs is precisely its 'decomposed' character: when the result of the causative event is encoded separately as an adjective it is easier to modify and elaborate, e.g. by means of the comparative form, by a modifier, by coordination, or by a combination of these possibilities:

(5)   What <u>makes</u> Sweden <u>so special</u> and Swedes <u>so very Swedish</u>? (JPM p 40)   Vad är det som <u>gör</u> Sverige <u>så</u> <u>väldigt speciellt</u> och svenskarna <u>så</u> <u>väldigt svenska</u>?

(6)   Varför hade man förresten lagt ner så mycket arbete på att <u>göra</u> husets första våning <u>så stor och elegant</u>, och lämnat allt som det var i övervåningen? (LG p 32)   And why had they put in so much work to <u>make</u> the ground floor <u>so</u> <u>grand and elegant</u> and left everything as it was on the upper floor?

As a result, translations using synthetic verbs are rare in both languages when the source is an A construction with an 'elaborated' adjective complement, as can be seen in Table 7.

The A construction is also more common in translations when the causee is an extraposed clause (e.g. *make it possible/easier to* ...), since a synthetic verb requires a conversion of the clause into a noun phrase (e.g. *facilitate sth*), which may not always be possible in the context. This tendency is noticeable in the translations in both directions.

While the A construction is often the unmarked choice in both languages, the synthetic option is more restricted. In many cases no synthetic verb is

Table 7. Translations of analytical constructions with an 'elaborated' adjective complement

Type of elaboration	Swedish translations		English translations	
	Congruent	Synthetic verb	Congruent	Synthetic verb
Comparative	21	1	9	0
Modification	8	1	5	1
Coordination	4	1	6	0
Combinations	6	0	9	0
Total elaborated	39	3	29	1
% elaborated	49	12	43	3
Total	79	26	68	29

available in either language (cf. Eng. *he happied her, Sw. *han besvek henne) and when there is one, it is often more specific in meaning (cf. Sw. *aktivera – göra aktiv*, Eng. *enrich – make rich*) or more formal (cf. Sw. *möjliggöra – göra möjlig*, Eng. *legalize – make legal*) than the analytical alternative. However, in many cases the synthetic variant is the most natural choice (cf *surprise – make surprised, persuade – ?make persuaded*) or even the only possibility (e.g. *disinherit – *make disinherited/inheritanceless*). English in particular has a wide range of synthetic causative verbs that are normally preferred to their analytical counterparts, both in the English source texts (e.g. *astonish, disappoint, surprise, puzzle, upset, worry*) and in the English translations of analytical Swedish counterparts (e.g. *göra illa → hurt, göra ren → clean, göra generad → embarrass*). Hence, the choice between the analytical and synthetic constructions is determined by such factors as availability, currency and appropriateness.

The selection of other causative alternatives is determined by similar factors. In both languages the choice is sometimes collocationally restricted (e.g. *drive* NP *crazy* rather than *make* NP *crazy, hälsa* NP *välkommen* rather than **göra NP välkommen*) or subject to other selection restrictions (e.g. Swedish *komma* which typically requires a nonpersonal or 'non-controlling' subject). Other constructions are textually useful because they allow the order of the causative elements to be reversed for end-weight or end-focus, or because they emphasise the result or leave the cause unspecified. Nominalising the result can offer other advantages, such as more convenient quantification or modification.

There are thus many reasons for selecting one causative variant rather than another. It has only been possible to touch on these briefly here, but it is obvious that corpus-based contrastive studies can do a great deal to uncover and clarify the many conditioning factors involved in the choice of causative construction in different languages. This exercise is of great linguistic as well as pedagogical value and will be an important task for future research.

10. Combining bilingual and learner data

The main conclusion that can be drawn from this contrastive study is that, on the whole, English and Swedish have a very similar range of causative options. In both languages, the dominant choice is the analytical construction with equivalent high-frequency verbs (*make* and *göra*), but there are also a number of competing alternatives – synthetic verbs, other causative verbs and grammatically 'reorganised' causatives – all of which tend to be lexically, grammatically or stylistically restricted and therefore more difficult for learners. In spite of these similarities, the study reveals that periphrastic causative structures with *göra* are more dominant than corresponding structures with *make* in English, which face greater competition from alternative causative expressions, notably synthetic verbs.

Learners' overuse of a target structure can be explained as being the result of overgeneralisation of an L2 pattern (intralingual influence) or the result of transfer from L1 (interlingual influence). As we have seen, the analytical construction can be regarded as the 'unmarked' causative in English. It is therefore reasonable to assume that learners – even advanced learners – will tend to overgeneralise this construction at the expense of more 'marked' alternatives. The problem with this explanation is that French-speaking learners do not overuse this construction in their L2 writing, as would be expected if intralingual influence had been the decisive factor. Consequently, we have to turn to transfer as a more plausible explanation.

Transfer can also be linked to the notion of markedness. As we have seen, the analytical construction can also be regarded as the unmarked form in Swedish. According to Hyltenstam (1984:43), learners are likely to substitute unmarked categories from their native language for corresponding marked categories in the target language, whereas marked structures are seldom transferred, especially when the corresponding target category is unmarked. This prediction is clearly applicable to the Swedish learners' overuse of the analytical construction in English. Chinese ESL learners provide another illustration of this tendency. Chinese, being poor in derivational morphology, has no synthetic causative verbs. As a result, Chinese learners tend to transfer the analytical Chinese *shi* 'make' construction to their L2, greatly overusing *make* causatives in their English (see Wong 1983 and Juffs 1996: 152).

Transfer can also be explained by the concept of prototypicality and by learners' judgements of the similarity between L1 and L2. What they perceive as prototypical and semantically transparent in their L1 determines what they transfer to their L2 (see Ellis 1994: 326 and Kellerman 1983, 1986). This perception does not seem to be affected by their experience of or proficiency in L2, which would explain why advanced Swedish learners tend to overuse the analytical construction, while French-speaking learners do not. To Swedish learners there is an obvious similarity between the prototypical causatives in English and their L1, to French-speaking learners there is not. This 'psychotypology' – to use Kellerman's term – can also be expected to retard second language development. Categories that are perceived as prototypical, unmarked or transparent are usually adopted early by learners and run the risk of becoming linguistic 'teddy bears' that continue to be favoured in later stages of learning at the expense of less common and more differentiated target alternatives (cf. Hasselgren 1994).

The contrastive picture that emerges from this study thus suggests that the Swedish learners' overuse of causative *make* with adjective complements is the effect of transfer supported by cross-linguistic similarity. Learners who are unfamiliar with less common causative alternatives in English are likely to overuse the dominant target pattern, especially if it is easy to transfer from their native language.

The aim of this study has been to use contrastive data to try and interpret Swedish learners' overuse of causative *make* with adjective complements. It remains to be seen if their overuse of causative *make* with infinitive complements has similar support in contrastive data. This is probable, but until such a study has been carried out it can only be a hypothesis. However, what I hope the present study has demonstrated is the usefulness of parallel corpora in cross-linguistic and interlanguage research. Apart from uncovering cross-linguistic 'paradigms' that would be impossible to discover in monolingual corpora, bilingual corpora offer an invaluable empirical resource for testing assumptions derived from learner data. By supplementing interlanguage research in this way, parallel corpora can give important contributions to what Granger (1996: 43) has called 'Contrastive Interlanguage Analysis'.

Notes

1. For a description of the *International Corpus of Learner English (ICLE)* and the methodology of corpus-based interlanguage research, see Granger (1993, 1998).

2. Statistically significant differences between each learner group and the native speaker control corpus are marked with an asterisk in the table.

References

a. Primary sources from the ESPC (texts quoted only)

LG Gustafsson, Lars (1991). *En kakelsättares eftermiddag.* Stockholm: Natur och Kultur. Translated by Tom Geddes as *A Tiler's Afternoon.* London: Harvill, 1993.

JL Lovelock, James (1988). *The Ages of Gaia.* Oxford: Oxford University Press. Translated by Folke Günther as *Gaia.* Stockholm: Natur och Kultur, 1991.

JPM Phillips-Martinsson, Jean (1991). *Swedes as Others See them.* 2 ed. Lund: Studentlitteratur. Translated by Mona Lagerström and Suzanne Sjöqvist as *Svenskarna som andra ser dem.* Lund: Studentlitteratur, 1992.

b. Secondary sources

Aijmer, K., Altenberg, B., & Johansson, M. (Eds). (1996). *Languages in contrast. Papers from a symposium on text-based cross-linguistic studies.* Lund: Lund University Press.

Aijmer, K., Altenberg, B., & Johansson, M. (1996). Text-based contrastive studies in English. Presentation of a project. In K. Aijmer et al. (Eds.) (pp. 73–85).

Altenberg, B. (1999). Adverbial connectors in English and Swedish: Semantic and lexical correspondences. In H. Hasselgård & S. Oksefjell (Eds.), *Out of corpora. Studies in honour of Stig Johansson* (pp. 249–268). Amsterdam: Rodopi.

Altenberg, B., & Granger, S. (2001). The grammatical and lexical patterning of *make* in native and non-native student writing. *Applied Linguistics, 22,* 173–194.

Ebeling, J. (1998). The Translation Corpus Explorer: A browser for parallel texts. In S. Johansson & S. Oksefjell (Eds.), (pp. 101–112).

Ellis, R. (1994). *The study of second language acquisition.* Oxford: Oxford University Press.

Granger, S. (1993). The International Corpus of Learner English. In J. Aarts, P. de Haan, & N. Oostdijk (Eds.), *English language corpora: Design, analysis and exploitation* (pp. 57–69). Amsterdam: Rodopi.

Granger, S. (1996). From CA to CIA and back: An integrated approach to computerized bilingual and learner corpora. In K. Aijmer et al. (Eds.), (pp. 37–51).

Granger, S. (1998). The computerized learner corpus: a versatile new source of data for SLA research. In S. Granger (Ed.), *Learner English on Computer* (pp. 3–18). London/New York: Addison Wesley Longman.

Hasselgren, A. (1994). Lexical teddy bears and advanced learners: a study into the ways Norwegian students cope with English vocabulary. *International Journal of Applied Linguistics, 4*, 237–260.

Hofland, K., & Johansson, S. (1998). The Translation Corpus Aligner: A program for automatic alignment of parallel texts. In S. Johansson & S. Oksefjell (Eds.), (pp. 87–100).

Hyltenstam, K. (1984). The use of typological markedness conditions as predictors in second language acquisition: The case of pronominal copies in relative clauses. In R. Andersen (Ed.), *Second language: A crosslinguistic perspective* (pp. 39–58). Rowley, MA: Newbury House.

Johansson, M. (1996). Fronting in English and Swedish: A text-based contrastive analysis. In C. Percy, C. F. Meyer & I. Lancashire (Eds.), *Synchronic corpus linguistics* (pp. 29–39). Amsterdam/Atlanta: Rodopi.

Johansson, S. (1998). On the role of corpora in cross-linguistic research. In S. Johansson & S. Oksefjell (Eds.), *Corpora and cross-linguistic research: Theory, method, and case studies* (pp. 3–24). Amsterdam/Atlanta: Rodopi.

Johansson, S., & Oksefjell, S. (Eds.). (1998). *Corpora and cross-linguistic research: Theory, method and case studies.* Amsterdam: Rodopi.

Juffs, A. (1996). *Learnability and the lexicon. Theories and second language acquisition research.* Amsterdam/Philadelphia: John Benjamins.

Kamimoto T., Shimura A., Kellerman, E. (1992). A second language classic reconsidered – the case of Schachter's avoidance. *Second Language Research, 8*(3), 251–277.

Kellerman, E. (1978). Giving learners a break: native language intuitions as a source of predictions about transferability. *Working Papers on Bilingualism, 15*, 59–92.

Kellerman, E. (1983). Now you see it, now you don't. In S. Gass & L. Selinke (Eds.), *Language transfer in language learning* (pp. 112–134). Rowley, MA: Newbury House.

Kellerman, E. (1986). An eye for an eye: Crosslinguistic constraints on the development of the L2 lexicon. In E. Kellerman & M. Sharwood-Smith (Eds.), (pp. 35–48).

Kellerman, E., & Sharwood-Smith, M. (Eds.). (1986). *Crosslinguistic influence in second language acquisition.* New York: Pergamon Institute of English.

Quirk, R., Greenbaum, S., Leech, G., & Svartvik, J. (1985). *A comprehensive grammar of the English language.* London: Longman.

Percy, C. E., Meyer, C. F., & Lancashire, I. (Eds.). (1996). *Synchronic Corpus Linguistics.* Amsterdam and Atlanta: Rodopi.

Schachter, J. (1974). An error in error analysis. *Language Learning, 24*, 205–214.

Schmied, J. (1996). Approaching translationese through parallel and translation corpora. In C. E. Percy, C. F. Meyer & I. Lancashire (Eds.), (pp. 41–56).

Song, J. J. (1996). *Causatives and causation. A universal-typological perspective.* London: Longman.

Wong, S. C. (1983). Overproduction, underlexicalisation, and unidiomatic usage in the 'make' causatives of Chinese speakers. *Language Learning and Communication, 2*, 151–163.

Modality in advanced Swedish learners' written interlanguage

Karin Aijmer
Göteborg University, Sweden

Chapter overview

In this chapter, Aijmer uses computer learner corpora to compare the range and frequency of some key modal words in native English writing and English L2 writing of advanced level university students. Although the primary focus of her investigation is Swedish L2 writers, she regularly conducts comparisons with French and German L2 writers, in an attempt to ascertain whether features of Swedish L2 writing are likely to be L1-induced or more generally shared by L2 writers of different language backgrounds.

One valuable feature of the study, based on c. 52,000-word samples from each native and learner variety, is that it takes into account not only modal auxiliaries but also a wider range of modal devices, such as adverbials and lexical verbs with modal meaning, which are now acknowledged as being widely used for expressing modality in English.

Her study reveals a global overuse of modal auxiliaries by all the L2 writers, a tendency which may be partly developmental, partly interlingual. Aijmer also finds evidence of 'register–interference', where the learners seem to transfer patterns of use from spoken English into the written medium, and notably a high degree of topic sensitivity in the use of particular modals. In conclusion, Aijmer argues for the need to present classroom learners with a wider range of modal expressions including modal phrases, collocations and larger sentence patterns.

1.   Introduction

As has been much discussed in the literature (Leech 1998; Granger 1998c; Horvath 2001), one of the chief contributions of computer learner corpora is that they make it possible to investigate aspects of learner language which have previously been difficult or impossible to explore. In many cases, these investigations are comparative: authentic learner output is compared with native speaker output of a similar type, a process which falls within the domain of contrastive interlanguage analysis (CIA) (see Granger 1998b). Modality is just one example of an area of learner language which has not previously been well described and where computer learner corpora can make a contribution, as this article attempts to illustrate.

Several non-corpus-based studies of modal verbs have shown that non-native speakers of English seem to have difficulty using modal verbs appropriately and that they overvalue or under-represent certain modal meanings or forms (Hinkel 1995:326; DeCarrico 1986). The present study sets out to compare modal forms, meanings and uses in compositions produced by non-native speakers (NNS) and native speakers (NS). The corpora are analysed using various search tools, through which the frequency and range of modal elements can be determined. The description of the use of modal categories and patterns by non-native writers which this learner corpus approach makes possible can be expected to have important pedagogical implications.

2.   A corpus-based approach to the study of modality

2.1   A contrastive interlanguage methodology

At the heart of studies using a contrastive interlanguage methodology are different types of comparison:

- comparing native language and interlanguage
- comparing different types of interlanguage (the language of different subcorpora) with each other

The aim of the first type of comparison is to establish distinctive features of a particular interlanguage. This approach gives rise to a 'brand-new field of study' (Granger 1998b:13), making it possible to investigate the phenomenon of overuse and underuse (rather than simply misuse) of linguistic items, which has the potential to reveal radically different distributional patterns from comparable native language. These different distributional patterns can help explain why a text which may contain no overt grammatical/lexical errors nevertheless creates the impression that it has not been written by a native speaker.

The second type of comparison, which involves comparing different types of interlanguages, makes it possible to look for strategies shared by all learners or by several learner groups and those which seem to be particular to one learner group. However, it is important not to jump to hasty conclusions when making statements about the universality of learner strategies based on the evidence of one corpus analysis. In most cases, results need to be tested out on different types of data and different types of learners before strong statements can be made. When the corpus analysis provides possible evidence of transfer from the L1, then corpus-based contrastive analysis (CA) is an important way of supplementing the learner corpus evidence (for an example of this approach, see Altenberg, this volume).

The use of the 'raw' corpus involves manual analysis because of the need for disambiguation (e.g. distinguishing between the noun *can* and the auxiliary). Fully automatic linguistic research requires an annotated corpus. By tagging the corpus for parts of speech it would, for instance, be possible to extract automatically all the examples of modal auxiliaries avoiding homonyms. However, in the present research, importance has been attached to considering a wide range of modal devices which writers have at their disposal for expressing modal notions and not only modal auxiliaries (Hoye 1997:52; Perkins 1983) and it is clearly not possible to automatically retrieve an open category of this type. Modality may, for instance, be expressed by functionally equivalent adverbs (*probably, possibly*) and lexical verbs with modal meaning (*I think, I feel*). The fact that writers have a wide repertoire of devices for expressing modality means that a method involving a combination of manual and automatic analysis seems more appropriate.

In this research, concordancing software was used to investigate the range and frequency of some key modal words in the corpora that were compared. An advantage of this method is that it highlights a variety of lexico-grammatical devices and shows the preferred modal collocations, for example combinations of modal auxiliaries and adverbs or of modal auxiliaries and lexical verbs with modal meaning.

Given the considerable agreement among linguists about the centrality of the modal auxiliaries in English, it was this category of modality that formed the starting point of the investigation. It was also possible to compare results with existing information on how modals are used in standard corpora gained from previous studies. Mindt (1995) for example is a corpus-based grammar providing frequency data and distributional information on modal verbs. It offers a detailed analysis of the verb phrase structure the modals occur with and describes their semantic profiles in quantitative terms on the basis of several available corpora.

Other corpus-based data concerning the range, frequency and contextual distribution of modal expressions have led to new insights that also show why modality is a difficult area for learners. Holmes (1988) investigated the relative frequencies of over 350 lexical items expressing certainty and uncertainty in written and spoken corpora and used the data to evaluate the treatment of epistemic modality in EFL textbooks. It turned out, for instance, that many textbooks devoted an unjustifiably large amount of attention to modal verbs and neglected alternative linguistic strategies for expressing doubt and uncertainty (Holmes 1988: 40). As information about native speaker usage Holmes used the learned section of the Brown Corpus of American English and the matching section from the LOB (Lancaster-Oslo/Bergen) Corpus of written English.

A comparison with the NS standard also makes it possible to examine if NNSs choose the appropriate stylistic variants. For instance, it may be that non-native speakers use modal expressions that are closer to the informal register and to speech and that native speakers are more formal. The London-Lund Corpus of Spoken English (LLC) is an obvious source for testing the hypothesis that non-native speakers in general choose modal expressions which are influenced by speech. The London-Lund Corpus contains representative samples of present-day standard English speech. It consists of half a million words and covers a variety of topics and situations and represents several degrees of formality.

Hoye (1997) used both spoken and written corpus data for his study of combinations of adverbs and modality in English. In order to compare native speakers of English with Spanish learners he conducted an experiment in the form of a completion test where native speakers were asked to insert a modal word or a phrase which were then compared with the modal and adverb categories independently established by speaker assessment. When the test was administered to the Spanish informants Hoye found that the speakers consistently neglected the potential for modals and adverbs to combine and that 'there are points of contrast and equivalents between the L1 and the L2 which may lead to 'negative transfer' or interference and actively impede the learner's level of performance in the L2' (Hoye 1997: 251).

2.2 Corpus material used in the study

Learner corpora are still in their infancy, a surprising fact given their potential importance for second language acquisition research. The corpus used for this research is the ICLE corpus (for a full description, see Granger 1998b). The learner corpus contains several sub-corpora representing different learner varieties. The sub-corpora analysed in this study are the Swedish component (SWICLE), which forms the main focus of the analysis and the German and French components. Each of the sub-corpora consists of 200,000 words of argumentative texts written by university students having reached a relatively advanced level of proficiency.

Given that the interpretation of the modal meanings and patterns in the texts requires extremely time-consuming analysis, this study is based on samples of approximately 52,000 words taken from each corpus, as shown in Table 1 below. The learner material is compared with the essays from LOCNESS (Louvain Corpus of Native English Essays).[1] As LOCNESS contains only student, ie non-professional writing, comparisons are also carried out with other NS standards such as the British LOB Corpus, in particular the academic prose (Section J) and editorial (Section B) section, and the 'corpus findings' in the *Longman Grammar of Written and Spoken English* (LSWE).

A comment is in order about the topics of the essays. The argumentative topics on which the Swedish advanced learners wrote, dealt with such (sometimes contentious) subjects as the integration and assimilation of immigrants in Swedish society, equality of opportunity, problems in Swedish education and the environment. The British university student native writers on the other hand, wrote on a range of literary and argumentative topics. The literary topics dealt with works by Camus, Sartre and Hugo. The argumentative topics, which constituted about one quarter of the total NS corpus, dealt with contemporary French education, French industrial relations and the President's role in the Fifth Republic.

Although the NS and NNS samples have been regarded as sufficiently similar to be used for this exploratory analysis into the range of ways in which

Table 1. Size of corpus samples used for the analysis of modal expressions.

Corpus	No. of words
LOCNESS (NS corpus)	52,877
ICLE-Swedish	52,191
ICLE-French	52,267
ICLE-German	52,249

learners express modality, the difference in topics (cf. Barbaresi 1987; Fairclough 1995) and above all, text type (literary vs argumentative), means that some of the quantitative results must be interpreted with caution, as indicated by Dagneaux (1995), who studies this particular issue. In her investigation of French learners' use of modal expressions in English, Dagneaux found that native English writers used more modal auxiliaries expressing possibility or probability than French writers when the topic was argumentative while the native writers used fewer auxiliaries when they wrote on literary topics (cf. Dagneaux 1995: 101). Hinkel (1995: 333) has also demonstrated the importance of topic in influencing the frequency of particular modals. In essays written on education, she found that non-native writers (native speakers of Chinese, Japanese, Vietnamese, Korean, Indonesian) overused *must* and *should*, whereas *must* was not encountered in non-native writer essays written on politics.

Topic will almost certainly be only one of a range of factors explaining differences in the expression of modality. The over- or under-representation of a certain structure or word in the NNS corpus may be due to transfer of mother tongue patterns or constitute general learner strategies. The learners' problems in choosing the 'right' modal items may also be related to the different distribution of the modals in the spoken or written mode (Kennedy 1998: 130) and in different text types (Biber 1988; Biber & Finegan 1988, 1989). It is also likely that teachers pay undue attention to infrequent modal meanings and that the use of modals in textbooks differs from their use in authentic English.

There may be other, more complex factors. For example, the modal patterns in the running text may be due to the transfer of language-specific cultural norms, to different rhetorical traditions or methods of teaching composition and even reflect different attitudes towards the writing task.

3.   Results and analysis

3.1 Use of modal auxiliaries

In the analysis which follows, the NS essays provide the backdrop against which characteristic features in the learners' use of modal expressions and patterns can be evaluated. When modal forms or meanings are more frequent in the NNS corpus than in the comparable NS component this has been described as overuse.

Table 2 shows the overall frequencies of modals in the Swedish learner and native writer material.

Table 2. Overall frequency of modal verbs in SWICLE and LOCNESS. SNNS= Swedish non-native speaker; NS= native speaker.[2]

Type of modal	SNNS	NS	χ^2
will (*'ll*)	224**	138	21.5
can	198	192	0.1
would	169*	125	7.2
could	72	66	0.3
must	67**	30	14.6
have (got) to	132**	41	49
should	130**	55	31.3
may	51	35	3.2
might	67**	8	47.2
ought to	10	3	3.9
shall	5	2	1.3
Total	1125	695	105.5

The most striking finding in Table 2 is that the category of modal auxiliaries as a whole is highly significantly overused. Within the global category, it is *will*, *might* and the group of modals *should/have (got) to/must*, and *might*, which stand out particularly.

Could the overuse of *will* by the Swedish writers be due to transfer of conversational uses to academic genres or the writers' inability to distinguish between informal spoken and academic written forms (Hyland & Milton 1997: 192)? An analysis of *will* in a corpus of spoken English (the London-Lund Corpus) and the LOB revealed that it is more frequently used in speech than in writing (Kennedy 1998: 130). The difference may also reflect differences in text type (the higher percentage of argumentative essays in the Swedish component). It is interesting that in Section B (editorials) of the LOB Corpus, *will* is more frequent than *would*, whereas in the LOB as a whole, the order is reversed (cf. Kennedy 1998: 130; Krogvig & Johansson 1981: 42).

The rank order of the possibility modals in the SNNS material was *can-could-might-may*. The distribution of *can* and *could* (with the meaning possibility or probability) was almost the same in texts by native and non-native speakers but *might* was over-represented, the difference being highly significant. The distribution of the possibility modals in the NS corpus (*can, could, may, might*) with the tentative/past time member ranked after the unmarked member of the pair conforms to the pattern reported for the LOB Corpus and the LSWE Corpus as well as for corpora of other language varieties (e.g. the Brown Corpus for American English).[3]

Table 3. Comparison of French, German, Swedish and British speakers' use of possibility modals[4] (* indicates significant difference (p < 0.01), ** highly significant difference (p < 0.005) from the NS corpus)

Modal	FNNS	GNNS	SNNS	NS
Can	238	287**	198	192
Could	75	103*	72	66
May	80**	41	51	35
Might	32*	27*	67*	8
Total	425**	458**	388**	301

One possible explanation for the overuse may be transfer from the L1. By comparing several NNS varieties with NS essays we can investigate the potential influence of the L1, whether different mother tongues leave different fingerprints in the learner texts. In Table 3, NS essays are contrasted with NNS essays written by German, French and Swedish learners.

Table 3 shows that all the learner groups under investigation here overuse the category of possibility modals in general, but that there is variation in the use of individual modals. *Can* and *could* for instance, were significantly overused only by German learners, *may* was only overused by French learners. *Might* on the other hand, is overused by all learner groups, although the Swedish learners used it more often than either the French or German learners, the difference in each case being highly significant.

Why then this generalised overuse of *might*? One possible explanation is that it stems from the learners' uncertainty in arguing in English. In the following example from the Swedish learner corpus, the possibility expressed by *might* appears to be too weak to convey persuasion and the writer therefore appears 'equivocal, diffident or naive' (cf. Hyland & Milton 1997: 186).

1. University studies will give you advantages all through life; it is an investment in your life. You will have more opportunities in several areas of life. You <u>might</u> get the opportunity to get your dream job later on in life because of the knowledge that you received at university, and at that particular time you <u>might</u> thank yourself for the long hours of studying that you endured. Or, you <u>might</u> find later in life that you get more out of discussions and reading, and that you see things differently and more clearly because you have the knowledge that it takes to widen your perspective. Or, you <u>might</u> find that the friends you made at university still are your friends and still give you intellectual stimulation. (SWICLE)

It may also be that different cultural groups have different preconceptions about the degree of directness and certainty required in academic writing, a hypothesis which receives some support from studies which have identified variation in the certainty with which arguments are expressed in different languages (Hyland & Milton 1997:186). According to these studies, Finns, Japanese, Malays and Chinese seem to favour a more indirect style in their academic writing than, for instance, German or Czech writers (Hyland & Milton ibid.). Speakers often overuse *might* where tentativeness is inappropriate as in (2):

2. The influence of astrology on people in today's is not always good, though. There is of course a risk that some people <u>might</u> live their lives after what their horoscopes say, doing things they normally would not do. There are, for example, often advice about taking or not taking risks in horoscopes. People <u>might</u> thus miss out on opportunities or take unnecessary risks because it is in their horoscope. Most people do not, of course, take astrology that seriously. (SWICLE)

Yet another possible explanation for the overuse of *might* may be influence from speech (note also the speech-like rhetorical structure of (1) above). Holmes (1988:29) showed, for instance, that *might* was more likely to occur in spoken than in written language. The relatively high frequency of *might* by non-native speakers may also reflect the fact that they are not using other epistemic modal devices expressing possibility preferred by native writers.

3.2 Categories of meaning in NS and NNS essays

It is clear that modal choice relates directly to the type of meaning created or expressed. Modals such as *must, may, should* and *might* have at least two prototypical meanings (epistemic and root). Both root and epistemic modality are important in argumentative writing although they belong to different argumentative styles (Kennedy 1998; Hyland & Milton 1997). Modals express degrees of likelihood (the system of epistemic modality) or degrees of obligation, necessity, permission, volition, etc (the root /deontic use). For some of the modals, the root meaning is more frequent while with others, the epistemic meaning predominates (cf. Kennedy 1992:351). *Must, have to, should* and *ought to* usually express root meanings (Kennedy ibid.). In 53% of the uses in the London-Lund Corpus, *must* had obligation/necessity meaning, compared with 46% of the cases with epistemic meaning (percentages according to Kennedy).[5] In the LOB Corpus, the root use was more than twice as frequent.

However, Kennedy's information (based on Coates 1983) could be compared with the finding in LSWE that '*must* in conversation is used most of the time to mark logical necessity [ie epistemic meaning]' (§6.6.4.2). *Must* in academic prose is 'somewhat more common marking personal obligation than logical necessity' (LSWE, ibid.). The distribution of the meanings of *must* in NS and SNNS writing is shown in Table 4.

Apparently neither the native nor the non-native writers use a large number of epistemic *must*. However, the root meaning of *must* was overused in SNNSs' writing.

May, on the other hand, was always epistemic in the learner corpus and was almost twice as frequent in the SNNS as in the NS compositions (see Table 5). Root possibility can be paraphrased as 'it is possible for' or as 'circumstances allow that'. It was found in NS texts in examples such as:

4.   Despite this the terrorists' moral approach invites admiration. Kaliayev is presented in a more favourable light than Stepan – the latter is seen to kick Kaliayev when he is down while the rest of the group tend to back Kaliayev. This may suggest that Camus is endorsing a moral approach to achieving political aims. (LOCNESS)

Root *may* is formal, which may explain why it is frequent with the impersonal passive:

5.   Caligula is seen to be logical in his approach and since he is sympathized with even by those who believe he is wrong, a greater sense of sympathy for him may be felt. A certain sense of sympathy may also be evoked because Caligula is shown to be slightly paranoid at times. (LOCNESS)

In the London-Lund Corpus, only 4% of the occurrences of *may* were root uses to be compared with 74% of epistemic *may* (Kennedy 1992:351).[6] In the case of the LOB corpus, root *may* occurred in 22% of the examples to be compared

Table 4. The distribution of the root and epistemic use of *must*

Root		Epistemic	
SNNS	NS	SNNS	NS
52	14	15	16

Table 5. The distribution of the root and epistemic use of *may*

Root		Epistemic	
SNNS	NS	SNNS	NS
0	10	46	25

with epistemic *may* in 61% of the cases.[7] It is necessary to also consider the influence from register. In the academic prose section in the LSWE Corpus, 'three of the permission/possibility modals (*could*, *may*, and *might*) are used almost exclusively to mark logical possibility [the epistemic meaning]'. *May* was found to be extremely common in this function (LSWE §6.6.4.1).

May was also one of the most frequent items expressing epistemic modality in English compositions by Cantonese speaking Hong Kong students, occurring almost twice as often as in the NS control corpus (Hyland & Milton 1997: 189).

One of the functions of modal elements in the compositions is to influence the reader's beliefs and attitudes by providing arguments. By overusing root *must* and other necessity/obligation modals (*should*, *have to*) the NNSs seem, for whatever reason, to be adopting a direct and emphatic style of persuasion, which in some essays seemed to be clearly topic-related. According to Biber (1988: 150), 'features, such as necessity modals … can mark the speaker's attempts to persuade the addressee that certain events are desirable or probable (e.g. *you should go*)'. Thus in SNNS essays on Swedish immigrant policy, there was a high number of *should* and *must*. *Should* and *must* stress that some action is desirable, advisable, or obligatory. *Should*, in particular, refers to cultural norms of behaviour or a moral code which may be specific to the learner, as illustrated in example (6) below.

6. When immigrants come to Sweden, they <u>should be</u> offered (or maybe even made to take) an introductory course in the swedish language as well as some short guide to how things are done in Sweden, with regards to going to the bank or post office, using public recreation grounds etc. Also, the swedish school system <u>should be</u> explained, so they willnot be afraid to send their children to school. As much as possible, Sweden shall provide education in their mother tongue and also in their culture, which I feel <u>should be</u> integrated in the schools in any case. (SWICLE)

The same didactic style, with frequent use of *must* and *should*, was also adopted in essays on environment and pollution, where students also clearly had strong opinions about desirable future courses of action.

7. There is little doubt man has to think twice about Mother Earth. We cannot afford to ignore the lifesaving resources nature offers. Most countries and their peoples agree we <u>must</u> stop polluting earth and space. To put toxins in our common ground and perforate the ozone layer is not the key to our species' success. In fact, the human race is on the endangered-species list.

So, what do we do? Well, except starting to save what is left and disinfect the wounds we have already made, we <u>must</u> gain access to existing knowledge of how nature actually works. We <u>must</u> learn to be constructive instead of destructive. (SWICLE)

It is revealing that of the 130 total occurrences of *should*, 59 (45.4%) were in the essays on integration and assimilation (which represented only 18.8% of the corpus (9857 words)). By contrast, another group of essays representing 35.5% of the corpus (18,520 words) contained only 19 instances of *should* (14.6%). These figures highlight the sometimes highly striking effect of topic on modal use.

3.2.1   *Ways of expressing epistemic meaning*
Will, would, may, might, could are the principal epistemic auxiliaries. *Will* is used to predict what will occur in the future with some certainty (predictive persuasion). *May* expresses a lower degree of certainty (what may or may not occur).

8.   However, this concept of family has changed very much in recent times. To many people the word has got a wider meaning. It is today common that parents get a divorce and the close unit of a core family is split as a married couple separate. Furthermore the parents <u>may</u> get a new wife or husband and perhaps also other children. A child of divorced parents <u>will</u> therefore get another sense of the word "family" as his new sisters and brothers <u>will</u> also belong to his or her family. (SWICLE)

Several writers have commented on the difficulties L2 writers from different cultures have mastering 'the appropriate degree of qualification and confidence in expressing claims' (Hyland & Milton 1997: 185; cf. also Holmes 1988).

Epistemic modality is a fuzzy area which includes a number of ways of expressing doubt and certainty. Epistemic modals have many grammatical and functional equivalents. Some meanings and forms are more prototypical and frequent than others. For example, modal verbs represent the most typical or 'grammaticalised' way of expressing modal meanings in English. Adverbial equivalents of *may* are illustrated in examples b and c:

    a.   He may be at home
    b.   He's probably at home
    c.   Perhaps he is at home

These are not simply stylistic variants but represent alternative patterns of modality. We have to consider when and how often they are used, whether they have the same function as the modal verb, etc.

It has been shown above that learners have a tendency to overuse modal verbs, the most grammaticalised way of expressing modality, a tendency which could be induced by teaching. As Holmes points out (1988:40), many textbooks devote an unjustifiably large amount of attention to modal verbs, neglecting alternative strategies. The next question is whether the learners in fact neglect alternative strategies.

In Swedish, the modals are less central than in English as indicated by their lower frequency in contrastive studies of epistemic modality; they are used with adverbial support or are replaced by an adverbial synonym (Aijmer 1999; cf. Løken 1997).

In Table 6, the figures refer to Swedish translations of *may* and *might* as adverbs/particles or as combinations of modals and adverbs/particles. Løken's Norwegian results are given in parentheses.

When use of these adverbs of (un)certainty was investigated in the corpora, it was found that they were also overused by learners, as Table 7 illustrates.

Table 6. Swedish and Norwegian translations of *may/might*

	may	*might*
adv/part	46.2% (34.5%)	30.3% (9.1%)
modal + adv/part	11.4% (0%)	22.9% (15.1%)

Table 7. Distribution of epistemic modal adverbs

MODAL	SNNS	NS	χ^2
UNCERTAINTY			
Perhaps	32	26	0.7
Probably	32**	9	13.2
Possibly	1	–	–
Maybe	19**	2	14
CERTAINTY			
Of course	60**	9	38.3
Certainly	18**	3	10.9
Indeed	7	13	1.7
Surely	6	3	1
TOTAL	175	65	

The greatest difference lies in the higher frequencies of *probably, maybe, of course* and *certainly* in the SNNSs' language than in the NS corpus.

3.2.2   *Combinations of epistemic modality in NS and NNS compositions*

In addition to modal verbs and adverbs, different patterns of modal and adverb combination are found in English. Modal combinations can be used to express more certainty and authority or more subjectivity or speaker involvement. In modally harmonic combinations (e.g. *may perhaps)*, the modal forms have the same meaning (Lyons 1977:807). The meaning of a modal verb can also be 'interfered with' by other modal elements. In collocations which are 'disharmonic', the adverb serves to reinforce (e.g. *may certainly*) or modify (e.g. *will perhaps*) the modal meaning of the verb.

Several different combinations are possible. Hoye (1997:9), for instance, distinguished the following categories of Possibility (ordered in terms of strength of speaker assessment): *could conceivably, could possibly, could maybe, could perhaps, might conceivably, might possibly, might perhaps, may conceivably, may possibly, may perhaps.*

As Table 8 shows, there are considerable differences between SNNSs and NSs in the use of combinations of modal verbs and adverbs.

Table 8. Harmonic combinations of modals and adverbs

	SNNS	NS
Will		
will probably (probably will)	10	1
will (most) certainly	7	–
will of course	2	–
perhaps will	1	–
will indeed	1	–
will undoubtedly	1	1
Would		
would probably	10	2
would perhaps	2	1
would of course	2	–
would surely	2	–
would indeed	1	–
Should		
should of course	2	–
perhaps should	1	–
probably should	1	–
certainly should	1	–
surely should	1	–

Table 8. *(continued)*

	SNNS	NS
Can		
can perhaps	1	–
can probably	1	–
Could		
could perhaps	1	–
May		
may of course	1	–
Might		
might perhaps	1	–
Must		
must of course	1	–
Total	51	5

Yet again, for this category of modal expressions, the Swedish learner writers used more examples and more combinations than the native writer group (Table 9).

The small number of types of combinations in the native writer corpus is predicted by Palmer (1990: 67), who finds that 'there are very few adverbs that may occur with epistemic modals (or even modals in general)'. The high number of types and tokens of combinations in the SNNS compositions might be due to a combination of different factors. The influence from spoken language is again likely to play an important role (Holmes 1988: 34f). As Hoye points out (1997: 272), 'it is generally the case that co-occurrence is more frequent in the spoken than the written language.... This is particularly noticeable in the case of the more frequent modals CAN, COULD and WOULD, where combinations are roughly twice as frequent as in the written language.'

Moreover, the frequency of modal and adverb combinations with the meaning of possibility or probability may be due to transfer from Swedish (Aijmer 1999). *Kan* ('can') is only weakly grammaticalised in its epistemic meaning and therefore needs adverbial support or is replaced by an adverb in the translation. It is not implausible that a factor contributing to the high fre-

Table 9. The distribution of examples (=tokens) and combinations (=types) in SNNS and NS essays

	Tokens	Types
SNNS	51	24
NS	5	4

quency of *would probably* in Swedish learners' texts is negative transfer of the combination modal+particle in Swedish (e.g. *kommer nog* 'will probably'). *Of course* corresponds to the Swedish particle *ju* ('as you know') which is frequent both on its own and in modal collocations.

Will and *would* have the widest collocational range and are connected both with possibility and certainty adverbs, perhaps because predictions are difficult. The modal meaning varies between certainty, probability and possibility depending on the collocate (*of course, undoubtedly, obviously, certainly, probably, perhaps*). However, there is a strong tendency for *will* and *would* to combine with adverbs of probability. *May* (and *must*) cooccurred with *of course*; *might* was used harmonically in combination with *perhaps* to express a cautious opinion.

In disharmonic combinations, the adverb does not simply reinforce the modal but it may have a different scope:

9.   This may of course be great fun, but it has nothing to do with Christmas. (SWICLE)
     This sentence can be paraphrased as 'It is of course the case that this may be great fun'.

The Swedish non-native speakers overuse modals and adverbial 'satellites' (in particular *probably, of course*, and *certainly*) and use collocations which are not used by the native speakers (*can/could perhaps, can probably, probably should*). About half of the combinations used by the Swedish non-native speakers contained an adverb of certainty 'boosting' the writer's subjective conviction. Interestingly, a study by Hyland and Milton into epistemic combinations in Chinese learners' essays (which incidentally found a global underuse of these combinations) also found that the Chinese learners often misjudged the effect of the clusters they used, with the result that their claims expressed inappropriate conviction (Hyland & Milton 1997: 199). The question remains as to whether this use of emphatic devices is the result of insufficient mastery of the written medium in L2, or the result of different rhetorical principles governing the use of emphatic devices (cf. the results of Lorenz 1998: 64). *Of course* (*obviously, surely, certainly*) have the rhetorical function of 'easing the receiver's approach to the argument' and 'knocking down the bulk of the entire argument into acceptable doses' (Barbaresi 1987: 21). *Should of course*, as used in (10) below for instance, has more persuasive force than the single *should*.

10. New influences from all over the world should of course be seen as assets, and some thing we could benefit from. (SWICLE)

Another possible type of combination is that of epistemic lexical verb + modal verb. When two of the most common epistemic lexical verbs (*I think* and *I believe*) were investigated, it was found that both were used almost exclusively by the non-native writers (see Table 10).

The use of these verbs in combination with modal verbs (cf. Table 11) may be due to influence from L1 since there were no examples in NS writing. It may also be due to novice writer effect.

Hedges are also found with modals which are not epistemic:

11. I think that the change must start with the children. (SWICLE)

The overuse of *I think* is an example of the overuse of features indicating Writer/Reader visibility (involvement). On the basis of four learner corpora (French, Dutch, Swedish and Finnish) and a corpus of comparable native English, Petch-Tyson (1998:110) demonstrated that all the non-native speaker groups used more features of W/R visibility. Several scholars have commented on the overuse of *I think* in particular. For instance, Granger (1998a) found that learners preferred active 'discourse frames' ('sentence builders') to passive ones (cf. Ringbom 1998; Altenberg 1998). Thus *I think* was used 72 times by French non-native speakers but it was only found in three examples in the native speaker corpus. Arguably, the overuse of *I think* is due to influence from spoken language. *I think* was one of the most frequent phrases in the London-Lund Corpus occurring 51 times per 10,000 words (Aijmer 1996:9).

Table 10. Distribution of epistemic modal verbs

	SNNS	NS
I think	43	3
I believe	24	2
TOTAL	67	5

Table 11. Hedges and modals in Swedish learners' writing

I think ... should	3
I think ... would	2
I think ... might	1
I think ... can	1
I think ... have to	2
I think ... will	3
I think ... must	2

4. Conclusion

This preliminary investigation into modality in advanced learner writing has revealed a generalised overuse of all the formal categories of modality examined: modal auxiliaries, modal adverbials and harmonic and disharmonic modal combinations. It was only at a functional level that any underuse was detected, with the learner writers failing to use *may* at all in its root meaning. It is important to point out however, that the study was non-exhaustive and although it considered a variety of modal expressions, the ways of expressing modality are so numerous that it would require a completely manual study, using a corpus manually tagged for every kind of modal expression, before any firm statements could be made about global use of modality in learner writing. It could be for instance, that whilst the non-native writers overuse the categories investigated in this study (eg. modal auxiliaries and adverbs) they underuse others which have not been considered (such as modal nouns and adjectives). In this respect, Dagneaux's (1995:97–98) study is of interest, as it shows that French learners use a much higher proportion of epistemic auxiliaries than of other epistemic devices (adjectives, adverbs and nouns). However, even without an exhaustive study, the findings of the present investigation are of interest, both in what they reveal about modality in learner writing, and in the research avenues they open up.

First of all, there is a striking overuse in the learner corpora of the categories of modal expressions investigated. This may in part be the result of learners adopting a more speech-like style in their writing than the native writers represented in the LOCNESS corpus. The LSWE reports for example, that *will, would* and *have to* are all preponderant in speech. The overuse may also be indicative of the tendency of learners noted by Lorenz (1998) to use pleonastic expressions in their writing.

In the case of the Swedish learner writers at least, it seems possible that this tendency is reinforced by interlingual factors. Whereas in English, modal meanings are prototypically and frequently expressed by modals, in Swedish, the epistemic modal meaning is more often realised as an adverb or as an adverb plus a modal verb. Transfer from the mother tongue may thus reinforce a tendency which is already present in interlanguage to use modal support or to express modality pleonastically. Swedish learners therefore need to be made aware that modal auxiliaries are a weak category in Swedish and that adverbs or combinations of modals and auxiliaries have a more central position than in English.

The distribution of expressions of modality clearly has an important function in establishing the style and tone of a piece of writing. Certain modal expressions are more frequent in speech than in writing and if they are used in writing with the frequency typically associated with speech, this will necessarily be a factor in creating a more spoken-like style. That this is in fact what happens in the learner writing under investigation should come as no surprise to anyone familiar with other research studies connected with the ICLE project, many of which have revealed that aspects of the language in the corpus are more speech-like than comparable native English writing (eg. Altenberg & Tapper 1998; Granger & Rayson 1998; Meunier 2000). As regards tone, significant use of modals expressing tentativeness or certainty will have a corresponding influence on the rhetorical effect of the text and the mixed use of contradictory strategies found in this study (e.g. combining tentativeness with absolute certainty) contributes to the impression sometimes given by a text that it has not been written by a native speaker, more so perhaps than use of a speech-like style, which is also typical of novice writers.

The study also found topic to be an extremely important factor in influencing the learners' use of modal auxiliaries. It is also likely, although not proven here, that there is significant text-book/teacher induced influence on the learner product. There is clearly no single factor explaining learner-specific modal realisations or patterns but factors of different type and strength combine to explain the differences in modal patterns.

Various implications for pedagogy suggest themselves. For example, linguistic discussions of modality have often tended to focus on modal auxiliaries, to the detriment of other categories. It is clearly essential that a wide definition of modality be adopted, taking into account the wide variety of structural categories which can express modality. The findings of the present study also point strongly to the need to place the study of modals firmly within a discourse perspective, one which takes into account tone and register as well as semantics.

Non-native writers would also undoubtedly benefit from being made aware that ways of talking about the world or presenting opinions may vary crosslinguistically and that modal devices function within different systems of cultural values, norms and expectations. *Indeed* and *certainly* were, for instance, overused especially by the French learners both singly and in combinations with modals to express a high degree of commitment to the argument, suggesting that this may be an important rhetorical strategy for this group.

In future work on modality in learner writing it would be desirable to control more tightly for topic, as this has been shown to be a key factor in modal use (cf. the use of root modals discussed in 3.2). It would also be fruitful to study a wider variety of learner corpora: the findings of this study suggest that some tendencies in modal use, such as the pleonastic use of expressions of modality, are shared by a number of learner groups, but before it is possible to speak of universal tendencies, more learner groups and perhaps also different proficiency levels should be investigated. Research up to the present has only scratched at the surface of modality, which is a rich and promising field highly worthy of further investigation.

Notes

1. ICLE (The International Corpus of Learner English) contains argumentative writing by non-native learners of English representing fourteen different nationalities. LOCNESS (the Louvain Corpus of Native English Essays) consists of essays which are both argumentative and literary written by British and American university students. See Granger (1998b: 13).

2. Chi-square has been used as a measure of significance in statistical differences. * marks the difference as significant ($p < 0.01$); ** indicates that the difference is highly significant ($p < 0.005$).

3. However in the Cobuild Corpus on CD-ROM the pattern is *could, can, may, might* (Chen 1998: 27).

4. The French and German samples had the same size as the SWICLE corpus.

5. 1% was categorized as 'other'

6. 16% of the cases were classified as permission uses and 6% as 'other'.

7. 6% of the cases were permission uses and 11% were classified as 'other'.

References

Aijmer, K. (1996). *I think* – an English modal particle. In T. Swan & O. J. Westvik (Eds.), *Modality in Germanic languages. Historical and comparative perspectives* (pp. 1–47). Berlin: Mouton de Gruyter.

Aijmer, K. (1999). Epistemic possibility in an English-Swedish contrastive perspective. In H. Hasselgård & S. Oksefjell (Eds.), *Out of Corpora* (pp. 301–323). Amsterdam & Atlanta, GA: Rodopi.

Altenberg, B. (1998). On the phraseology of spoken English: the evidence of recurrent word combinations. In A. P. Cowie (Ed.), *Phraseology: theory, analysis, and applications* (pp. 101–122). Oxford: Oxford University Press.

Altenberg, B., & Tapper, M. (1998). The use of adverbial connectors in advanced Swedish learners' written English. In S. Granger (Ed.), (pp. 80–93).

Barbaresi, L. M. (1987). 'Obviously' and 'certainly': Two different functions in argumentative discourse". *Folia Linguistica, XXI*, 3–24.

Biber, D. (1988). *Variation Across Speech and Writing*. Cambridge: Cambridge University Press.

Biber, D., & Finegan, E. (1988). Adverbial stance types in English. *Discourse Processes, 11*, 1–34.

Biber, D., & Finegan, E. (1989). Styles of stance in English. *Text, 9*(1), 93–124.

Biber, D., Johansson, S., Leech, G., Conrad, S., & Finegan, E. (1999). *Longman Grammar of Spoken and Written English*. [LSWE].

Chen, H.-J. Howard (1998). Underuse, overuse, and misuse in Taiwanese EFL Learner Corpus. *First International Symposium on Computer Learner Corpora, Second Language Acquisition and Foreign Language Teaching. 14–16 December, 1998. Symposium Proceedings*, pp. 25–28.

Coates, J. (1983). *The Semantics of Modal Auxiliaries*. London & Canberra: Croom Helm.

Dagneaux, E. (1995). *Expressions of epistemic modality in native and non-native essay-writing*. Unpublished MA dissertation. Département d'Etudes Germaniques, Université Catholique de Louvain.

DeCarrico, J. (1986). Tense, aspect and time in the English modality system. *TESOL Quarterly, 20*, 665–82.

Fairclough, N. (1995). *Critical Discourse Analysis. The Critical Study of English*. London: Longman.

Granger, S. (1998a). Prefabricated patterns in advanced EFL writing: Collocations and formulae. In A. P. Cowie (Ed.), *Phraseology: Theory, analysis, and applications* (pp. 145–160). Oxford: Oxford University Press.

Granger, S. (1998b). The computer learner corpus: a versatile new source of data for SLA research. In S. Granger (Ed.), (pp. 3–18).

Granger, S. (Ed.). (1998c). *Learner English on Computer*. London & New York: Longman.

Granger, S., & Rayson, P. (1998). Automatic profiling of learner texts. In S. Granger (Ed.), (pp. 119–131).

Hinkel, E. (1995). The use of modal verbs as a reflection of cultural values. *TESOL Quarterly, 29*(2), 325–343.

Holmes, J. (1988). Doubt and certainty in ESL textbooks. *Applied Linguistics, 9*, 21–44.

Horvath, J. (2001). *Advanced Writing in English as a Foreign Language. A Corpus-Based Study of Processes and Products*. Pecs: Lingua Franca Csoport.

Hoye, L. (1997). *Adverbs and Modality in English*. London & New York: Longman.

Hyland, K., & Milton, J. (1997). Qualification and certainty in L1 and L2 students' writing. *Journal of Second Language Writing*, 6(2), 183–205.

Kennedy, G. (1992). Preferred ways of putting things with implications for language teaching. In J. Svartvik (Ed.), *Directions in Corpus Linguistics. Proceedings of Nobel Symposium 82, Stockholm, 4–8 August 1991* (pp. 334–373). Berlin: Mouton de Gruyter.

Kennedy, G. (1998). *An Introduction to Corpus Linguistics*. London: Longman.

Krogvig, I., & Johansson, S. (1981). *Shall, will, should* and *would* in British and American English. *ICAME News, 5*, 32–56.

Leech, G. (1998). Learner corpora: what they are and what can be done with them. In Granger (Ed.), xiv–xx.

Løken, B. (1997). Expressing possibility in English and Norwegian. *ICAME Journal. Computers in English Linguistics, 21*, 43–59.

Lorenz, G. (1998). Overstatement in advanced learners' writing: stylistic aspects of adjective intensification. In S. Granger (Ed.), (pp. 53–66).

Lyons, J. (1977). *Semantics* (I & II). Cambridge: Cambridge University Press.

Meunier, F. (2000). *A computer corpus linguistics approach to interlanguage grammar: noun phrase complexity in advanced learner writing.* Unpublished PhD thesis. Centre for English Corpus Linguistics. Université catholique de Louvain, Louvain-la-Neuve.

Mindt, D. (1995). *An Empirical Grammar of the English Verb: Modal Verbs.* Berlin: Cornelsen.

Palmer, F. R. (1990). *Mood and Modality.* Cambridge: Cambridge University Press.

Perkins, M. R. (1983). *Modal Expressions in English.* London: Frances Pinter Publishers.

Petch-Tyson, S. (1998). Writer/reader visibility in EFL written discourse. In S. Granger (Ed.), (pp. 107–118).

Ringbom, H. (1998). Vocabulary frequencies in advanced learner English: a cross-linguistic approach. In S. Granger (Ed.), (pp. 41–52).

A corpus-based study of the L2-acquisition of the English verb system

Alex Housen

Vrije Universiteit Brussel & Fund for Scientific Research – Flanders

Chapter overview

In this chapter, Housen presents the results of a cross-sectional, corpus-based study into the acquisition of the basic morphological categories of the English verb system, intended to test empirically current hypotheses. Using annotated oral corpus data from learners grouped into four different levels of proficiency, plus native speaker baseline data, Housen addresses four issues: how learners acquire these basic forms; what stages of development can be seen in their acquisition; how L2 learners map these forms onto their appropriate *temporal*, *aspectual* and *grammatical meanings*, and what stages can be observed in the development of these form-meaning relations.

At the broadest level, the study mostly confirms the general order of emergence of the formal morphological categories posited by previous studies, but reveals significant variation at the level of individual learners and that formal variation precedes functional use, with learners fluctuating between overuse and underuse as they fine-tune the form-meaning associations. In conclusion, Housen calls for studies based on large corpora of longitudinal data, to investigate the key issue of variation more thoroughly.

Introduction

This chapter reports on a corpus-based investigation of how second language (L2) learners of English acquire the forms and functions of the English verb system.[1] The choice of the verb system as the focus of study in second language acquisition (SLA) is based on the assumption that this is a centrally important area for the structure of any language which is moreover likely to pose major learning problems for learners of any age (Harley 1986; Palmer 1975).

It is believed that computer-aided language learner corpus research provides a much needed quantificational basis for current hypotheses about the extent and nature of these problems and about the ways in which learners try to resolve them over time, which should be of theoretical interest for SLA researchers and of practical value for educators. The data analysed here are oral English interlanguage data drawn from the *Corpus of Young Learner Interlanguage* (CYLIL), described in Section 2. The data of this corpus have been transcribed and annotated in CHAT format and subsequently analysed with the aid of the CLAN software. The CHAT and CLAN tools were obtained from the CHILDES organisation (MacWhinney 1995). Choice of these tools was largely determined by the linguistic domain under investigation, the research questions that guided the investigation and the theoretical hypotheses tested. These will therefore be outlined first in Section 1. Section 2 describes the methodology, including subjects, data collection, data processing and corpus construction, and the analytic procedures used. Sections 3 and 4 present the results of the analyses of the formal and functional development of the verb system respectively.

1.   The verb in SLA

Even in English, which by many accounts is a morphologically 'simple' language, over 200 grammatically possible verb forms or combinations of forms can be distinguished (Joos 1964:74). Collectively, these forms express an equally extensive range of semantic meanings (tense, aspect, mood), grammatical relations (agreement, voice) and discourse-organizational functions (grounding), many of which are crucial to effective communication. Learners of English face the difficult task of identifying the correct verb forms and mapping them onto their appropriate meanings and functions, a task which is greatly complicated by the lack of structural congruity and of isomorphy of form and meaning in this linguistic subsystem.

1.1   Form-oriented research

Much research on SLA and IL (interlanguage) has been primarily concerned with studying verb *forms* at a specific point in time or their development over

Table 1. Hierarchy of development of verb morphemes in English-L2 acquisition (based on Dulay, Burt & Krashen 1982; Ellis 1994).

Stage	Verb form
1	• Present Participle (*Ving*) • Irregular Present of copula *Be* (*am, is, are*)
2	• Progressive *Aux/Be* + *Ving* • Irregular Preterit of copula *Be* (*was, were*)
3	• Irregular Preterit (*Ven*) of lexical verbs
4	• Regular Preterit (*Ved*) of lexical verbs
5	• Regular Present (*Vs*) of lexical verbs
6	• Irregular Present (*does, has*) • Present Perfect *Aux Have* + *Ven/ed*

time. Examples in case are the well-known *morpheme studies* which sought to establish the general order in which the major grammatical morphemes of a language (including verb morphemes) were acquired by learners of different age categories and in different learning contexts (cf. Dulay, Burt & Krashen 1982; Pica 1984). The general sequence in the development of the English verb system which emerged from this research is shown in Table 1. It is significant, from the point of view of the present study, that all these studies found -*ing* to be the earliest acquired grammatical morpheme (e.g. Hakuta 1976). In contrast, the Simple Present -*s* form invariably came late.[2]

Several conceptual and methodological limitations detract from the findings of this type of *form-oriented* SLA research (see Sato 1990; Larsen-Freeman & Long 1991 and Ellis 1994). Particularly problematic is its equation of linguistic *form* with *function*. It assumes that the concept of function precedes the acquisition of form so that 'acquisition of form' implies 'acquisition of function'. Recent studies suggest this may not always be true.

1.2 Form-function research

Wagner-Gough (1978) was one of the first to recommend looking at both form and function when asserting that a language learner has 'acquired' a particular linguistic structure. She showed how her subject *Homer*, a five-year-old speaker of Assyrian learning L2-English, used the *Ving* form to refer to all tenses and aspects, and even the imperative. Can one say that Homer had actually acquired the English progressive? Cases such as these point very clearly to the need for both formal and functional considerations in the explanation of grammar acquisition. Accordingly, the approach to studies in SLA has gradually shifted from descriptions of the formal properties of IL to the broader question of the forces which drive the construction of form-function relations (Pfaff 1987; Sato 1990). This research suggests that the process of form-function mapping is a complex one. When new grammatical categories like English -ed and -ing first appear in learner language, they do not do so with all verbs or in all target contexts of use simultaneously. Nor are they used with the full range of meanings and functions which they express in the target language. Instead, new forms appear to follow a systematic pattern of successive integration as the interlanguage form-meaning mappings are modified until they ultimately assume their target-like values. Opinions in the literature differ, however, as to how this process can best be described and explained.

One influential view, known as the *Aspect Hypothesis*, holds that the emergence, early use and subsequent development of verb morphology in language acquisition is strongly influenced by the *inherent semantic properties of the lexical verb* which the learner selects to refer to a particular event (Andersen & Shirai 1996; Bardovi-Harlig 1999). The relevant semantic properties are most commonly defined in terms of Vendler's (1967) model of lexical verb aspect. Briefly, this model distinguishes four verb types – states, activities, accomplishments and achievements – on the basis of whether the lexical verb denotes an event which is either stative or dynamic, punctual or durative, and telic or atelic (i.e. whether or not it has an inherent goal or natural endpoint). An adapted version of this model appears in Table 2.

Table 2. Inherent semantic features of lexical verb types (after Andersen 1991)

	dynamic	telic	punctual	examples
State	–	–	–	*know, feel, want, hate*
Activity	+	–	–	*think, laugh, run, work*
Accomplishment	+	+	–	*explain, prepare, grow up*
Achievement	+	+	+	*start, fall, die, shoot, break*

The theoretical underpinnings of the Aspect Hypothesis need not concern us here (but see Andersen & Shirai 1996; Bardovi-Harlig 1999). The concrete predictions of the Aspect Hypothesis for the acquisition of English are:

a. Learners first associate and use the imperfective aspect marker -*ing* with prototypical dynamic-durative verbs (or *activities*) like *work* and *laugh*, regardless of the required grammatical tense, aspect or agreement values;

b. Perfective past and perfect tense markers (*-ed*, *-en*) are initially restricted to telic-punctual verbs (or *achievements*) like *drop* and *stop,* regardless of the required grammatical tense, aspect or agreement values;

c. The simple present tense marker *-s* is first predominantly used with stative verbs (or *states*) like *know* and *like*, again regardless of the required tense, aspect or agreement values;

d. In subsequent stages, the strong initial distributional bias of each morpheme towards its prototypical verb type gradually relaxes as learners extend its use to other verb types, following a systematic pattern of lexical diffusion displayed in Table 3.

Only in the last stage, when they are no longer bound to the inherent semantics of the verb, can the respective morphemes be put to their full functional use as markers of tense, aspect or agreement.

Andersen & Shirai (1996) point out that these distributional biases should not be taken in absolute terms but as relative tendencies based on frequency. In other words, what one should expect in the early stages of acquisition is not an *absolute restriction* of a specific morpheme to one specific class of verbs but a statistically *significant trend*. It is appropriate, therefore, that the extent and nature of the predicted distributional biases should be explored via a quantitative distributional analysis of verb morphology in a corpus of interlanguage data which is sufficiently large for such trends (if any) to appear. Several previous studies fail to meet this requirement, judging by the information provided in Bardovi-Harlig's (1999: 354–356) recent survey of tense-aspect research in SLA.[3]

Table 3. Predicted functional development of English verb morphemes

	Imperfective aspect marker *-ing*				Past and perfect tense marker *-en/ed*				Present tense marker *-s*			
	STAT	ACT	ACC	ACH	STAT	ACT	ACC	ACH	STAT	ACT	ACC	ACH
stage												
0	V	V	V	V	V	V	V	V	V	V	V	V
1	V	V-ing	V	V	V	V	V	V-p	V-s	V	V	V
2	V	V-ing	V-ing	V	V	V	V-p	V-p	V-s	V-s	V	V
3	V-ing	V-ing	V-ing	V	V	V-p	V-p	V-p	V-s	V-s	V-s	V
4	(V-ing)	V-ing	V-ing	V-ing	V-p	V-p	V-p	V-p	V-s	V-s	V-s	V-s

1.3   Aims of the present study

The present study aims to investigate the formal and functional development of selected verb categories through a *cross-sectional* comparison of their distributional patterns in the interlanguage speech of 46 young L2-learners from two first language (L1) backgrounds (Dutch and French) representing four different stages in L2 acquisition. One of the aims of the study is to check the findings from a previous longitudinal study (Housen 1995, 1998a, 2000) against a larger corpus of cross-sectional English IL data.

The acquisition of the entire English verb system lies well beyond the scope of this study, which will deal with only the following general questions:

(1)   a.   How do L2-learners acquire the basic morphological categories of the English verb system, i.e. the base form *Vø* , the Simple Present form *Vs*, the Present Participle form *Ving*, the regular Preterit/Past Participle form *Ved* and the irregular Preterit/Past Participle form *Ven*?

   b.   What stages of development are evident in the acquisition of these forms?

(2)   a.   How do L2-learners map these forms onto their appropriate *temporal, aspectual* and *grammatical meanings*, such as present, past or anterior time, imperfective, progressive, or habitual aspect, and person and number agreement?

   b.   What stages are evident in the development of these form-meaning relations and what are the causal factors that shape it?

The next section describes the methodology and corpora used.

2.   Method

The analyses are based on data taken from the *Corpus of Young Learner Interlanguage* (CYLIL). Construction of this corpus started in 1990 at the *Vrije Universiteit Brussel*. It consists of English oral interlanguage data elicited from European School pupils at different stages of development and from different L1 backgrounds (Dutch, French, Greek and Italian). The total CYLIL corpus currently amounts to 500,000 words. For the present study only data from Dutch- and French-speaking learners were used. This subcorpus amounts to 230,000 words.[4]

2.1 Learning context

The data were collected through interviews with 23 Dutch- and 23 French-speaking pupils of the L2-English section of the European Schools in Brussels and Mol (Belgium). Pupils in the European School system receive their basic education in one of 11 different mother tongue sections. They all learn a second language (either English, French or German) as a subject from the first grade of primary school onwards. The European School curriculum and method of L2 teaching in the early grades of primary school are grafted on communicative and functional-notional principles of foreign language teaching and learning, emphasizing oral-aural skills. A more structural approach to L2 teaching is started in grade 5 of primary school, including instruction on selected aspects of the L2 verb system. From grade 3 of primary school onwards the L2 is also increasingly used as a medium of instruction for other school subjects. In addition, pupils can use their L2 as a vehicular language with peers from other first language backgrounds, though this depends very much on the specific context and individual pupil involved. Further information about the European School model of multilingual education can be gained from Housen (2002a).

2.2 Subjects and data collection

Six of the 46 learners (three for L1-French, three for L1-Dutch) were studied longitudinally over a period of three years (grades 3–5). They were interviewed on five occasions at five-month intervals, creating a total of 30 data sets. The remaining 40 pupils were sampled from grades 3, 5, 7, 9 and 11 (roughly corresponding to the ages of 9, 11, 13, 15, and 17 respectively). They were interviewed on one occasion only, producing 40 data sets. (Although the data includes both longitudinal and cross-sectional data, the approach taken in this study will be only cross-sectional. For analysis of the longitudinal data, see Housen (1995, 2000, 2002b)). Similar data were also collected from eight native speakers (NSs) from the English language section of the European School in Brussels (four each from grades 5 and 7) to serve as baseline data in some of the analyses. Table 4 shows the distribution of the informants together with an estimation of the accumulated amount of formal classroom contact with English at the end of each of the five grades involved.

The oral interviews consisted of both informal free conversation and semi-guided speech tasks and were designed to elicit use of various features of the English verb system, including tense, aspect, modality, agreement and verb phrase syntax. Pupils were asked to talk about past experiences and future

Table 4. Informants

Grade level	Cross-sectional					Longitudinal	
L2-contact hrs.	3	5	7	9	11	3–5	
	250	370	1045	2095	2670	250–370	*total*
L1-Dutch	4	4	4	4	4	3	23
L1-French	4	4	4	4	4	3	23
L1-English		4	4				8

plans, to describe pictures, retell films they had seen, and retell three picture stories involving a variety of characters and actions. One of the picture stories is the well-known *Frog story*, which has been used in various other studies on L1 and L2 acquisition (e.g. Berman & Slobin 1994).

2.3 Data processing

The data collected were processed (i.e. transcribed, segmented, coded and annotated) in CHAT format to allow for computer-aided analysis with the help of the CLAN software. CHAT (*Codes for the Human Analysis of Transcripts*) and CLAN (*Computerized Language Analysis*) are two tools that have been especially developed for the study of language learner speech by the CHILDES organisation. As the name already indicates, the CHILDES system (for *Child Language Data Exchange System*) was originally developed for the study of child language and first language acquisition but it is increasingly used by SLA researchers, speech pathologists and discourse analysts. In addition to a standardised transcription and coding system (CHAT) and an associated analytic software package (CLAN), the CHILDES system also contains an archive of electronically available corpora on child language, interlanguage, bilingual speech, and speech disorders, all of which are in CHAT format. At the moment of writing, the CHILDES archive contained 20 corpora with data from L2 learners or bilingual speakers. The CYLIL corpus used in the present study will eventually also be added to the CHILDES archive. CHILDES is an open-ended, dynamic system, which means that new corpora are regularly added to the archive and that additions and modifications to the CHAT system and CLAN software are made on a regular basis (though the core of CHAT and CLAN has been stable for many years).

Access to the three components, viz. the CHILDES data base, the CHAT conventions and the CLAN software, is free. Permission to use them can be obtained via http://childes.psy.cmeu.edu or, for Europe, via http://atila-www.uia.ac.be/childes/.

The CHAT transcription and coding conventions have been designed to be compatible with a wide variety of speech data and a wide range of transcription and analytic needs. However, the accompanying CLAN software imposes some restrictions on the form of the transcription. The CLAN package currently includes over 30 programs that have been written in the *C* programming language and which can be compiled for a variety of operating systems, including UNIX, Macintosh, and Windows. Most of the programs can be run on any type of (extended) ASCII file though they run best on CHAT files. There are CLAN programs for transcript and corpus management (e.g. CHECK, CHSTRING, COLUMNS, FLO), for frequency counts (e.g. FREQ), for string searches (KWAL, COMBO), for computing indices of grammatical development and complexity (e.g. MLU, DSS), for co-occurrence analysis (COOCCUR), for interactional and discourse analyses (e.g. CHIP, CHAINS), as well as a semi-automatic morpho-syntactic parser (MOR). Each of these programs depends closely on particular aspects of CHAT.

A detailed discussion can be found in MacWhinney 1995 (updated copies of which are also available from the above internet addresses). The next two sections briefly exemplify aspects of CHAT and CLAN relevant for the CYLIL corpus in general and the present study of the verb system in particular.

2.3.1   Transcription and segmentation

Each interview in the present study was audio-recorded and transcribed in a separate text (ASCII) file, producing a total of 78 data sets (40 cross-sectional IL transcripts, 30 longitudinal IL transcripts, 8 native speaker transcripts). Following the CHAT guidelines, each transcript starts with a *@Begin* code and ends with a *@End* code. General information relating to the transcript as a whole is indicated at the beginning of the transcript (e.g. identification of the interlocutors, setting, etc.). For the CYLIL corpus, both the informants' and the interviewer's utterances were transcribed in standard English orthography on separate lines, called the main or independent tiers. These are prefixed with an asterix and a three-letter speaker code. Each main tier ends with one of a clearly specified set of utterance terminators (e.g. +... for trailing off). The general format of a CHAT transcript from the CYLIL corpus is illustrated in the following example:

```
@Begin
@Participants:  EMA Learner, INV Interviewer
@Coder: Alex Housen.
@Coding:  CHAT 1.0.
@ID:    EMA.
@Language:      Lan1 dutch.
@Education of Ema:      grade 4.
@Age of EMA:    9;
@Age of INV:    27;
@Sex of EMA:    female.
@Sex of INV:    male.
@SES of EMA: middle.
@Date: 19-DEC-1991.
@Tape Location: Tape 13, side a .
@Location:      Small classroom, European School, Brussels,
                Belgium.
@Room Layout:   desks, picture books.
@Situation:     INV and EMA are sitting next to one another
        with one small tape-recorder placed visibly on the
        other end of the desk, surrounded by picture books,
        boxes with crayons and small pots. A second tape-
        recorder is placed on a small chair opposite of EMA
        but largely concealed from her view. EMA comes in
        announcing that she has been ill.
*INV:   well when did it start # your illness?
*EMA:   uh maandag@d [= monday] [//] monday # monday+evening.
%com:   EMA sneezes.
*INV:   monday+evening?
*INV:   well what [/] what was wrong?
*EMA:   uhm # I was uhm +...
*EMA:   I don't know +...
*EMA:   [c] how you say it.
*EMA:   I was uhm turning around in my head all <the time> [>].
*INV:   <oh really> [<]?
*EMA:   and I had cold and hot at the same time.
*INV:   that's pretty scary.
@End
```

Sound strings were partitioned according to the word boundaries of the target language, with the exception of some complex strings which were clearly
grammatically unanalyzed, such as the formula *I + don't + know*. The plus signs
indicate that the entire string has the status of a single lexical unit. Plus signs
were not used for smaller unanalyzed units like *she's* or *that's* (e.g. *she's is hot*;
that's is a dog). Their special status was noted separately.

Phonetic transcription was used only to disambiguate severe mispronunciation or homographs (e.g. [red] vs. [ri:d] for *read*).[5] Particular attention was also paid to potential cases of phonetic assimilation, such as *I like/liked to go there* or *He say/said to me*. In such cases it was often impossible to decide whether the learner had supplied an inflectional marker or not. Forcing a decision could have had far-reaching analytic consequences and therefore these cases were clearly marked in the transcripts and, as a rule, excluded from further analysis. Particularly the learners' speech was transcribed in minute detail, including performance phenomena such as direct speech, incomprehensible speech, word and utterance fragments, pauses, fillers, retracings, repetitions, laughter, gestures and overlapping with the interviewer's speech. CHAT provides clear guidelines for indicating such features. Also indicated were non-English speech segments (mainly from Dutch, French, Greek and Italian) and idiosyncratic interlanguage expressions. In addition to the speech data, the transcripts also contain meta-data, i.e. annotations and comments necessary for a correct interpretation of the utterances. For example, deliberate modifications in speech rate, tone and pitch of voice were marked, referents of deictics identified, and relevant gestures or extra-linguistic sounds (laughter, sighs) indicated. Most of such clarificational information was rendered in UPC format (*Utterance-plus-Clarification*) and placed on a dependent tier (prefixed with *%com:*) beneath the main tier (Edwards 1995).

After transcription, all learner utterances were segmented into workable units for analysis. For our current purposes, segmentation was done on the basis of *clausal units*, following von Stutterheim (1986), Hickman (1990) and Slobin (1993). Each clausal unit was transcribed on a separate main tier. A clausal unit is defined here as a semantic unit consisting of at least one major argument (e.g. an agent, patient, recipient, instrument) and a predication about the argument (cf. Ochs 1979). In practice, a clausal unit usually corresponds to a predicate, which typically consists of a copula or a main verb (finite or non-finite) with its arguments. However, clausal units can also be verbless (e.g. due to ellipsis or errors of omission) while others may contain elaborate verb complexes (e.g. periphrastic constructions with auxiliaries and catenatives like *try/want/like* + *V*). Instances of clause linking (subordination) in matrix sentences were indicated with [*c*].

2.3.2   *Coding and annotation*

For the analysis of the verb system, all clauses with an overt verbal predicate were extracted from the corpus with the help of the CLAN program KWAL. Certain types of clauses were excluded, such as echolaic clauses and highly frequent non-analyzed formulaic utterances.[6] The refined database contained approximately 29,000 learner clauses and 7,000 native speaker clauses (with an average of 400 and 870 predicates per transcript respectively).

To investigate the development of the verb system, these 36,000 clausal units were coded for the following structural and semantic parameters:

a. the morpho-syntactic form of the verb phrase ($VERB): e.g. main, copula or auxiliary element, inflectional morphs (-ing, -s, -ed, -en), contractions and negations;
b. agreement values ($AGR): e.g. 1, 2, 3 person, singular vs. plural number;
c. tense semantics ($TENS): e.g. past, present, future, anterior;
d. aspectual semantics ($ASP): e.g. imperfective, progressive, dynamic;
e. inherent aspectual semantics or *Aktionsart* ($AA): state, activity, accomplishment, achievement.

This analytic information was annotated in *SPS* format (*Segment-Plus-Specification;* cf. Edwards 1995) on a separate tier (prefixed with *%cod:*) and labelled as to type (prefixed with $).[7] An example of a fully annotated extract is provided below.[8]

```
(1)  *EVA:  well he was rowing.
     %cod:  $VERB:AUX:PRET:BE:MAIN:Ving:was+rowing
            $AGR:3:SG:
            $TENS:PAST:SIM:
            $ASP:PROG:
            $AA:ACT:row

     *EVA:  and he lost one uh oar.
     %cod:  $VERB:MAIN:Ven:lost
            $AGR:3:SG:
            $TENS:PAST:SIM:
            $AA:ACH:lose+x

     *INV:  uhuh.

     *EVA:  and so he couldn't row anymore.
     %cod:  $VERB:AUX:Ven:NEG:CONTR:CAN:MAIN:V:could+not+row
            $AGR:3:SG:
            $TENS:PAST:SIM:
            $AA:ACT:MOD:row
```

Although CHAT comes with a large number of predefined codes, many of the analytic codes used in the present study were especially created for the specific analytic tasks at hand. New codes or symbols can be added as long as they are explicitly defined in a special file in the library of the CLAN package (the *depfile*) so that the CLAN programs can recognise them.

The coding of the formal and semantic properties was performed in two independent steps, to avoid circularity of analysis. Part of the coding of the formal aspects of the verb system ($VERB) was performed with the help of the MOR program in CLAN.[9] The coding of the semantic aspects ($AGR, $TENS, $ASP, $AA) had to be done by hand. (It is unlikely that the investigation of meaning in learner language will become amenable to automatic analysis in the foreseeable future). Two general remarks with respect to the coding system are in order here. First, some redundancy was deliberately built in to the coding system to allow for the extraction of rich information even with analyses focusing on a limited set of coding categories, thus obviating the necessity of performing multiple analyses. Secondly, like other coding systems of this kind, the coding system used here makes particular assumptions about formal and semantic categories of language, some of which are not uncontroversial. Moreover, their application in the analysis of genuine speech data requires that the analyst must make what may sometimes seem as crude and overly categorical decisions. This particularly holds for semantic categories such as past, imperfective, anterior, dynamicity. Although great efforts were made to keep the semantic coding as objective as possible through the use of several independent coders, the use of standardised diagnostics proposed in the literature on verb semantics (e.g. Dowty 1986), and the exclusion of overly ambiguous cases, it is important to acknowledge that coding for meaning in language is a problematic undertaking. (For a more detailed discussion of these and related problems, see Housen 1994, 1995, 1998b, 2002b.)

2.3.3   *Grouping of the data*

For the purpose of cross-sectional comparison, the 70 learner transcripts were regrouped in terms of proficiency level.[10] English proficiency was operationalised in terms of two lexical and two grammatical indices, each computed for 200 consecutive clauses of learner discourse. The lexical indices are the *Index of Guiraud*, a derivative of the type/token ratio, and the *Number of Verb Types* (Menard 1983; Broeder, Extra & van Hout 1993; Dietrich 1990). These measures were calculated with the help of the FREQ program which generates word lists and computes type and token frequencies. The grammatical indices were the *Target-Like Usage (TLU)* score, which measures a speaker's morphological accuracy against the target norm (Stauble 1978; Pica 1984), and the *Syntactic Diversity* index, which is based on the number and type of subordinate clauses produced in a given speech sample (Reilly, Bates & Marchman 1998).

Table 5. Grouping of data sets by proficiency level

Proficiency level	Number of data sets	Target-like usage	Guiraud	Number of verb types	Syntactic diversity
L	21	0–35 *(31)*	5–8 *(6.3)*	8–19 *(15)*	0–4 *(1)*
LI	21	36–55 *(46)*	8–10 *(9.2)*	20–29 *(26)*	5–9 *(6)*
HI	17	56–75 *(63)*	10–12 *(10.9)*	30–39 *(34)*	11–18 *(15)*
H	11	76–100 *(86)*	12–15 *(13.8)*	40–53 *(47)*	24–72 *(53)*
NS	8	n.a.	13.9–17.3 *(15.1)*	42–71 *(56)*	33–88 *(59)*

Numbers in columns 3-6 reflect range of scores; numbers in parentheses are mean group scores.
TLU scores were not calculated for the NSs as they can be expected to fall in the 95-100% range.

Four groups of learners were thus distinguished, representing a low (*L*), lower intermediate (*LI*), higher intermediate (*HI*) and high (*H*) level of proficiency. We will assume that these four proficiency levels correspond to four broad consecutive stages of interlanguage development. Table 5 shows the resulting classification and gives an indication of the range of scores and mean values obtained by each group on the four proficiency measures used. Note that most of the Francophone data sets fall in the L and LI groups, while the HI and H groups mainly consist of data from the Dutch-speaking learners.

2.4 Analytic procedures

Further analysis of the data proceeded in three steps. First, the relative proportion of major verb forms and patterns was calculated for each transcript with the aid of the FREQ program. These figures were then used as the denominators for more detailed explorations of verb form production and development (see Section 3).

Second, all clauses in the learner transcripts were analysed for the under-/overuse of the English inflectional verb categories (*Vø, Ving, Ved, Ven, Vs*) in target-like and non-target-like contexts with the help of the KWAL and FREQ programs (see Section 4.1). In this analysis the concern was not so much the errors in the *formation* of verb categories as with issues pertaining to the correct or incorrect *use* of these categories, whether correctly or incorrectly formed.

Third, to investigate the possibility of an inherent semantic basis for the development of verb morphology as predicted by the Aspect Hypothesis, all affirmative declarative non-modal clauses containing a lexical verb were extracted from the learner and native speaker data with the help of KWAL and coded for inherent semantic aspect. After exclusion of all ambiguous cases some 15,000 clauses were retained for further analysis (see Section 4.2). Further analysis of the data was done with the aid of the FREQ and COMBO programs.[11]

3.   Formal development of the verb system

3.1   Global patterns

This section discusses the development of the repertoire of verb forms as it emerges from a general cross-sectional analysis of the corpora. I will first discuss the overall distribution of the major English verb forms in the learner and native speaker data.

Tables 6 and 7 show the proportion of various verb categories to the total number of verb phrases in each of the five subcorpora (L, LI, HI, H, NS). Several relevant trends can be noted. First, the vast majority (i.e. more than 80%) of lexical verbs in the L and LI corpora appear as uninflected base forms (*Vø*), whether they occur in finite position (as main or auxiliary verb) or non-finite position (as participles). This is illustrated by examples (1) to (3).[12]

(1)   Lf1: uh mister Neil # say # uh me +...

(2)   Lf1: uh mister Neil have give me # the uh # <la lettre>.

(3)   Lf4: and [/] and he go uhm # to her grandmother...

The predominance of *Vø* forms in the L and LI group data steadily decreases in the data of the HI and H groups as other morphological categories appear. The first inflected form of lexical verbs to emerge is the present participle *Ving*. In fact, *Ving* is the only other inflected form to occur with any frequency alongside the uninflected base form *Vø* in the data of the L and LI groups. However, as examples (4–6) below indicate, the ability to produce the *Ving* form at these early stages of development does not imply mastery of the grammatical category of the Progressive. The function of the *Ving* form is clearly still incompletely analysed as it is randomly used in both finite and non-finite contexts, and both with and without an auxiliary element. In contrast, in the data of the HI and H learners *Ving* is used mostly correctly as a participle of *Be* in the formation of the Progressive (cf. table 7 and examples 7–8).

(4)   Lf1: what you doing?

(5)   Lf4: and he eating the grandmother.

(6)   Lf4: yes # I have understanding.

Table 6. Percentage distribution of main verb complexes and auxiliaries

	Main verbs — Simple						Main verbs — Complex					Total N	Catenatives						Do				Have				Be			Modal verbs			Total N
	Vo	Ving	Ved	Ven	Vs	Be	Do+V	Have+V	Be+V	V+V	Other	N	Vo	Ving	Ved	Ven	Vs	N	Vo	Vs	Ven	N	Vo	Vs	Ven	N	Pres.	Pret.	N	Vo	Ven	N	N
L (n=21)	44	7	0	2	1	22	3	3	6	8	2	3710	70	30	0	0	0	93	100	0	0	126	100	0	0	126	99	1	446	100	0	212	1003
LI (n=21)	41	2	0	4	4	26	6	3	3	10	1	8419	90	3	0	0	7	7	89	11	0	369	94	5	2	301	81	9	273	97	3	541	1722
HI (n=17)	26	0	2	6	6	25	6	7	13	10	0	9947	77	4	4	4	12	147	86	5	9	632	84	14	3	725	43	57	1213	83	17	796	3513
H (n=11)	18	0	3	11	7	26	5	3	15	12	0	6945	60	1	16	13	10	163	55	13	32	376	67	15	18	323	69	31	1010	73	27	524	2396
NS (n=8)	16	0	3	8	6	28	7	4	14	15	0	6961	59	0	17	10	14	232	58	13	28	472	63	15	22	481	72	28	960	55	45	599	2744

Do+V: formulaic I+don't+know excluded.

Be+V: includes occurrences of Progressive and of going/gonna + V with overt auxiliary Be.

V+V: verbal complexes with modal, aspectualizer and catenative verbs.

Other: idiosyncratic verb constructions and those containing an L1 element (e.g. is + tombé, have + speel).

* Percentages are calculated for each category separately

Do: Vo= do(n't); Vs = does(n't); Ven = did(n't)

Have: Vo= have(n't); Vs = has(n't); Ven = had(n't); includes occurrences of modal Have + Vinf

Be: Pres. = am,are,is; Pret. = was,were,been; includes occurrences of Be + go/going/gonna + V

Modal: Vo= can, must, will, shall; Ven = could, would, should.

Table 7. Percentage distribution of verb form categories in finite and non-finite positions

| | Finite positions | | | | | | | | | Nonfinite positions | | | | | | | | | | | |
| | main & auxiliary verbs | | | | | | Be (aux. & cop) | | | participles of Aux-*Have* | | | | | | participles of Aux-*Be* (incl. Be-passives) | | | | | |
	Vø	Ving	Ved	Ven	Vs	N	Pres.	Pret.	N	Ving	Ved	Ven	Vø	Vs	N	Ving	Ved	Ven	Vø	Vs	N
L (n=21)	85	11	0	3	1	2620	96	4	359	8	2	2	89	0	51	48	0	1	50	1	88
LI (n=21)	80	3	0	8	8	5775	74	26	808	4	2	7	87	0	79	61	2	4	32	1	95
HI (n=17)	72	0	4	13	11	6213	52	48	998	4	14	23	55	3	192	87	2	1	9	1	302
H (n=11)	52	0	8	25	15	4110	65	35	1131	1	12	71	16	0	69	91	3	3	2	0	351
NS (n=8)	53	0	9	23	14	4064	71	29	2891	0	15	73	12	0	261	86	8	4	2	0	87

(7)   HId6: because Hans was <u>moving</u> uh very much.

(8)   Hd3: they were all <u>laughing</u> at me.

The next inflected form to make its entry in the verb system of these learners is the irregular *Ven* form. The first verb to appear in the *Ven* form is *Be*. The form *was* becomes a fairly regular feature of the informants' speech from the LI group onwards (cf. example 9). It is followed by the *Ven* forms of other high-frequency verbs such as *have (had)* and *do (did)* (cf. examples 10 and 11). *Ven* forms of lexical verbs (cf. examples 12 to 14) are still underextended in the data of the L, LI and HI learners when compared to the H and NS group data where *Ven* constitutes 27% of all finite verbs and more than 70% of all participles of *Aux-Have*. Overall, the *Ven* forms appear first mainly as simple verbs in the L and LI data; from the HI group onwards they also appear as participles in the formation of Perfect tenses (cf. examples 13 and 14 *vs.* example 1 above).

(9)   LIf6: and then he <u>was</u> happy.

(10)   LId17: <my mother> [/] my mother uhm <u>had</u> that one time.

(11)   LIf6: uhm # I <u>did</u> uh # pancake.

(12)   HId4: but then <the co(ws)> [//] uh the bull &s uh <u>saw</u> that.

(13)   HId7: uh no uh the doctors <u>said</u> that.

(14)   HId5: uh misses Bristow have <u>said</u> it.

Regular *Ved* appears later than its irregular counterpart and does not become a regular feature of the speech of these informants until the HI level. And even then, *Ved* forms are relatively infrequent compared to the *Ven* forms, even in the native speaker data (i.e. ±9% of finite forms, ±15% of participles of *Have*). This is in accordance with the general trend in native English that *Ved* forms have high type frequency but low token frequency while the reverse holds for *Ven* forms (Francis & Kucera 1982).

(15)   LId17: I was in Brussels in the [/] in # the Flemish school [c]
         but I <u>stopped</u> it [c] as I uh was # five [/] six year old.

(16)   LId6: and you have <u>putted@il</u> # uh the lights out.

(17)   HId9: and then uh we <u>eated@il</u> [c] and <u>watched</u> # uhm Perfect+Strangers.

Examples (16) and (17) illustrate one of the most conspicuous grammatical errors in learner language, namely overgeneralization of the *-ed* morpheme to irregular verbs. In this study, 14.3%, 19.4% and 13.7% of all *Ved* forms in the LI, HI and H data respectively involve such overgeneralizations. They do not occur in the L data (where *Ved* forms are still virtually absent). This type of over-regularization is considered to be indicative of the language learner's growing morphological capacity (cf. Marcus et al. 1992). Interestingly, 6 instances (2%) of over-regularization were also found in the native speaker data (e.g. *teached*, *catched* and *ranned*).

The last major inflectional category of the English verb, *Vs*, is also a relatively late occurrence, with most learners at least. Its use is either infrequent or erratic in the L and LI data. Unlike the other inflectional categories, *Vs* hardly ever occurs in non-finite participle position (as in example 21).

(18)   Lf4: no # she can <u>speaks</u> english # and # neerlandais@f .

(19)   Lf4: mais@f we <u>speaks</u> french.

(20)   LIf6: there's some children [c] who <u>goes</u> to missus Bristow.

(21)   LId17: and then we don't <u>has</u> # so much time for this.

Tables 6 and 7 conceal the considerable individual variation in the use of *Vs* among the L and LI learners. The relatively high percentage of *Vs* forms in the LI group (8%) is almost entirely attributable to a few informants only who use this form frequently while it is virtually absent from the data of other members of that group. Other significant instances of individual variation not apparent from Tables 6 and 7 include the use of simple *versus* compound verb forms in the early stages of acquisition. Some learners clearly show an early and consistent predilection for compound, Perfect Perfect-like constructions (cf. examples 22–23), while other learners avoid this form altogether in favour of the simple Preterit-like form, which they also overextend to contexts where native speakers of English would use a compound Perfect form (cf. examples 24–25).

(22)   LId15: uh you mean # what I <u>have done</u> yesterday?

(23)   LId16: oh yes # I <u>have done</u> it many time.

(24)   Hd2: you didn't <u>sleep</u> yet?

(25)   Hd2: it was the best camp I ever <u>had</u> till now

3.2 A composite developmental picture

The development of verb form categories as apparent from the quantitative analysis of these cross-sectional data is largely congruent with the picture that emerged from the longitudinal study in Housen (1995, 1998a). It can be summarised in terms of three broad stages of development:

Stage 1: Invariant default forms. Verbs appear in a first stage as unique, invariant forms. These are typically unmarked base forms (*Vø*) like *see* and *play* but morphologically marked forms can also be observed, particularly high frequency *Ven* forms like *got* and present participles like *dancing*. These invariant forms function as *default forms* in all contexts, regardless of the intended or required tense, aspect or agreement values. This first stage of development is represented by the data of the L corpus.

Stage 2: Non-functional 'allomorphic' variation. The onset of morphological variation marks the second stage of development, represented here by the data from the LI and HI corpora and illustrated by examples (26) to (30) below. The overall order in which the various morphological categories emerge is as follows:

Vø > Ving; *was* > Ven > Ved; *going* + Vinf > *have* + V; Vs; *will* + V

The first categories to appear after the baseform are *-ing* and irregular *Ven* forms, particularly *was* and *had*. Regular *Ved* appears later, followed by *Vs*, compound Perfect-like forms and *be* + *going* + V constructions (including variants like *go/gonna* + *V*). Some learners, however, show an early preference for a compound Present Perfect-like form (*Aux.Have* + V) rather than for inflectional Preterit forms. Other analytic and periphrastic forms like *will* + V are also late developments.[13]

(26)   [the interviewer asks the informant whether her friend speaks any French]
       LIf6: no uh ... she speaking uh Nederlands@d .

(27)   [the interviewer asks the informant whether she speaks any English at school]
       LIf6: uh yes ... in class we speak English uh by mister Neil.

(28)   [the informant is describing a picture of trees which have lost their leaves]
       LIf6: the leaves is going away from the trees.

(29)   [the informant is asked to describe a picture of a man falling from a ladder]
       INV: and what is he doing here?
       LIf6: uh she fall.

(30)   [the interviewer asks the informant what she did during the weekend]
       LIf6: uh we went again to the sea.
       INV: uhuh ... so uh the house has not been sold yet?

> LIf6: uh no but my father and mother <u>go</u> there # [c] to speak with uh people.

The order of emergence presented here should not be interpreted too strictly. There is considerable individual variation and it is possible that with more data analysis, the order may have to be modified somewhat. Perhaps more important than the order in which the various verb forms emerge, is the observation that 'new' forms are not yet functional for encoding the tense, aspect or agreement meanings of the target language. The formal contrast between *speak* and *speaking* in examples (26) and (27), for instance, does not signal perfective versus imperfective meaning in any consistent way, nor does the contrast between *went* and *go* in (30) seem to signal past vs. present tense. At this stage the variants behave like allomorphs as they appear first in random variation and then in complementary distribution. Their use is both underextended and overextended, that is, they are not consistently used in all the contexts where a native speaker would use them (cf. the omission of *-ing* in (29)), and conversely, they are used in contexts where native speakers would not use them (cf. the use of *-ing* in (26)). It seems then, that form precedes function in the acquisition of the verb system or, as Klein et al. (1993) have remarked, *formal variation precedes its functional use.*

Stage 3: Distributional restructuring, functional specification and increasingly target-like use of verb morphology to encode tense, aspect and agreement. Further development consists of the learners trying to determine the target-like meanings and functions of each verb form. This marks the final stage in the development of the verb system, a stage which only a few of the most advanced informants in the H group reach. This stage will be discussed in Section 4.

The developmental pattern for the acquisition of verbal morphology observed in the present study is congruent – at least in outline – with those observed in other studies involving older L2-learners from different first language backgrounds, learning different target languages in different learning contexts (Dietrich et al. 1995; Giacalone Ramat 1992; Housen 1994; Vogel 1989). Similar patterns have also been observed in first language acquisition (Fletcher & Garman 1986). Such similarities have been taken as evidence for the operation of universal mechanisms of language development. One such hypothesis, the Aspect Hypothesis (Andersen 1991; Andersen & Shirai 1996), will be tested in the next section.

4.   The functional development of the verb system

This section presents the findings from the investigation of the relation between meaning, function and form in the informants' use of verbal categories, with special attention to the predictions of the Aspect Hypothesis (see Section 1.2).

4.1   Patterns of usage

The previous analysis showed that new grammatical forms like English -*ed* and -*ing* are initially under- and/or overextended in IL. This is indicative of the learner's tendency to hypothesise restricted or over-general form-meaning mappings. Our next step then, consisted of investigating the patterns of use (underuse, overuse, correct use, accurate use) of each of the five basic English verb form categories (*Vø* , *Vs, Ving, Ved, Ven)* in the four learner corpora by examining their distribution across target-like and non-targetlike grammatical and temporal-aspectual contexts as specified on the $AGR, $TENS and $ASP coding tiers (cf. 2.3.2).

Overuse was operationalised as the ratio of the number of times a form is incorrectly supplied to its total number of uses. An *underuse* score was calculated as the ratio of the frequency with which a form is omitted from obligatory contexts to the total number of obligatory contexts for use. *Correct usage* is expressed as the ratio of the number of correct uses of a form in obligatory contexts to the total number of uses. The *accuracy of use* of a form was measured by the TLU score, which is the ratio of the number of correct uses of form to the sum of the number of correct uses, incorrect uses and omissions. These ratio scores (multiplied by 100) are shown in figures 1a–1e.

These figures reveal that the various verb categories do not show the same patterns of variation in their use and development. The base form *Vø* is initially not only often underused but also, and particularly, overused in contexts where native English would require some inflected form of the verb (cf. Fig. 1a and examples 1–3 above). This reflects its status as the main default verb form in the early and intermediate stages of IL development.

Graph 1b shows that the *Vs* form is massively overextended and especially underextended (i.e. omitted) at the L and LI levels of development, suggesting extensive random variation in its use (cf. examples 18–21). It is not until the H level that use of *Vs* approaches target-like criterion levels.

Figure 1c shows that the *Ving* form is not only underextended in the early and intermediate stages of acquisition (as could perhaps be expected) but also frequently overextended, both to semantic contexts that do not easily allow

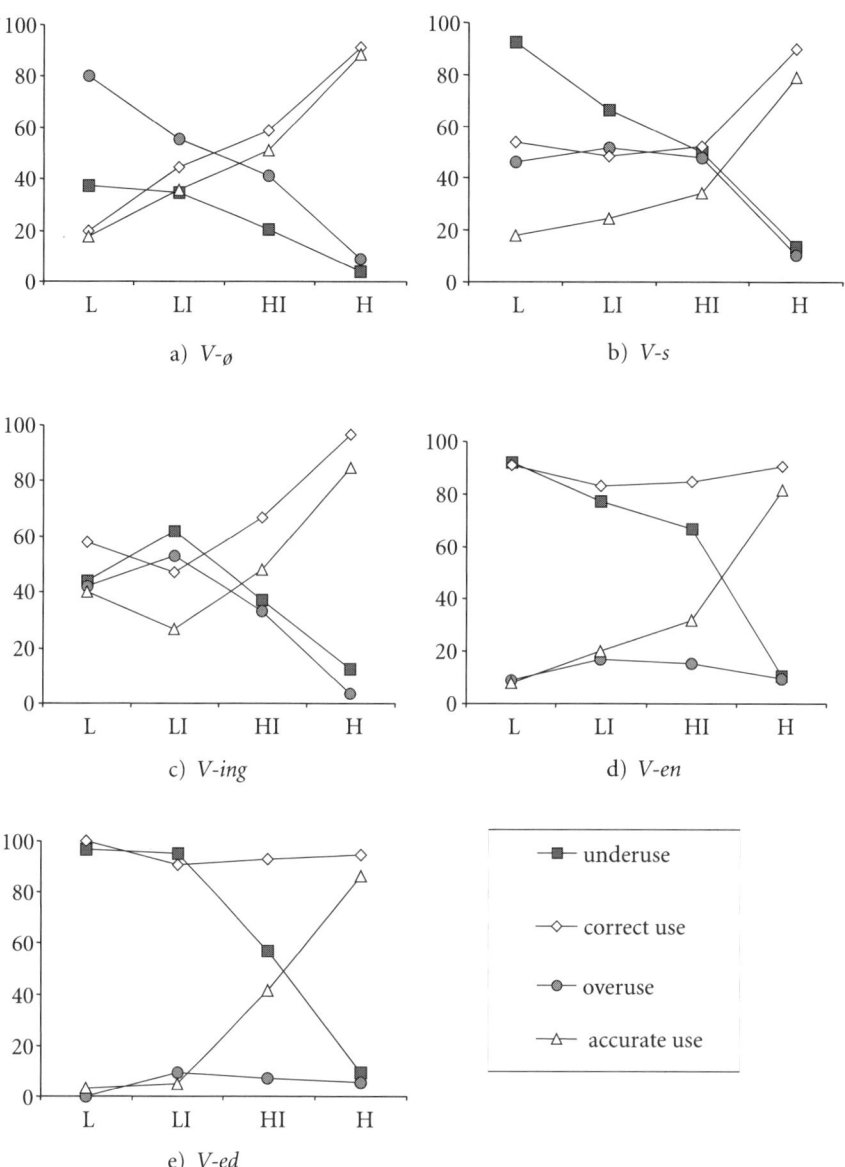

a) *V-ø*

b) *V-s*

c) *V-ing*

d) *V-en*

e) *V-ed*

- ■ — underuse
- ◇ — correct use
- ● — overuse
- △ — accurate use

Figure 1. Patterns of over-, under-, correct and accurate use (in %)

for an imperfective reading or to grammatical contexts that would require another verb form. For example, these learners say *I'm going to Ostend* [LId17] (for *I went to Ostend), He can not dancing* [Lf12], and even *I wasn't knowing it*

[HId8]. Interestingly, over- and underextension of *Ving* increases from the L to the LI level to drop again from the HI level onwards, thus showing a learning curve reminiscent of the famous *U-shaped* pattern in the development of the English *Ved* and *Ven* forms described in the literature (cf. Ellis 1994).

Irregular *Ven* forms are initially also overextended occasionally to non-past or non-perfect contexts (e.g. *I always took a book with me when I'm coming to school.* [LId17]) but less frequently so than *Ving*.[14] In contrast, regular *-ed* is hardly ever overextended (< 1%); it is only underextended, especially at the L and LI levels, where *Ved* forms are still rare. But whenever *-ed* is used, it is nearly always used appropriately in either a Past or Perfect tense context. Thus, these learners will not say, for example, *"Tomorrow I visited my grandmother"*. This is probably not a trivial observation and I will return to it in the discussion.

To summarise, the patterns of use of the various verb form categories by the different groups discussed suggest that learners fluctuate between overuse and underuse as they fine-tune form-meaning associations. The questions which now arise are, first, in what kinds of contexts are the respective verb forms over- and/or underextended, and secondly, how can this be explained? As discussed in Section 1.2, the Aspect Hypothesis provides a possible answer to these questions.

4.2 Interdependency between inherent semantics and morphological form

Following the procedure described in Section 2.4, some 15,000 clauses (an average of 190 per transcript) were retained for the analysis of the hypothesised interdependency between verb form and inherent semantics of the verb. The native speaker data were also analysed to provide a baseline for comparison.

The bar-charts in figures (2) to (4) display the distributional-combinatorial patterns of the three major verb categories (*Ving*, *Vs*, *Ven/ed*) across the four semantic verb classes (states, activities, accomplishments, achievements) in each of the five subcorpora. (Numbers in bars are percentages; numbers in parentheses underneath each bar are the corresponding token frequencies). Examples (32) to (61) illustrate the relevant trends.

4.2.1   *Aspect morphology (-ing)*
The analysis appears to support the predictions of the Aspect Hypothesis for the development of the English aspect marker *-ing*. The first two graphs in Figure 2 show that, at the L level, use of *-ing* is mainly restricted to inherently atelic-dynamic-durative verbs (*activities*) like *dancing* and *fighting* (cf. 32–34). This distributional bias, however, is not (or perhaps no longer) absolute, as

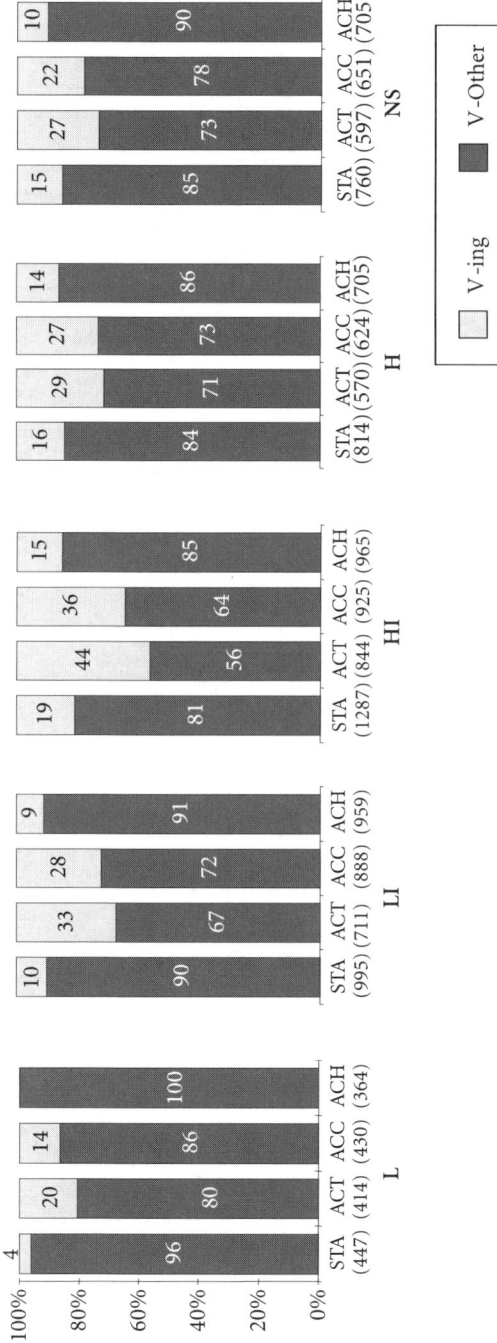

Figure 2. Distribution of the aspect marker across semantic verb categories: percentage distribution of *V-ing* tokens

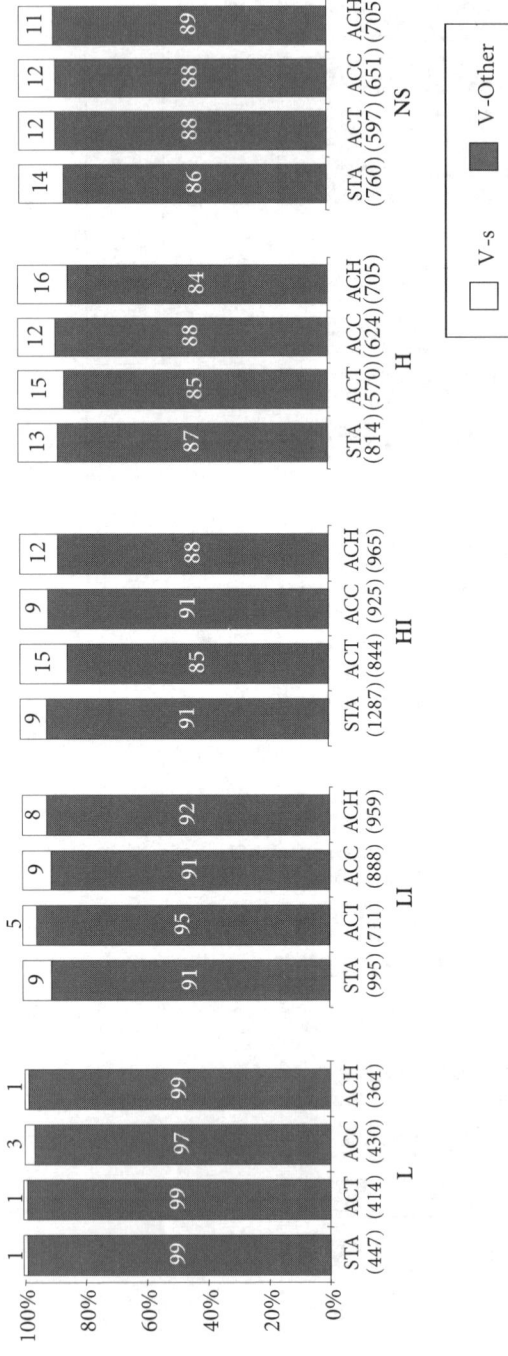

Figure 3. Distribution of Present tense marker across semantic verb categories: percentage distribution of V-s tokens

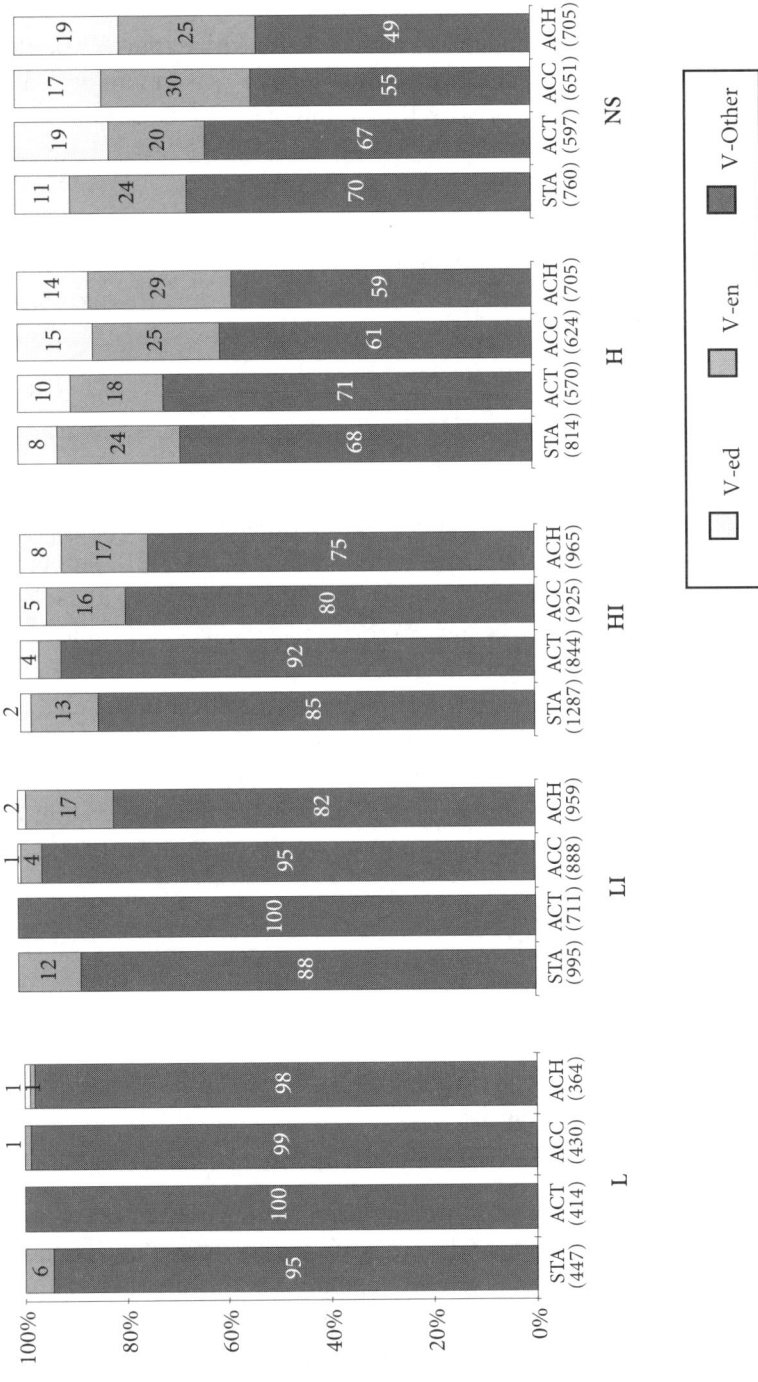

Figure 4. Distribution of *Past/Perfect morphology* across semantic verb categories: percentage distribution of *V-en* and *V-ed* tokens

telic-dynamic-durative verbs (*accomplishments*) like *going + to + location* also occur with the *-ing* marker, though less so than the activity verbs (cf. 35). Also as predicted, state and achievement predicates tend to remain uninflected at this stage, whether the context is perfective or imperfective (cf. 36–39).

(32)   Lf2: she's <u>dancing</u>.   [activ.]

(33)   Lf2: the boy uh <u>fighting</u>.   [activ.]

(34)   Lf3: and the people is <u>laughing</u>.   [activ.]

(35)   Lf8: he's <u>going</u> to the car.   [accompl.]

(36)   Lf2: I <u>want</u> a red uh sweet.   [state]

(37)   Lf2: the boy <u>hear</u> the frog.   [state]

(38)   Lf1: he <u>fall</u> uh for the dog.   [achiev.]

(39)   Lf2: the man <u>take</u> the watch. [achiev.]

From the LI level onwards, the initial bias of *-ing* towards activity verbs gradually relaxes as it extends to achievements and states (cf. (40)–(42)). This indicates that the use of *-ing* gradually frees itself from the constraints of the inherent semantics of the verb and, as such, becomes increasingly more functional as a marker of imperfective aspect.

This development, however, is initially accompanied by overextended usage of *-ing*. With some learners it even leads to overextension of *-ing* to highly stative verbs like *seem, know, want,* and *be* (cf. (43)–(46)). Interestingly, this type of overextension has not been attested in L1 acquisition and even in L2 acquisition it appears to be a rare phenomenon (Andersen & Shirai 1996).

(40)   LId15: the boy <u>falling</u>.   [achiev.]

(41)   LId16: the car is <u>crashing</u>.   [achiev.]

(42)   LId16: the boy is <u>standing</u> uh on a stone.   [state]

(43)   HId7: because it was just <u>seeming</u> fantastic.   [state]

(44)   HId7: and then the king and queen were <u>wering</u> angry.   [state]

(45)   HId8: I wasn't <u>knowing</u> that.   [state]

(46)   HId8: and then the bull was <u>wanting</u> to run after him.   [state]

The learners in the H group seem to have acquired the specific restrictions on the semantic scope of the English *-ing* form: they no longer overextend it to stative verbs of cognition and perception. On the whole the H group uses *Ving* more economically than the LI and HI groups and its pattern of distribution closely resembles that of the native speaker group. Interestingly, the distributional bias of -*ing* towards dynamic-durative verbs (activities, accomplishments) does not completely disappear, not even in the NS data. This lends credence to the Distributional Bias Hypothesis which holds that the strong distributional bias of verb morphemes towards certain verb types in learner language is a reflection of a similar though less outspoken distributional bias in the speech of native speakers, which serves as input for the language learners (Bowerman 1989; Andersen & Shirai 1996; Housen 1998a).

4.2.2   *Present tense & agreement marker -s*

The use and development of the Present tense/ agreement marker -*s* does not show the hypothesised link with the inherent semantics of the verb predicate (cf. Figure 3). From the start, i.e. from the L level onwards, -*s* appears with any verb type, including achievements and accomplishments like *break* and *go + location*, instead of being restricted to states such as *mean*. This is shown in the examples (47) to (50), all taken from the *L* corpus.

(47)   Lf8: what [/] what's <u>means</u> uh 'garden'?   [state]

(48)   Lf8: uh I <u>looks</u> television.   [activ.]

(49)   Lf9: she <u>goes</u> to a [//] the forest.   [accompl.]

(50)   Lf5: and he <u>breaks</u> the ball.   [achiev.]

Development of -*s* beyond the L level does not reveal any particular interdependence with inherent verb semantics either. *Vs* more or less evenly spreads across all verb categories and becomes gradually more native-like as development proceeds.

4.2.3   *Past/Perfect markers -en/-ed*

The Aspect Hypothesis predicts that Preterit/Perfect forms first emerge with achievement verbs before gradually extending, from right to left through the Vendlerian matrix, to other verb classes until all verbs in past and perfect tense contexts are properly marked (cf. Table 3). This is not the pattern which emerges from the graphs in Figure 4. Although some inflected achievements and accomplishments do occur in the L data (cf. 51–52), Preterit/Perfect morphology on lexical verbs appears first and foremost with states like *had* and *saw* (cf. 53–55). Note that these cases all involve highly frequent *Ven* forms.

(51)   Lf12: I <u>forgot</u> it.   [achiev.]

(52)   Lf14: and he <u>lost</u> the uh thing.   [achiev.]

(53)   Lf9: and I <u>saw</u> a reportage@f.   [state]

(54)   Lfl1: we <u>had</u> much snow this winter.   [state]

(55)   Lf10: and he <u>heard</u> sleeping the wolf.   [state]

Closer analysis of the graphs in Figure 4 reveals that regular *Ved* forms not only appear later than *Ven* forms but their distribution also seems to show a closer link with the inherent semantics of the verb than their irregular counterparts. *Ved* first appears with achievements in the LI data before spreading in the following stages to accomplishments, activities and states, in that order (cf. examples 56–61).

(56)   LIf4: she <u>died</u>.   [achiev.]

(57)   LIf8: and he <u>finished</u> it.   [achiev.]

(58)   LId17: and she <u>sewed</u> it again .   [accompl.]

(59)   LId16: you have <u>walked</u> to the uh # that # the door.   [accompl.]

(60)   Hid7: I only <u>looked</u> a little bit to the pictures.   [activ.]

(61)   Hd6: I <u>liked</u> it very much.   [state]

Unfortunately, because of the low token frequencies of *Ved* in the present data (e.g. a mere 3 and 15 *Ved* tokens could be included for the analysis of the L and LI corpora respectively), we cannot state with certainty that regular *Ved* follows the pattern of development predicted by the Aspect Hypothesis more closely than the irregular *Ven* forms.

4.3 Discussion

Why do the verb markers investigated here show different patterns of distribution? Why are only the *-en* and *-ed* markers mainly underused but hardly ever overused? Why does the use and development of *-ing* (and perhaps also *-ed*) show a stronger link with inherent verb semantics than *-en* and *-s*? At the current stage of research, one can only speculate as to the answers to these questions.

The absence of a significant association between *-s* and inherent verb semantics may have to do with the fact that the primary function of *-s* is that of a marker of grammatical agreement rather than of grammatical present (or non-past) tense. Inherent verb semantics may well serve as a guiding principle in the acquisition of temporal-aspectual form-meaning relations but not, or less so, in the acquisition of grammatical functions such as syntactic agreement. Inherent lexical verb semantics and grammatical tense and aspect meanings are said to share the same ontological basis (Lyons 1977); no such clear conceptual resemblance exists between lexical verb semantics and grammatical concord. This then could explain why no supporting evidence was found for the predictions of the Aspect Hypothesis for the 'Present tense' marker -s.[15]

This explanation cannot satisfactorily account for the different patterns observed for *Ving*, *Ven* and *Ved*, whose major functions *are* as markers of tense and aspect. A possible explanation for these differences may be found in psycholinguistics. Psycholinguists have argued that different types of processing mechanisms operate in the acquisition of grammatical morphology. To simplify, *irregular* morphology would be mainly subject to the process of *associative* or *lexical* learning whereas the acquisition of *regular* morphology would mainly involve *productive morphological rule*-learning (Pinker & Prince 1994; Bybee & Slobin 1982). If we apply this to the current findings, we could hypothesise that primitive conceptual-semantic notions such as stativity, durativity and telicity may play a steering role in the process of morphological rule learning, which mainly affects regular morphology like -*ing*, but not, or less so, in associative learning, which mainly affects irregular forms like *went*, *got*, and *broke*. These irregular forms would be directly mapped onto a given conceptual scene and then stored as one specific form-meaning unit in associative memory. Additional evidence for this hypothesis could come from the observation that regular -*ed*, like -*ing*, also shows a significantly stronger link with inherent aspect than irregular -*en*. This is indeed suggested by the present analyses.

A final explanation draws on the notion of transfer from the learner's L1. Slobin (1991) has argued that L2-learners come to the acquisition of the grammar of their L2 predisposed by the basic grammatical distinctions of their L1 so that they will look in the input language for similar distinctions. If they find such similarities, they will use these as a basis for reconstructing the target language grammar. If they find no such similarities, i.e. when they encounter form-meaning relations in the L2-input which have no obvious counterpart in their L1, they will try first to construct such a system with the help of universals such as semantic prototypes. Applying this to the current case would mean that the Francophone and the Dutch-speaking learners both came to their L2-acquisition task in the expectation that the verb system of their target language, English, makes a primary distinction between past and non-past tense because this is basically what happens in their respective L1s. Moreover, this is basically also what happens in English (Dahl 1985; Comrie 1976). Their expectations thus being to some extent met, these learners were immediately drawn to analyze and use the *Ven* and *Ved* forms *mainly* in terms of this past/non-past contrast. This would explain why the informants rarely overextend these forms to present or future contexts in their own output (cf. Section 4.1). However, taking this view, the aspect marker *–ing* would be processed in a different way. The learners in this study may not have been prepared for their target language to mark aspectual distinctions to the same extent as they were prepared for the marking of tense distinctions, since in their respective first languages, grammatical aspect is either absent (in Dutch) or only a minor system (in French). Hence, these learners had no clear L1-based framework available within which to interpret the formal opposition between the *simple* and the *Ving* forms which they encountered in the input. They therefore analyzed the *-ing* morpheme in terms of universal *prototypical* meanings first, interpreting it as a marker of the inherent dynamic-atelic-durative nature of the verb, before gradually sorting out its targetlike values (e.g. through a process of metaphorical inferencing as proposed by Taylor 1989).

5. Conclusion

The study reported here can be considered an instance of what Granger (1998: 12) has called CIA – *Contrastive Interlanguage Analysis*. It combines the two major CIA approaches: first, an *IL vs. IL comparison* and, though this has not been fully exploited in the present report, an *IL vs. NL* [Native Language] *comparison*. Through a cross-sectional comparison of different learner corpora covering four different proficiency levels and two different L1 backgrounds, it has been possible to investigate aspects of the diachronic and cross-linguistic development of the English verb system in the process of SLA. The combination of a substantive annotated computer corpus with analytic software tools made it possible to empirically validate previous research findings obtained from smaller transcripts, as well as to test explanatory hypotheses about pace-setting factors in second language acquisition.

The findings of this study suggest that even for young L2 learners in an educational context, the acquisition of the forms and functions of the verb is a complex process which follows a route similar to that observed for older learners in naturalistic language learning contexts. Attempts to explain this process point to a complex interaction between general mechanisms of language processing, universal perceptual-conceptual predispositions, L1-based predispositions and the quantitative tendencies of the input language.

The explanatory scenarios proposed here must at the present state of the research remain tentative and general in their degree of specification. More detailed cross-linguistic research and additional data are needed to support them. We acknowledge, however, that cross-sectional comparisons of overall frequencies and patterns of distribution in multi-learner corpora cannot tell the whole story. The findings from longitudinal case studies (Housen 1995, 1998b, 2000b) suggest that there may be significant individual variation in the route of development, even between learners of the same proficiency level and L1 background. This variation manifests itself in the order of emergence of different formal categories, their accuracy of use, their patterns of distribution and the degree to which the learners are sensitive to the influences from their L1 or from universal factors such as the inherent semantic notions considered here. To investigate these issues more adequately, large corpora with *longitudinal* data from individual learners are necessary.

Notes

1. Following standard practice in second language acquisition research, the term *second language acquisition*, its abbreviation *SLA* and its various derivations (e.g. *L2-learner, L2-knowledge, L2-input*) are used as umbrella terms for such distinctions as *foreign* vs. *second* language acquisition, second language *acquisition* vs. second language *learning*, *second* language acquisition vs. *third/fourth* language acquisition, *formal/ instructed/ guided/educational* second language acquisition vs. *informal/ spontaneous/ naturalistic/ unguided* second language acquisition. One of the central questions of current language acquisition research is whether these various types of language acquisition are indeed different in terms of their route, rate, outcome and underlying mechanisms of learning. In addition, these distinctions often turn out to be of limited heuristic value, particularly for languages of wider currency such as English, where they become blurred. For example, it is not clear whether the learning of English in Brussels or Amsterdam would qualify as an instance of second or foreign language learning, given the pervasiveness of English in the media and the presence of sizeable English-speaking communities in these cities, providing learners of English with ample opportunity for naturalistic exposure to the target language (in addition to whatever classroom exposure they may have). In reality then, *non-primary* language acquisition is rarely purely guided or unguided, second or foreign; usually it is a combination of both, that is, *mixed*.

2. The following short-hand notations will be used for the different form categories of lexical verbs in English-based interlanguages: *Vø* : for bare stem-like forms (*go, work, can*); *Ving:* for present participle-like forms (*going, working*); *Ved* : for regular Preterit or past participle-like forms (*worked, eated*); *Ven* : for irregular Preterit or past participle-like forms (*went, seen, eaten*); *Vs* : for 3rd person singular-like forms (*goes, works*); *Aux + V* : for any compound verb phrase involving an auxiliary element (*have + going, is + fall, is + going + work*). These categories are based on the categories of the target language. However, assignment to a particular category is based on the structural properties of the verb forms only. It is neutral as to their functional or grammatical status.

3. The size of the data samples analysed in the literature varies considerably, ranging from a high of 8,554 verb forms (from 182 different learners) in Bardovi-Harlig & Reynolds (1995) to 534 predicates (from 2 learners) in Rohde (1996). The highest ratio of verb forms per learner is found in Robison (1990) with 553 predicates from 1 learner; the lowest is Bardovi-Harlig (1992) with 945 predicates from 135 subjects (or an average of 7 verb forms per learner). Obviously, these figures must be interpreted in the light of various other factors, such as the research design used (longitudinal vs. cross-sectional), the number of morphological categories analysed (e.g. some studies include all inflectional categories, others focus only on the past tense or progressive aspect) and the number of analytical categories across which the distribution of verb forms is investigated (most studies use Vendler's four categories but some use five or six).

4. These counts include L2 learner speech only, not the speech from the interviewers (although this too has been transcribed; see 3.3). These counts further include interjections (e.g. yeah, no, yes) and filled pauses (e.g. er, hmm, uhuh). Self-repetitions, retracings, self-corrections and indications of performance phenomena (e.g. laughter, gestures) are not included.

5. CHAT does not support the IPA alphabet but uses its own ASCII-based phonetic alphabet called UNIBET.

6. Only *identical* echoes were excluded. The form *ate* in the following example, for example, was considered an identical echo because this learner used either the base form *eat* or the interlanguage form *eated* on all other occasions:

```
*Hd4:  but he did [/] didn't eat her.
*INV:  well I think he ate her.
*Hd4:  <yeah [/] yeah he &i [/] &i > [//] yeah he ate@e her.
```

Non-identical echolaic expressions, however, were included. In the following example, the subject echoes the lexical verb *sweep* but not the verbal suffix. This was considered analytically relevant information:

```
*Lf3:  yeah she is uh # +...
*Lf3:  ah <il balaie> [:=f he sweeps] [gesture].
*INV:  sweeps [''] uh with a broom huh.
*Lf3:  he sweep@e the leafs.
```

As a rule, unanalyzed expressions were included in the analysis given their crucial role in the early development of L2 grammar (cf. Nattinger & DeCarrico 1992; Weinert 1995). A small set of formulaic expressions, however, were systematically excluded, the most conspicuous case being *I + don't + know*, which occurs with high frequency in particularly the data of the lower-level speakers. Thus, for the sake of consistency and to maintain some degree of comparability in the quantitative analyses, it was decided to exclude all occurrences of this expression for all learners. Also excluded was filler *you + know* (but variants such as *she don't know* were included).

7. CHAT allows for multiple coding tiers per main tier. The decision to place all coding categories on one or more coding tiers can have consequences for the application of some of the CLAN programs. Some operate on coding categories across different coding tiers, others only on categories within one coding tier.

8. There is no place here to discuss the descriptive framework that underlies the formal and functional coding of the verb system in these interlanguages. This has been presented elsewhere (Housen 1994, 1995, 1998). Suffice it to say that the coding categories are intended to be as theory-neutral and language-independent as possible. They draw on available work by scholars since Reichenbach (1947) and Vendler (1969), including Comrie (1976, 1985), Palmer (1975), Quirk et al. (1985), Mourelatos (1981), Dowty (1986), Hopper (1979), and Klein (1994).

9. Although the MOR program has gained considerably in accuracy and analytic detail since the coding of CYLIL corpus was started in 1993, it is still too crude for the specific purposes of our analysis.

10. Grade level proved to be an unreliable predictor of the learner's maturity in English and therefore inadequate as a grouping metric for cross-sectional comparison. Individual levels of L2-proficiency within each grade level varied considerably. This variation can be attributed partly to individual differences and partly to differences in L1 background, with the Dutch-speaking informants consistently outperforming their French-speaking peers. These L1-related differences can in turn be attributed in part to the typological differences that exist between Dutch and French *vis-à-vis* English, with Dutch being closer to English than French (at least in the domain of basic lexis and morphology) and in part to differences in the pupils' socio-psychological disposition towards learning a second language. Dutch-speaking European School pupils in general seem to be more favourably disposed towards English and learning English than Francophone pupils (Housen 1995, 1997).

11. The following illustrates some of the CLAN commands and the uses to which they have been put in the present study. The FREQ program performs frequency counts on specified strings and combinations of codes. It is a useful tool for determining whether and how often a particular coding category occurs in a given file or series of files. The following is a sample command (where * is a wild card):

```
freq SAH* +t*SAH +t%cod +s'$VERB*BE*' +f
```

This command searches through all the transcripts of the longitudinal learner SAH, picks out all of Sah's clauses (rather than, for instance, the interviewer's clauses) containing a code for the verb *Be* on the %*cod* coding tier, makes frequency counts and classifies them according to grammatical function (copula *vs.* auxiliary) and morphological form (i.e. Present vs. Preterit forms, *am* vs. *is* forms, etc.) and sends the output to a special file which can be consulted for further analysis. The FREQ routine was used in combination with COMBO to investigate hypothesised affinities between formal and semantic categories. COMBO provides for Boolean searching (combinatorial pattern-matching) on coding categories on the same coding tier. The following complex CLAN command was used to investigate the co-occurrence probability between the formal category of *Ving* and inherent aspect type (states, activities, accomplishments, achievements) in the second transcript of the longitudinal learner EMA:

```
combo +t%cod +g +s''Ving*^(STAT+ACT+ACC+ACH)'' +x +d EMA2.COD |
freq +t%cod +s''%STAT%'' +s''%ACT%'' +s''%ACC%'' +s''%ACH%''
```

This produces the following result for the distribution of *Ving* forms across inherent aspect classes:

```
* * * * * * * * * * * * * * * * * * * * * * * * * * * * * * * * * * * * * * *
From pipe input

14      acc
3       ach
31      act
4       stat
------------------------------
4  Total number of different word types used
52 Total number of words (tokens)
```

These data were then imported in data matrices for further statistical analyses.

12. The learner codes (e.g. Lf1, Lf4) used in these and the following examples are not standard CHAT speaker codes. The original CHAT codes (e.g. *EMA) were renamed to better identify the data sets from which the examples are taken. Capital letters indicate proficiency group (L, LI, HI, H, NS) and small letters first language background (French (f), Dutch (d)).

13. All major categories of the English verb are introduced in the course of the 4th and 5th grades of primary school in the European Schools, following the order of presentation of the textbooks used at the time of observation (Abb & Worrall 1984):

(1)   Simple Present of *be, have, do*

(2)   Simple Present Vø of lexical verbs

(3)   Simple Present *–s* of lexical verbs

(4)   Progressive Present

(5)   Simple Future (*will* + V)

(6)   Simple Past of *be* (*was, were*)

(7)   Simple Past regular of lexical verbs

(8)   Simple Past irregular of lexical verbs

(9)   Progressive Past

(10)   Present Perfect (*Have* + Ven/Ved)

This reveals that *teaching order* and *learning order* are only partially isomorphic (e.g. the early teaching *vs.* late emergence of Simple Present *–s*).

14. This is particularly true after exclusion of instances of *got* in the highly frequent *have+got* construction. This construction is also used in non-past contexts in native British English, the dominant input variety to which our informants are exposed.

15. This explanation is mainly inspired by two cognitive operating principles: (a) the *Relevance Principle* (Bybee 1985; Slobin 1985) and (b) the *Congruence Principle* (Andersen 1993). Space precludes a fuller discussion of these principles here (yet see Andersen & Shirai 1996: 554ff; Bardovi-Harlig 1999: 372; Housen 2002b).

References

Abb, B., & Worrall, A. (1984). *Jigsaw: a Three-Year Elementary English Course for Young Beginners*. Harlow: Longman.

Andersen, R. (1991). Developmental sequences: the emergence of aspect marking in second language acquisition. In T. Huebner & C. Ferguson (Eds.), *Cross-Currents in Second Language Acquisition and Linguistic Theories* (pp. 305–324). Amsterdam: John Benjamins.

Andersen, R. (1993). Four operating principles and input distribution as explanations for underdeveloped and mature morphological systems. In K. Hyltenstam & A. Viborg (Eds.), *Progression and Regression in Language* (pp. 309–339). Cambridge: Cambridge University Press.

Andersen, R., & Shirai, Y. (1996). The primacy of aspect in first and second language acquisition: The pidgin-creole connection. In W. Ritchie & T. Bhatia (Eds.), *Handbook of Second Language Acquisition* (pp. 527–570). London: Academic Press.

Bardovi-Harlig, K. (1992). The relationship of form and meaning: a cross-sectional study of tense and aspect in the interlanguage of learners of English as a second language. *Applied Psycholinguistics, 13*, 253–278.

Bardovi-Harlig, K. (1999). From morpheme studies to temporal semantics: Tense-aspect research in SLA: The state of the art. *Studies in Second-Language Acquisition, 21*, 341–382.

Berman, R., & Slobin, D. (Eds.). (1994). *Relating Events in Narrative: A Crosslinguistic Developmental Study*. Hillsdale, NJ: Erlbaum.

Bowerman, M. (1989). Learning a semantic system: what role do cognitive predispositions play? In M. L. Rice & R. L. Schiefelbusch (Eds.), *The Teachability of Language* (pp. 133–169). Baltimore: Paul H. Brooks.

Broeder, P., Extra, G., & Van Hout, R. (1993). Richness and variety in the developing lexicon. In C. Perdue (Ed.), *Adult Language Acquisition: Cross-Linguistic Perspectives* (Vol. I) (pp. 145–163). Cambridge: Cambridge University Press.

Bybee, J. (1985). *Morphology – A Study of the Relation between Meaning and Form*. Amsterdam: Benjamins.

Bybee, J., & Slobin, D. (1982). Rules and schemes in the development and use of the past tense. *Language, 58*, 265–289.

Comrie, B. (1976). *Aspect: An Introduction to the Study of Verbal Aspect and Related Problems*. Cambridge: Cambridge University Press.

Comrie, B. (1985). *Tense*. Cambridge: Cambridge University Press.

Dahl, Ö. (1985). *Tense and Aspect Systems*. Oxford: Oxford University Press.

Dietrich, R. (1990). Nouns and verbs in the learner's lexicon. In W. Dechert (Ed.), *Current Trends in European Second Language Acquisition Research* (pp. 13–22). Clevedon, Multilingual Matters.

Dietrich, R., Klein, W., & Noyau, C. (1995). *The Acquisition of Temporality in a Second Language*. Amsterdam: John Benjamins.

Dowty, D. R. (1986). The effects of aspectual class on the temporal structure of discourse: semantics or pragmatics. *Linguistics and Philosophy, 9*, 37–61.

Dulay, H., Burt, M., & Krashen, S. (1982). *Language Two*. Oxford: Oxford University Press.

Edwards, J. (1995). Principles and alternative systems in the transcription, coding and mark-up of spoken discourse. In G. Leech, G. Myers & J. Thomas (Eds.), *Spoken English on Computer* (pp. 19–34). London: Longman.

Ellis, R. (1994). *The Study of Second Language Acquisition.* Oxford: Oxford University Press.

Fletcher, P., & Garman, M. (Eds.). (1986). *Language Acquisition.* Cambridge: Cambridge University Press.

Francis, N., & Kucera, H. (1982). *Frequency Analysis of English Usage: Lexicon and Grammar.* Boston: Houghton Mifflin.

Giacalone Ramat, A. (1992). Grammaticalization processes in the area of temporal and modal relations. *Studies in Second Language Acquisition, 14,* 297–322.

Granger, S. (1998). The computer learner corpus: a versatile new source of data for SLA research. In S. Granger (Ed.), *Learner English on Computer* (pp. 3–18). London: Longman.

Hakuta, K. (1976). Becoming bilingual: A case study of a Japanese child learning English. *Language Learning, 26,* 321–351.

Harley, B. (1986). *Age in Second Language Acquisition.* Clevedon: Multilingual Matters.

Hickman, M. (1990). *The Development of Discourse Cohesion: Coding Manual.* Nijmegen: Max Planck Institute for Psycholinguistics.

Hopper, P. J. (1979). Aspect and foregrounding in discourse. In T. Givón (Ed.), *Discourse and Syntax. Syntax and Semantics,* Vol. 12 (pp. 213–241). New York: Academic Press.

Housen, A. (1994). Tense and Aspect in Second Language Learning: the Dutch interlanguage of an adult native speaker of English. In C. Vet & C. Vetters (Eds.), *Tense and Aspect in Discourse* (pp. 257–293). New York/Berlin: Mouton-De Gruyter.

Housen, A. (1995). It's About Time – The Acquisition of Temporality in English as a Second Language in a Multilingual Educational Context. Free University of Brussels: unpublished Ph.D dissertation.

Housen, A. (1998a). Facteurs sémantico-conceptuels et discursivo-fonctionnels dans le développement des systemes temporo-aspectuels: aperçus de l'acquisition de l'anglais comme langue étrangère". In S. Vogeleer, A. Borillo, C. Vetters & M. Vuillaume (Eds.), *Temps et Discours* (pp. 257–279). Louvain-la-Neuve: Peeters.

Housen, A. (1998b). Inherent semantics versus discourse-pragmatics in the L2-development of Tense-Aspect. In L. Dìàz & C. Pérez (Eds.), *Views on the Acquisition and Use of a Second Language* (pp. 299–312). Barcelona: Pompeu Fabra Press.

Housen, A. (2000). Verb semantics and the acquisition of Tense-Aspect in L2 English. *Studia Linguistica, 54*(2), 249–259.

Housen, A. (2002a). Processes and outcomes in the European Schools model of multilingual education. *Bilingual Research Journal, 26*(1), 43–62.

Housen, A. (2002b). The development of Tense-Aspect in English as a second language and the variable influence of inherent aspect. In Y. Shirai & R. Salaberry (Eds.), *Description and Explanation in the Acquisition of Tense-Aspect.* London: John Benjamins.

Joos, M. (1964). *The English Verb: Forms and Meanings.* Madison, WI: University of Wisconsin Press.

Klein, W., Dietrich, R., & Noyau, C. (1993). The acquisition of temporality. In C. Perdue (Ed.), *Adult language acquisition: Cross-linguistic perspectives,* Vol. 2, The Results (pp. 73–118). Cambridge: Cambridge University Press.

Klein, W. (1994). *Time in Language*. London: Routledge.

Larsen-Freeman, D., & Long, M. (1991). *Introduction to Second Language Acquisition and Research*. London: Longman.

Lyons, J. (1977). *Semantics*. Cambridge: Cambridge University Press.

MacWhinney, B. (1995). *The CHILDES Project: Computational Tools for Analyzing Talk*. Hillsdale, NJ: Lawrence Erlbaum.

Marcus, G., Pinker, S., Ullman, M., Hollander, M., Rosen, T., & Xu, F. (1992). *Overgeneralization in Language Acquisition*. Monographs of the Society for Research in Child Development, serial No. 228, Vol. 57, No. 4.

Menard, N. (1983). *Mesure de la Richesse Lexicale – Théorie et Vérifications Expérimentales*. Paris: Slatkin-Champion.

Mourelatos, A. (1981). Tense and aspect. Reprinted in P. Tedeshi & A. Zaenen (Eds.), *Syntax and Semantics, 14*, 191–212. New York: Academic Press.

Nattinger, J., & DeCarrico, J. (1992). *Lexical Phrases and Language Teaching*. Oxford: Oxford University Press.

Ochs, E. (1979). Transcription as theory. In E. Ochs & B. Schieffelin (Eds.), *Developmental Pragmatics* (pp. 201–228). New York: Academic Press.

Palmer, F. R. (1975). *The English Verb*. London: Longman.

Perdue, C. (Ed.). (1993). *Adult Language Acquisition: Cross-Linguistic Perspectives* (2 vols). Cambridge: Cambridge University Press.

Pfaff, C. (Ed.). (1987). *First and Second Language Acquisition Processes*. Rowley, MA: Newbury House.

Pica, T. (1984). Methods of morpheme quantification: Their effect on the interpretation of second language data. *Studies in Second Language Acquisition, 6*, 69–78.

Pinker, S., & Prince. A. (1994). Regular and irregular morphology and the psychological status of rules of grammar. In S. D. Lima, R. L. Corrigan & K. Gregory (Eds.), *The Reality of Linguistic Rules* (pp. 321–351). Amsterdam: John Benjamins.

Quirk, R., Leech, G., Greenbaum, S., & Svartvik, J. (1985). *A Comprehensive Grammar of the English Language*. London: Longman.

Reichenbach, H. (1947). *Elements of Symbolic Logic*. New York: MacMillan.

Reilly, J., Bates, E., & Marchman, V. (1998). Narrative discourse in children with early Focal Brain Injury. *Brain and Language, 61*, 335–375.

Robison, R. (1990). The primacy of Aspect – Aspectual marking in English interlanguage. *Studies in Second Language Acquisition, 12*, 315–330.

Rohde, A. (1996). The Aspect Hypothesis and emergence of tense distinctions in naturalistic L2 acquisition. *Linguistics, 34*, 1115–1137.

Sato, C. (1990). *The Syntax of Conversation in Interlanguage Development*. Tubingen: Gunter Narr.

Slobin, D. I. (1985). Crosslinguistic evidence for the language-making capacity. In D. I. Slobin (Ed.), *The Crosslinquistic Study of Language Acquisition* (pp. 1157–1257). Hillsdale, NJ: Erlbaum.

Slobin, D. I. (1991). Learning to think for speaking: native language, cognition and rhetorical style. *Pragmatics, 1*, 7–25.

Slobin, D. I. (1993). Coding child language data for linguistic analysis. In J. Edwards & M. Lampert (Eds.), *Talking Data: Transcription and Coding in Discourse Research* (pp. 207–219). Hillsdale, NJ: Lawrence Erlbaum.

Stauble, A. (1978). The process of decreolization: a model for second language development. *Language Learning, 28*, 29–54.

Taylor, J. R. (1989) *Linguistic Categorization: Prototypes in Linguistic Theory.* Oxford: Clarendon Press.

Vendler, Z. (1967). Verbs and times. In Z. Vendler (Ed.), *Linguistics in Philosophy* (pp. 79–121). Ithaca: Cornell University Press.

Vogel, T. (1989). Tempus und Aspekt im natürlichen Zweitsprachenerwerb. In B. Ketteman, P. Bierbaumer, F. Alwin & A. Karpf (Eds.), *Englisch als Zweitsprache* (pp. 123–147). Tübingen: Gunter Narr.

von Stutterheim, C. (1986). *Temporalität in der Zweitsprache.* Berlin: Mouton de Gruyter.

Wagner-Gough, J. (1978). Comparative studies in second language learning. In E. Hatch (Ed.), *Second Language Acquisition: a Book of Readings* (pp. 155–171). Rowley, MA: Newbury House.

Weinert, R. (1995). The role of formulaic language in second language acquisition: A review. *Applied Linguistics, 16*, 180–205.

III. Corpus-based approaches to foreign language pedagogy

The pedagogical value of native and learner corpora in EFL grammar teaching

Fanny Meunier
Université catholique de Louvain, Belgium

Chapter overview

In this chapter, Meunier attempts to give a critical evaluation of the pedagogical value of native and learner corpora in EFL grammar teaching. In part one, she examines the field of EFL grammar teaching from an SLA perspective, considering current thinking and current practice within the SLA research community. In part two, she discusses the link between corpus research and English grammar, concentrating first on the contribution of native corpus research to the description of English grammar. She then assesses the influence of native and learner corpus research on EFL grammar teaching, distinguishing between three domains of application: curriculum design, reference tools and classroom EFL grammar teaching – and in each case giving examples of how researchers have suggested that corpora might be used, or how they have in fact implemented their use. In conclusion, Meunier discusses what has actually been achieved to date using corpora in EFL grammar teaching, ways of overcoming current difficulties and future challenges for corpus research in EFL grammar teaching.

1. EFL grammar teaching: Current thinking and practice in SLA

The value of EFL grammar teaching has always been much debated in SLA literature. Three schools of thought are generally recognised as characterising the interface between grammar teaching and acquisition of a non-native language, which Ellis (1993) and Hulstijn and De Graaf (1994) speak of as the *strong in-*

terface, the *no interface* and the *weak interface*. All three address the same question – whether or not grammar teaching enhances the acquisition of a non-native language – and whereas proponents of the strong interface say 'yes definitely', those of the no interface say 'not at all' and those of the weak interface say 'yes, but only indirectly'. While the strong interface advocates exclusive *focus on formS*, the weak interface recognises the need for a certain degree of focus on the formal aspect of language and is rooted in the more general (and topical) cognitive language awareness and consciousness-raising approaches (Hawkins 1984; Van Lier 1995): explicit knowledge helps people, especially adults (see Schmidt 1990), acquire a variety of skills as diverse as swimming, computer programming and language learning.

A large number of empirical SLA classroom studies have demonstrated that drawing students' attention to form (including rule giving or discovering) gives better results than implicit learning. Hulstijn and Hulstijn (1984) showed that the acquisition of Dutch word order patterns by adult learners was easier for those who could formulate the rules but that those who could not formulate the rules also benefited from focussing their attention on word order. Rutherford (1987) demonstrated that corrective feedback could raise the learner's consciousness. VanPatten and Cadierno (1993a & 1993b), N. Ellis (1995) and Robinson (1996) have all shown that explicit teaching improves accuracy. Dewaele (1996), in a study of L2 French, concluded that a lack of formal instruction affected morphosyntactic accuracy in interlanguage. Other studies which point in the same direction include Lightbown and Spada 1990; White et al. 1991; Fotos 1993 and Spada and Lightbown 1993; Beheydt 1993 and 1996; Westhoff 1998.

Evidence that focus on form is useful has not led to a return to exclusive focus on forms (strong interface) but rather to the idea that grammar teaching should be integrated <u>within</u> a communicative framework. Rogers (1996:38) for example also argues that 'the reinstatement of grammar as part of the communicative competence need not lead back to syllabuses which are driven by wholly formal considerations, nor to teaching methods which return to de-contextualised rote learning'. A number of possible teaching methods for integrating focus on form within communicative-oriented activities have been put forward (see Doughty & Wiliams 1998). These methods vary in their degree of explicitness, obtrusiveness on the part of the teacher and use of metalanguage: from complete implicitness to detailed explicitness, and from unobtrusively attracted to obtrusively directed attention, but the shared characteristic of the new teaching paradigms is the 'emphasis on induction in the learning process' (Todd 2001:92).

Another noticeable fact is that while teachers and SLA researchers' interests do not always converge, there are currently 'calls from all sectors of education to bring grammar back into the classroom' (Joyce and Burns 1999: 10). There is a certain degree of divergence about how this focus on grammar should actually be implemented, and the proportion of classroom time it should take, whether focus on form should also include focus on formS, whether or not implicit focus can be sufficient or whether more explicit focus is needed, etc., but the intrinsic value of focus on form is largely attested.

Building on the consensus in favour of focus on form in teaching, I will show in the second section how the results of corpus research can be incorporated into form-focused instruction, thereby validating Todd's comment (2001: 93) that 'a further impetus behind the growing interest in induction is the increasing use of corpora and concordancing in language teaching'.

2. Corpus research and English grammar

Before examining the actual benefits of corpus research for EFL grammar teaching (see Section 2.2) I will first address the contribution of native corpus research to the description of English grammar.

2.1 Native corpus research and the description of English grammar

Analysis of raw and grammatically annotated native corpora using the methods and tools of corpus linguistics has led to a much better description of the English language in general (see Kennedy 1998, for an introduction to corpus linguistics data, tools and methods). The benefits for grammatical description are numerous and will be approached here by means of (interconnected) keywords. The first of these is **frequency**. Analysis of large quantities of authentic language has given us insights into the frequency of grammatical or function words,[1] parts-of-speech, grammatical phenomena and syntactic structures, and hence provided access to scientifically measurable (vs. previously introspective) evidence of frequency. The second keyword (albeit two words) is **grammatical patterns.** Corpus research has highlighted the patterned nature of language, both lexically (collocations, recurrent word combinations) and grammatically or syntactically. These grammatical patterns range from simple lexico-grammatical combinations (e.g. verb complementation) to complex syntactic patterns (e.g. zero relative clauses).

The focus on grammatical patterns in language (see Partington 1998; the Collins Cobuild Grammar Patterns series – e.g. Verbs 1996) combined with analysis of the various text types represented in large corpora has led to one of the most striking contributions of corpus research to grammatical description, i.e. the discovery of what Byrd (1997: 3) calls the '**grammatical signatures**' of different types of communication or, more explicitly, the systematic intertwining of grammar structures in various settings (ibid.: 5). These 'grammar structures' can vary from single grammatical word units (e.g. personal pronouns, relative pronouns) to increasingly complex grammatical patterns (passive constructions, complex noun phrases, etc.). The pioneering role of Biber (1988 and ensuing publications) is usually referred to as being typical of this trend. Many studies have confirmed the existence of grammatical signatures and some studies have even shown that samples of the same text type either intended for different audiences or produced by different authors shared the same basic grammatical signatures (see Byrd 1997, for narrative texts meant for young readers and for adult audiences with advanced literacy skills and Meunier 2000, for academic written texts produced by university students and professional writers).

English grammar is thus no longer seen as a monolithic entity (i.e. basically the grammar of written educated English) but rather as being comprised of several specific grammars: the grammar of written, spoken, narrative, argumentative texts types, etc. Many grammatical features are found in a wide range of text types but the main difference lies in their frequency of occurrence.

The extent to which this new way of describing English grammar has (or has not) revolutionised the field of EFL grammar teaching will be examined in the next section.

2.2   Native and learner corpus research and the teaching of EFL grammar

While only *native* corpus research has influenced the description of English grammar, one would reasonably expect both native *and* learner corpus research to have influenced EFL teaching. Their actual input into EFL teaching will be addressed in this section. As Granger (this volume) provides a comprehensive overview of exactly what learner corpus research encompasses, I will focus here on EFL grammar teaching specifically.

The influence of *native* and *learner* corpus research will be examined in three distinct domains: curriculum design, the production of reference tools and classroom EFL grammar teaching.

2.2.1   Curriculum design

The study of *native corpora* provides a precise description of grammatical and syntactic features of the target language, accompanied by frequencies and proportions which can be related to text type. The results of such studies can be incorporated into curriculum design by facilitating selection and gradation of the most common forms. A look at the literature shows that a number of ideas, insights and suggestions have been put forward but that the actual implementation of corpus research results in curriculum design is timid, if not absent. I shall examine three programmatic articles and comment on actual implementations.

Grabowski and Mindt (1995) analysed the use of irregular verb forms in the Brown and LOB corpora, following which they produced a frequency list of these verbs for learners of English. This enabled teachers, instead of presenting irregular verbs in alphabetical order, to sequence the study of irregular verbs in order of frequency and thus, arguably, relevance. However, while few counter-arguments can be found to challenge the authors' position, little is known about the actual implementation of the list in the curriculum of German or other learners.

Biber et al. (1994) investigated the frequency of various noun phrase postmodification structures and showed that frequency was not reflected in EFL grammars, as the most frequent postmodifying structure (prepositional phrases) was often presented last and was allocated the smallest number of pages. However important frequency is, it is essential to bear in mind that it is not the only variable that should be taken into account for curriculum design. Within an EFL framework it is important to strike a balance between frequency, difficulty and pedagogical relevance. That is exactly where learner corpus research comes into play to help weigh the importance of each of these. *Learner corpus research* offers further refinement in identifying those forms which are problematic for learners. It also makes it possible to take into account the learners' mother tongue and hence provide more focused and appropriate teaching. As Granger (this volume) argues: 'when there is a clash between the insights derived from native and learner corpora, it is always the learner angle which should be given priority'. The value of combining native and non-native data is brought out by Meunier's study (2000) of postnominal modifiers in the written English of native speakers and French learners (summarised in Granger, this volume). The main problem, however, is not giving priority to the learner angle, it is simply gaining access to this learner angle. Learner corpus research is still in its infancy and little is known about the learners' grammar. The link between corpus research and curriculum design is still programmatic, and major changes in EFL curriculum design have not yet taken place.

One of the most extreme views of the influence that corpus research should have on curriculum design has been expressed by Byrd (1997). She claims that the traditional 'divide-up-the-grammar curriculum' used in the United States for the different proficiency levels of ESL students is based on ideas about the easiness or difficulty of certain structures for learners. Figure 1 illustrates the traditional curriculum.

Byrd claims that such a division is inauthentic, unrealistic and inapplicable to work on authentic texts. She suggests a combination of task-based and genre-based curriculum design based on the results of corpus research which reveals the grammar system underlying genres and tasks. The first task would be to select the communication type that the learners at a particular level need (e.g. conversation) and then concentrate, among other things, on the grammatical features of the relevant text type: e.g. for conversation: present tense, contractions, fragments rather than complete sentences, questions, *you* and *I(we)*. Byrd advocates a real commitment to putting grammar in context and illustrates her views by saying that 'rather than teaching students about conditional sentences as if the main issue involves getting the right verb tenses in the right clauses, we need to teach students that they are trying to build combinations that will convince the reader of the truth of their argument. The persuasive purpose comes first – then getting the tense right is part of a larger obligation of the writer to take meaning and audience into consideration.' This view is also in line with what Celce-Murcia (web doc) calls 'the current need in the ESL/EFL discipline to re-analyze virtually all of English grammar at the discourse level', the sentence-based view of grammar (both in its description and in its teaching) being inconsistent with the notion of communicative competence.

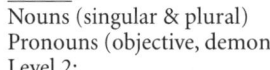

```
Level 1:
Nouns (singular & plural)
Pronouns (objective, demonstrative)
Level 2:
Noun phrases (count, non-count with articles)
Pronouns (reflexive and impersonal 'you')
Level 3:
Nouns (collective and abstract)
```

Figure 1. A traditional divide-up-the-grammar curriculum statement for an ESL composition sequence (adapted from Byrd, web doc)

Such changes, if applied, will imply a fundamental re-thinking of the curriculum but, here again, only the programmatic stage has been reached.

Corpus studies based on native and learner corpora are providing better descriptions of native and learner grammars. Whilst native language descriptions could typically be used to define the teaching agenda, the learner descriptions can be used to modify this agenda to take into account the needs of specific learner populations.

2.2.2   *Reference tools*[2]

Despite its relative lack of effect on curriculum design, corpus research has been highly influential in initiating profound changes in reference tools. Most striking perhaps are the changes in dictionaries which, in addition to the usual lexical and grammatical information, now also provide frequency and register information in the form of language/usage notes illustrating, among other things, differences between spoken and written language. Figures 2 and 3 show how the results of corpus research have been implemented in modern dictionaries, more specifically here in the Longman Dictionary of Contemporary English.[3] Figure 2 illustrates some of the words most commonly used with the noun *information* (LDOCE 1995:732). The information provided includes typical collocations (*additional/further information*) but also lexicogrammatical information (dependent prepositions: *information about/on*)

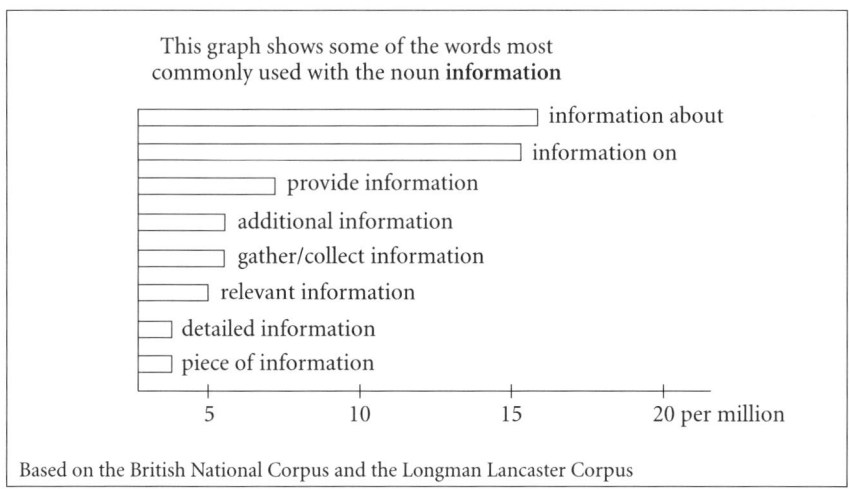

Figure 2. Some of the words most commonly used with the noun **information** (adapted from LDOCE 1995:732)

Figure 3a illustrates differences in the frequencies of the pronoun *that* in spoken and written English and figure 3b provides usage and grammar notes on the use of the conjunction *that* in speech and writing.

Grammar books have also benefited from corpus research. Collins Cobuild has for instance produced a number of grammars[4] based on the analysis of the Bank of English. The volume on verbs (Collins Cobuild 1996) presents a large number of verbal structures ranging from very simple (e.g. V-ing – *keep trying*, *avoid looking*, etc.) to more complex patterns (e.g. V n *about* n/-ing/wh – His father played fiddle and taught him about country music. He advises senior managers about getting the best out of their teams. I asked him about what his record company is like). Equally important in the volume are the links made between structures, usage and meaning. Sinclair, in the foreword to the book, illustrates the relationship between patterns and meaning with the verbs belonging to the < V *by* amount > pattern. These verbs belong to three closely related meaning groups: the 'increase and decrease' group (they expect the number to increase by 50%), the 'win and lose' group (the government lost by one vote) and the 'overrun' group (the meeting overran by more than one hour).

Probably closer to a typical comprehensive reference grammar is the new Longman Grammar of Spoken and Written English or LGSWE (Biber et al. 1999), which is the first reference grammar to adopt a corpus-based approach

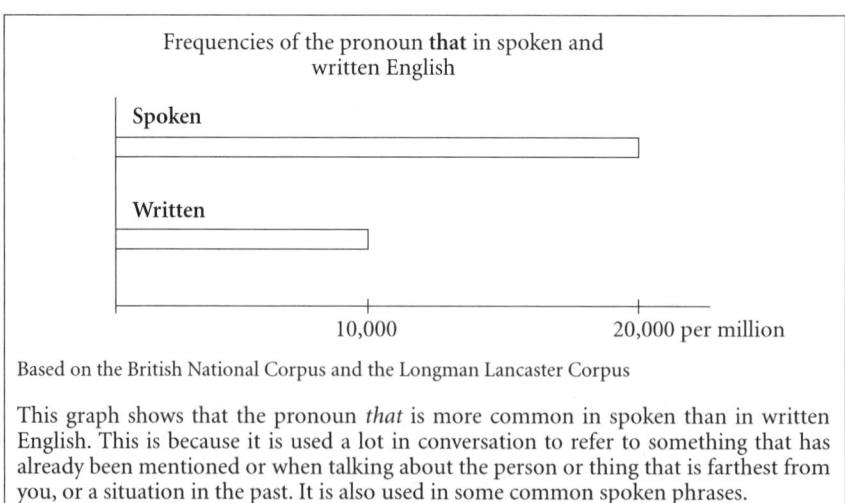

Figure 3a. Frequencies of the pronoun *that* in spoken and written English (adapted from LDOCE 1995: 1491)

USAGE NOTE: THAT

SPOKEN-WRITTEN

In conversation it is not usual for **that** to actually be used in a that-clause after a verb or adjective. This is especially true after the commonest verbs taking such clauses in spoken English – **think, say, know, see**, and after common adjectives like **sure, confident, afraid, sorry, aware, glad**: *I think Stuart's gone crazy* | *I'm afraid it could be there for six months.*

In written English there are differences between different styles of writing. **That** is hardly ever left out in academic writing, where in any case the commonest verbs are not the same as in spoken English, but are words like **show, ensure**: *Empirical data show that similar processes can be guided quite differently* | *It is important that both groups are used in the experiment.*

In newspapers **that** is used at least twice as much as it is left out: *The police say that they don't have time to worry about the marijuana.* But in fiction it is left out more often than it is kept in: *I'm sorry I hit you just now.*

GRAMMAR

That is more often left out when the subject of the *that* clause is the same as the subject of the main clause, or when it is a pronoun: *I think I'll make a shopping list* | *They were glad she'd gone out.* But, *I suspect that John was a bit drunk.*

That is usually put in if the main verb is passive, or where the *that* clause does not immediately follow the verb: *I was told that he had arrived* | *They warned him that it was dangerous.*

Figure 3b. Usage note: *that* (adapted from LDOCE 1995: 1491–1492)

to describe the actual use of grammatical features in different varieties of English. Its descriptions show that (Biber et al. 1999: 4) 'structure and use are not independent aspects of the English language' and that (ibid.) 'analysis of both is required to understand how English grammar really functions in the day-to-day communicative activities of speakers and writers'. The LGSWE includes a structural description and a description of patterns of use: frequency of different features, distribution of grammatical features across registers and distribution of grammatical features in relation to other features such as particular sets of lexical words or dialect differences. An illustration of the results in the case of the noun phrase is given below in Figure 4 where the link between text types and noun phrase complexity is clearly demonstrated: preponderance of simple noun phrases (no modifier) in conversation and much higher proportion of complex noun phrases with pre-, post- or both pre- and post-modification in academic writing.

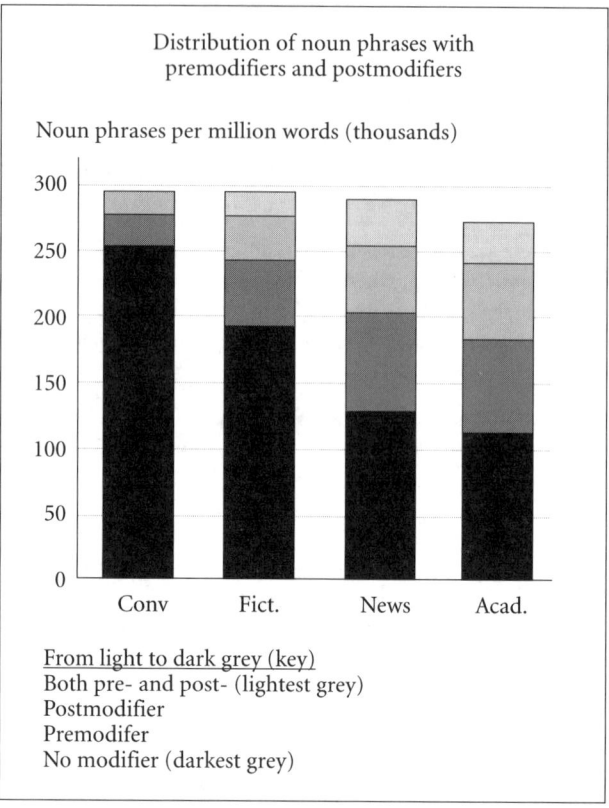

Figure 4. Distribution of noun phrases with pre- and postmodifiers, adapted from the Longman Grammar of Spoken and Written English (Biber et al. 1999:578)

Corpus research has undeniably influenced the content of recently published reference tools and, most of all, of dictionaries. Corpus-based grammars are only beginning to become available but the LGSWE will probably not remain the only one of its kind. It should be pointed out, however, that both the Cobuild pattern series and the LGSWE are better suited for advanced students with at least some basic knowledge of linguistics.

Having looked at curriculum design and reference books, I shall turn to the influence of corpus research on classroom EFL grammar teaching, making a distinction between textbooks and classroom methodology.

2.2.3 *Classroom EFL grammar teaching*

2.2.3.1 *Teaching textbooks.* Native corpora are a rich source of 'in context' authentic examples which can easily be included in textbooks. Carter, Hughes and McCarthy (2000) have used authentic examples from corpora for their grammar textbook, *Exploring Grammar in Context,* to 'reflect grammar as it is used today'. The examples, taken from written and spoken data, often contain several sentences to illustrate how grammar works beyond the boundaries of a single sentence or individual speaking turns. The book, designed for upper-intermediate and advanced students, also favours 'discovery procedures' and data-driven learning (see 2.2.3.2).

The use of authentic examples (and an enlarged context) is intuitively desirable and even officially[5] encouraged. It is also clear from the ongoing debate, however, that authentic examples are not the only source of information about grammar that students should receive. Authentic examples can be messy, some corpus findings can be 'pedagogically unwelcome' (Lorenz 2000), the input can be too complex for the level of the learners, the time needed to find examples of one particular aspect of description can be prohibitive, especially if one has to look for complex grammatical structures. The use of corpora to illustrate grammatical phenomena is to be recommended but should not become a dogma.

In Carter et al.'s book all the examples have been taken from native corpora. Parrott (2000), in his *Grammar for English Teachers,* makes extensive use of authentic native data too, but he also uses authentic *learner* data from time to time. These extracts, illustrated in Figure 5, are used for error correction exercises. Despite the fact that the presentation of erroneous output to learners is debatable and controversial, it must be recognised that most students like this type of exercise, find it useful and enjoy the 'correction' phase. They also comment on the fact that it is often easier to find errors in somebody else's text and that the active correction phase helps them remember problematic areas when they have to deal with them at a later stage.

Grammar textbooks including authentic corpus data are still limited in number but more are likely to appear. It is worth stressing that, once again, the books discussed here are designed for use with more advanced students and that the main input from corpus research is limited to the inclusion of authentic examples (produced mainly by native speakers and, occasionally, by learners), with larger contexts and taken from a number of different text types. The actual structure of the books, on the other hand, in terms of chapter headings or division into sections, is not innovative and remains fairly traditional.

Learners' English

In the first paragraph below, a learner of English has written about a trip to the cinema, and the second is about a TV programme she had seen. The numbers indicate mistakes and especially interesting instances of how she uses articles. In each case identify correct alternatives and speculate about her use of articles.

The (1) last week I decided to go to a (2) cinema. It was difficult to choose an interesting film which I could understand without a (3) problem. I looked in a (4) newspaper and found a film. It was "Cinema Paradiso". The actors played in (5) Italian Language. I don't understand the Italian language but fortunately the subtitles were written in English. It is a wonderful film about many interesting aspects of the world cinema and the (6) life.

I watched on a (7) TV about the (8) tuberculosis. It was (9) very interesting film. Many years ago they had to go in the (10) hospital. It was like a (11) jail. At this time many people were treated among the (12) family.

Figure 5. Learners' English (Parrott 2000: 53)

2.2.3.2 *Classroom methodology.* The greatest methodological influence that corpus linguistics has had on teaching is probably in the use of classroom concordancing, which has encouraged a more inductive approach to learning. The number of references in Tim John's classroom concordancing/data-driven learning bibliography[6] bears witness to the liveliness of the field. The term *data-driven learning* has been defined by Johns and King (1991: iii) as 'the use in the classroom of computer-generated concordances to get students to explore regularities of patterning in the target language and the development of activities and exercises.' Data-driven learning (DDL) is particularly well suited for consciousness-raising activities. One characteristic of DDL activities is that, so far, they have mainly addressed the fields of lexis and lexico-grammar. Figure 6 illustrates the use of concordance-based teaching and learning material. It has been copied from Tim Johns's Virtual DDL Library (searchable on the web at http://web.bham.ac.uk/johnst/ddl_lib.htm) and presents a sequence of materials which explores a notoriously difficult area of English grammar: article usage.

The second characteristic of current DDL is the almost exclusive use of native speaker data, the idea being that learners should be presented with as much authentic native data as possible. Granger and Tribble (1998), however, also suggest possible ways of combining native and learner data in the classroom. Figure 7 illustrates the use of parallel native and learner concordances for the study of error-prone items. In the exercise presented, learners are asked

Definite v. Zero Article II

There are in English a number of countable/uncountable pairs of words. Thus we have *process* (countable) v. *processing* (uncountable), which explains the use of *the* v. zero article in the following citations:

1. ow `a real possibility of affecting the ageing	process with biomedical intervention". The pr
2. terials allow operation of the chromatographic	process in the range pH 2–12. Biases in satel
3. which can affect the delays. During the design	process they simulated the delay of figures t
4. constructed a mathematical model of the drying	process which matches the moisture content of
5. cases the image is reduced in the lithographic	process, allowing the features on the mask to
6. es more expensive than wood, the manufacturing	process was less labour-intensive – despite c
7. s works continuously throughout the maturation	process and is active maximally in metaphase
8. t (APU) in Cambridge. She believes the reading	process, particularly in nonfiction and work-

1. his demonstrates interactions between auditory	processing and vocalization at the single-neu
2. r biologically significant organics. Catalytic	processing of small molecules within cell wal
3. 1970s and anticipating the revolution in data	processing that was to come ('The thinking ma
4. residues could become concentrated during food	processing. The Environmental Protection Agen
5. nsidered to play a central role in information	processing, because it is the target of all i
6. rogram instructions one at a time. In parallel	processing a task is split up and handled sim
7. red its Word for Windows software for word	processing with WordPerfect, made by WordPerf
8. technic of Milan are also using improved image	processing to study recent images of Mount Et

In this handout we look at 5 "key nouns" in English which may be countable or uncountable (industry, language, society, trade and religion), together with a sixth (literature) which is similar in the way it behaves, though there the difference in countability is not so clear. For each noun, 1–3 pairs of citations are given to hekp you try to work out the difference in meaning between the noun as countable and as uncountable, and 12 'gapped' citations to see if you have formed the correct hypothesis (key provided at the end).

industry

1. Last year output of the electronics **industry** rose 28 per cent on an employment rise of only 3 per cent.

2. The British film **industry** has always had a problem trying to film in the great British outdoors.

3. Further rises will mean deep trouble for Toyota, as for most of Japanese **industry**.

4. It opened in 1985 as the bequest of the prime minister, Andrei Kozygin, to the town and to Soviet light **industry**.

1. they would all get jobs in _____ British industry, Still more alarmist about the flow of ski

2. ne lead-free fuel. And _____ British car industry, in the face of mounting environmental and

3. ith the huge expansion in _____ chemical industry that took place after the Second World War

4. and on Hunt's knowledge of _____ modern industry, It is lavishly illustrated, partly in colo

5. research on new ideas in _____ European industry. One of the major aims of the shake-up is

6. for storage heaters). _____ electricity industry does not intend to make a habit of cutting

7. o seek firm proposals from _____ private industry to take over the government's remote-sensi

8. olic work. Glucose is used by _____ food industry mainly in the manufacture of confectionary

9. rea used to be the centre of _____ heavy industry. For 100 years after 1830, when the Cathol

10. ical profession and _____ pharmaceutical industry has tottered from crisis to crisis now for

11. management, such as _____ manufacturing industry, local authorities, reclamation and recycl

12. left _____ French information-technology industry in a mess – at least compared with America

language

1.In Gwynedd, a bedrock of the Welsh language, there are 25 film-making companies.

2.We must accept that the salvation of the French language involves learning one or more of the languages in neighbouring countries.

3.The research also showed increases in the frequency of bad language and sex on television.

4.Inspectors said behaviour was generally good, but features "such as free use of colloquial language and non-attendance at lessons are tolerated much more than in conventional schools".

1. proud of their command of _____ English language and engage in quite of lot of patting them

2. but it does not mean that _____ everyday language is bad: it is simply the way of things tha

3. cluded that cerebral dominance for _____ language is established before the age of five. Dur

4. abulary is one thing and _____ technical language is another, Vocabulary is words, lists of

5. avic-speakers. Orthodoxy and _____ Greek language remain the two markers of modern Greek ide

6. up an emaciated child, and in _____ sign language asked me to vaccinate the baby. There is o

7. t of a computer system for _____ Chinese language. In another move, Computer Applications to

8. ther splendid hope that _____ scientific language could provide a model for cultural discour

9. ng writers attemped to free _____ poetic language from the prev ailing romantic imitations o

10. phoneticised version of _____ Tsimshian langauge. To someone such as I, who had the vague b

11. ould be able to understand _____ natural language. The truth is that is is a much more diffi

12. was French. "Le own goal" entered _____ language. New Scientist, in an article by Stephen S

Key

Note that 'no article' is symbolized by the symbol for zero Ø.

industry1. Ø2. the 3. the 4. Ø5. Ø6. the 7. Ø8. food 9. Ø10. the 11. Ø12. the (IT is a specific technique).**language**1. the 2. Ø3. Ø4. Ø5. the 6. Ø(sign language is not a language such as English, Greek, etc.) 7. the 8. Ø9. Ø10. the 11. Ø12. the (ie French)

Figure 6. Concordance-based teaching and learning material (definite vs zero article – exercises for *industry* and *language*) Tim Johns's website http://web.bham.ac.uk/johnst/art.htm

Example task

Consider the two examples from native and non-native speaker writing given below.

1. *What grammatical structures appear to follow "accept"?*
2. *Do any grammatical forms only appear in the non native-speaker examples? If this is the case, check if the students are using an acceptable form.*
3. *Carry out the same investigation of "possibility" – again, do the non-native speaking writers use a form which is not found in the native speaker data set? If yes, is it an appropriate use of the word?*

(The Longman Activator provides useful advice on the appropriate use of "accept" and "possibility")

Native Speaker writing

not being able to accept	> that fulfilment of life is possible
be overcome? Why not accept	> the differences as an intentional
the act. Hugo cannot accept	> that the party line has changed
mothers and learn to accept	> their traditions.
with their emotions and try to accept	> that diversity.
If the peer group doesn't accept	> what the friend is wearing
of a woman, why not accept	> it and consider ways to use

Non-native Speaker writing

families, the parents accept	> that new visions of things
think that women must accept	> that some differences exist
nor the children accept	> to recognize that
the parents accept	> that new visions of things may
don't always accept	> that their children also
women have to accept	> the other side of the coin
young. He could never accept	> to be inferior
guinea-pig and accept	> to receive some viruses, some
Feminists have to accept	> to be treated as men
Johnny will not accept	> the Company's decision

Native Speaker Writing

from the two-fold possibility	> for joining the party: was
earth. There is no possibility	> of his dominant position in
and sensible possibility	> for solving international
There seems every possibility	> that the present Queen will
you die, there is no possibility	> of benefiting from that
deduces the possibility	> of a relatively increasing
mention the possibility	> that one of the motives for
47 that, there is no possibility	> of conversion from one
but there is a possibility	> of entry for those
popular because of the possibility	> for abuse. The second

Non-native Speaker Writing

January 1993 on, the possibility	> for workers of all kind to
is, however, a strong possibility	> that our society is still
European level, the possibility	> for students to move from
Students have the possibility	> to leave for another
of employees, the possibility	> for professional people to
self-confidence and possibility	> of identification. To follow
culture and have the possibility	> to practise their
to young people the possibility	> to enrich their
already explored the possibility	> of forming other such
argument against the possibility	> of an identity
there may be a possibility	> of reducing the
because we have the possibility	> to travel more freely all
of life, i.e. the possibility	> to be in harmony with

Figure 7. Parallel native and learner concordances (Granger & Tribble 1998: 202–203)

to compare the complementation of the words *accept* and *possibility* in native and non-native speaker data.

The use of learner (and hence erroneous) input for EFL purposes is controversial but it should be stressed that such exercises are based on attested problematic areas for learners, i.e. on learner corpus analysis and error analysis. Joyce and Burns (1999: 48) argue that 'by noticing the gap between their own and target language forms, learners are also better able to accelerate their acquisition'. The use of learner input should in no way replace the use of native input, but should only be used, here and there, to complement native data and to illustrate carefully selected L1 dependent characteristics, as well as universally problematic areas.

There are many advantages to DDL activities based on a comparison between native and non-native data:

- learners become researchers and discover the differences between their interlanguage and the target language (sense of discovery, of motivation),
- they have access to the errors or infelicities in their production but also to what is correct and valid,
- such activities also reinforce negotiation, interactivity and interaction (among learners and between learners and teachers)

Corpora are also a rich source of autonomous learning activities of a serendipitous kind (Bernardini 2000) and the analysis and use of corpora 'develops an understanding of the patterned quality of language which would alone be a desirable outcome of their learning process'.

Despite their advantages, DDL activities have some drawbacks: they are time-consuming (because of the interaction, negotiation and research procedure adopted by the students) and also require a substantial amount of preparation on the part of the teacher, who has to predefine the forms that will be focused on and make sure that interesting teaching material is provided. The various learning strategies (deductive vs inductive) that students adopt can also lead to problems. Some students hate working inductively and teachers should aim at a combined approach (see Hahn 2000 for a combined approach). Experience with classroom activities (Bernardini 2000) based on inductive learning has revealed that students are attracted by discovery and problem-solving activities but also that they can lack confidence, and that technical problems constitute a handicap. They sometimes also express an 'impression of vagueness' and 'frustration' because once they realise the way language works, they are no longer confident in their own output and intuition. Experience has also shown that such activities were usually more successful with more advanced students who already have some linguistic knowledge.

Classroom concordancing and data-driven learning can lead to rehabilitation of grammar (see Doughty & Williams 1998 for a description of Focus on Form activities in the classroom), to exciting, enjoyable problem-solving activities, but the trade-off between time (for material preparation and classroom exploitation), scientific interest, pedagogical interest and learning types should not be disregarded. Corpus activities should be used to complement other types of teaching methodologies, not to replace them altogether.

3. Discussion and conclusions

Corpus research has brought about profound changes in language description, at a lexical, grammatical, syntactic and discourse level. The so-called 'corpus revolution' has also triggered further revolutions such as the 'dictionary revolution', to name but one. While it would be highly presumptuous to speak of a 'teaching revolution', let alone a 'grammar teaching revolution', it should be noted that a number of changes are taking place.

The most obvious **development in the short term** is probably the use of concordances in the classroom for data-driven learning activities. Concordances offer an ideal (and visual) way of helping learners discover the patterned nature of language. Possibilities for useful exploitation of both native and learner data exist and have been illustrated in Section 2.2.3.2. However, despite the fact that Tribble and Jones's book, *Classroom Concordancing*, dates back to 1990 and the Collins Cobuild's Concordance Samplers series (Capel 1992; Goodale 1995) to the early nineteen nineties, concordances have not made their way into the classroom yet. One of the reasons for the discrepancy between what *can* be done and what actually *is* done is that many teachers are not aware of the possibilities offered by corpus work and classroom concordancing. These subjects should be part of both pre- and in-service teacher training. It is also worth stressing that there has been, especially over the last two decades, much less attention paid to form. The fact that new technologies are only now making their way into the classroom also accounts for the time shift between the 'possible' and the reality of everyday teaching practice.

There is, however, hope of a quick improvement as schools are being equipped with computers. The corpus should simply become a new reference tool in the classroom, in addition to the paper dictionaries and grammar books which are generally available. Learners would play an active role, work on authentic data and be involved in a heuristic process. Corpus work can be carried out:

- *'online'*: a number of sites offer the possibility of searching huge corpora online. All the user has to do is to enter a search word (or combination of words, or combination of word + part-of-speech) and press the 'search the corpus' or 'go and find it' button. The number of instances (or concordance lines) is often limited to forty or fifty, but this is more than enough for classroom use. Free access to corpus searching is offered, for instance, by Cobuild (The Cobuild Corpus Sampler, at http://titania.cobuild.collins.co.uk/form.html) and by the British National Corpus, at http://sara.natcorp.ox.ac.uk/lookup.html. These sites offer access to major standard corpora of native English.

- on *commercially available CD-Roms*: the BNC Sampler, for instance, contains one million words of spoken text and one million words of written text and is available at an affordable price. It includes 184 texts from many different genres of writing and modes of speech and contains a number of search engines.[7]

- on self-compiled *tailor-made corpora*: in addition to searching existing corpora, teachers can also decide to build their own native (or learner!) mini-corpora for their own purposes and analyse the corpora with text retrieval software. User-friendly (and inexpensive) text retrieval programs exist. They do not require powerful computers and can easily be used by the teacher (also for course preparation) and his/her students. One such program is WordSmith Tools.[8]

It should also be noted that focus on form activities can easily be incorporated into communicative activities. Doughty and Williams's *Focus on Form in Classroom Second Language Acquisition* (1998) and Joyce and Burns's *Focus on Grammar* (1999) are two excellent books, both of which provide the teacher with a mine of information and ideas on how to incorporate the teaching of grammar into more communicative activities. Corpus work can be made part of these activities and students can, for instance, use the computer to check specific constructions or minor points of grammar.

The **medium-term perspective** for grammar teaching should probably be an increased focus on form which would not only include the results of both native and learner corpus research, but also make use of the methods and tools of corpus linguistics. The problem is that, in addition to the usual technical challenges such as time, availability of computers, etc., a number of specific problems arise when dealing with grammar :

- very few fully part-of-speech and syntactically tagged corpora are available
- grammatical and syntactic analysis of corpora is extremely time-consuming and such analyses are only being made available for native corpora. They are almost non-existent for learner corpora
- despite the apparent consensus in favour of focussing on form, grammar is not always 'fashionable'. In French-speaking Belgium, the need for authentic material is repeatedly stressed in the official teaching programmes but the grammatical exploitation of texts in not on the agenda. In some other countries (e.g. Germany) where the teaching of grammar is very topical, DDL approaches making use of new technologies and corpus exploitation could be used to complement other teaching methods
- data-driven learning activities are also extremely time-consuming

While teachers may not always have time to create their own exercises, they can use *textbooks* which are based on the analysis of authentic material (from both natives and learners) and favour an inductive approach to learning, such as in Carter et al., 2000. Another possibility is the exploitation of existing *corpus-based web resources* specifically designed for teachers and learners (corpus-based exercises, teaching guidelines, answers to frequently asked questions, guidelines for ESP writing, etc.) such as *TeleNex* (http://www.telenex.hku.hk, cf. Allan this volume) or Tim Johns's site (http://web.bham.ac.uk/johnstf/homepage.htm). Other worthwhile sites include corpus-based *Internet Grammars*. The London Internet Grammar is based on the British component of the International Corpus of English (see http://www.ucl.ac.uk/internet-grammar/home.htm) and offers theory and exercises. It is not EFL-oriented, however, and does not include an inductive component. The Chemnitz Internet Grammar (http://www.tu-chemnitz.de/phil/ InternetGrammar/html), on the other hand, is written specifically for foreign language learners and contains both theory and exercises (see Hahn 2000). It is 'learner-centred, contrastive in the deductive component and data-based in the inductive component, interactive and learner-adaptive, e.g. providing immediate feedback and correction in the exercise component' (Schmied 2001:514).

The number of corpus-based grammar textbooks and internet sites is set to increase in the future. In the meantime, researchers and teachers should also be encouraged to make their own exercises or analyses available via the web to a large teaching community.

Some other exciting and challenging changes will require a massive amount of extra research and are therefore definitely situated in a **long-term perspective**. They include a fundamental rethinking of the EFL grammar curriculum based on a re-analysis of grammar at the discourse level, and the combination of task-based and genre-based curriculum design (see Section 2.2.1).

I would like to end this article with a word of caution. Stressing the validity and importance of corpus work for both EFL research and teaching does not imply that it should constitute the only approach to these areas. Corpus work is one methodology among many and is not suitable for all kinds of exercises. Granger (1999:200) argued that the authenticity of the data 'is no guarantee of pedagogical soundness'. She highlighted the danger of using a concordance format for the presentation of tenses (as in Goodale 1995) and showed that concordances offer access to limited context, not suitable for an approach to tenses which requires access to general principles of grammar at a textual level.

The aim of this article is to present teachers with new, and hopefully attractive, possibilities. Ultimately, what really makes the difference is not the method but the teacher's capacity to adapt and opt for the best approach for a given group of learners, at a given time, in a given context.

Notes

1. Grammatical or function words are opposed to lexical or content words.

2. This section deals exclusively with general reference tools such as dictionaries and grammar books. Pedagogical textbooks will be addressed in Section 2.2.3.1.

3. Corpus information used in the LDOCE was obtained from the British National Corpus.

4. The books in the Grammar Pattern series are called 'grammars' (cf. back cover of the books) because they 'present the structure of English in a fresh and innovative way'

(Sinclair's Foreword to *Collins Cobuild Grammar Patterns* 1996). It should however be pointed out that they differ from more traditional types of grammars in that each book deals with one part-of-speech (nouns, verbs, etc) and concentrates exclusively on the pattern aspect.

5. In French-speaking Belgium, the latest version of the official foreign language teaching guidelines ('Savoirs et compétences requis en langues germaniques') repeatedly stresses the need for authentic examples.

6. The bibliography is available at web.bham.ac.uk/johnstf/biblio.htm

7. These engines are: the Corpus Work Bench (from Arne Fitschen, IMS Stuttgart), Qwick, a Java application (from Oliver Mason, University of Birmingham), SARA, (the SGML-Aware Retrieval Application developed at Oxford) and WordSmith Tools (from Mike Scott at Liverpool University).

8. A demo version of the program can be downloaded free at: http://www1.oup.co.uk/elt/catalogue/Multimedia/WordSmithTools3.0/download.html. The whole WordSmith Tools suite of programs is made available but the user will not be able to see more than a sample of the results (about 25 lines of output) until he/she upgrades to the full version.

References

Beheydt, L. (1993). Grammatica's Nederlands voor anderstaligen. *Neerlandica Extra Muros, XXXIX*(3), 15–20.

Beheydt, L. (1996). Nederlandse grammatica voor anderstaligen op nieuwe wegen. *Neerlandica Extra Muros, XXXIV*(1), 41–50.

Bernardini, S. (2000). *Serendipity expanded: exploring new directions for discovery learning.* Paper presented at TALC 2000; Graz, Austria, August 2000.

Biber, D. (1988). *Variation Across Speech and Writing.* Cambridge: Cambridge University Press.

Biber, D., Conrad, S., & Reppen, R. (1994). Corpus-based approaches in applied linguistics. *Applied Linguistics, 15, 2*, 169–185.

Biber, D., Johansson, S., Leech, G., Conrad, S., & Finegan, E. (1999). *Longman Grammar of Spoken and Written English.* London and New York: Addisson Wesley Longman.

Byrd, P. (1997). *Grammar FROM Context: re-thinking the teaching of grammar at various proficiency levels.* Web document available at: http://langue.hyper.chubu.ac.jp/jalt/pub/tlt/97/ dec/ byrd.html

Capel, A. (1992). *Concordance Samplers 1: Phrasal Verbs.* London and Birmingham: Collins Cobuild.

Carter, R., Hughes, R., & McCarthy, M. (2000). *Exploring Grammar in Context. Grammar reference and practice.* Cambridge: Cambridge University Press.

Celce-Murcia, M. (undated). *Describing and teaching English grammar with reference to written discourse.* Web document available at: http://exchanges.state.gov /education/engteaching/pubs/BR/functionalsec5_13.htm

Collins Cobuild. Grammar Patterns 1: Verbs (1996). *The Cobuild Series from the Bank of English*. London: HarperCollins.

Dewaele, J. M. (1996). Effet de l'intensité de l'instruction formelle sur l'interlangue orale française de locuteurs néerlandophones. In D. Engel & F. Myles (Eds.), *Teaching Grammar: perspective in higher education* (pp. 167–194). London: Association for French Language Studies, in association with the Centre for Information on Language Teaching and Research.

Doughty, C., & Williams, J. (1998). Pedagogical choices in focus on form. In W. Doughty & J. Williams (Eds.), *Focus on Form in Classroom Second Language Acquisition* (pp. 197–262). Cambridge: Cambridge University Press.

Ellis, N. (1995). *Implicit and Explicit Learning of Languages*. London: Academic Press.

Ellis, R. (1993). The structural syllabus and second language acquisition. *TESOL Quarterly, 27*, 91–113.

Fotos, S. (1993). Consciousness-raising and noticing through focus on form: grammar task performance vs. formal instruction. *Applied Linguistics, 14*(4), 385–407.

Goodale, M. (1995). *Concordance Samplers 2: Phrasal Verbs*. London and Birmingham: Collins Cobuild.

Goodale, M. (1995). *Concordance Samplers 3: Tenses*. London and Birmingham: Collins Cobuild.

Grabowski, E., & Mindt, D. (1995). A corpus-based learning list of irregular verbs in English. *ICAME Journal, 19*, 5–22.

Granger, S. (Ed.). (1998). *Learner English on Computer*. London and New York: Addisson Wesley Longman.

Granger, S., & Tribble, C. (1998). Learner Corpus data in the foreign language classroom: form-focused instruction and data-driven learning. In S. Granger (Ed.), 1998: 199–209.

Granger, S. (1999). Use of tenses by advanced EFL learners: evidence from an error-tagged computer corpus. In S. Hasselgard & S. Oksefjell (Eds.), *Out of Corpora. Studies in Honour of Stig Johansson* (pp. 191–202). Amsterdam and Atlanta: Rodopi.

Hahn, A. (2000). Grammar at its best: the development of a rule- and corpus-based grammar of English tenses. In L. Burnard & T. McEnery (Eds.), *Rethinking Language Pedagogy from a Corpus Perspective* (pp. 193–206). Hamburg: Peter Lang.

Hasselgard, H., Johansson, S., & Lysvag, P. (1998). *English Grammar: theory and use*. Oslo: Universitetsforlaget.

Hawkins, Eric (1984). *Awareness of Language*. Cambridge: Cambridge University Press.

Hulstijn, J., & De Graaf, R. (1994). Under what conditions does explicit knowledge of a second language facilitate the acquisition of implicit knowledge? A research proposal. In J. Hulstijn & R. Schmidt (Eds.), *Consciousness in Second Language Learning. AILA Review, 11*, 97–112.

Hulstijn, J., & Hulstijn, W. (1984). Grammatical errors as a function of processing constraints and explicit knowledge. *Language Learning, 34*, 23–33.

Johns, T., & King, P. (Eds.). (1991). Classroom Concordancing. *English Language Research Journal* (New Series) 4. Special Issue. Birmingham: University of Birmingham.

Joyce, H., & Burns, A. (1999). *Focus on Grammar*. Sydney: National Centre for English Language Teaching and Research. Macquarie University.

Kennedy, G. (1998). *An Introduction to Corpus Linguistics.* London and New York: Addisson Wesley Longman.

Larsen-Freeman, D., & Long, M. (1991). *An Introduction to Second Language Acquisition Research.* London and New York: Longman.

Lightbown, P., & Spada, N. (1990). Focus on form and corrective feedback in communicative language teaching. Effects on second language learning. *Studies in Second Language Acquisition, 12*(4), 429–448.

Longman Dictionary of Contemporary English (1995). Harlow: Longman.

Lorenz, G. (2000). *Language corpora rock the base: standard English and linguistic authority in the face of seemingly adverse corpus evidence.* Paper presented at the TALC 2000 Conference, Graz, Austria, August 2000.

Meunier, F. (2000). *A Computer Corpus Linguistics Approach to Interlanguage Grammar: noun phrase complexity in advanced learner writing.* Université Catholique de Louvain: Unpublished PhD dissertation.

Parrott, M. (2000). *Grammar for English Language Teachers.* Cambridge: Cambridge University Press.

Partington, A. (1998). *Patterns and Meanings. Using Corpora for English Language Research and Teaching.* Amsterdam and Philadelphia: John Benjamins.

Robinson, P. (1996). *Consciousness, Rules and Instructed Second Language Acquisition.* New York: Peter Lang.

Rutherford, W. (1987). *Second Language Grammar: learning and teaching.* London and New York: Longman.

Schmied, J. (2001). Exploring the Chemnitz Internet Grammar: examples of student use. In Rayson, P., Wilson, A., McEnery, T., Hardie, A. & Khoja, S. (Eds.), *Proceedings of the Corpus Linguistics 2001 Conference*, UCREL Technical papers, Vol. 13, special issue (pp. 514–521). Lancaster: Lancaster University Press.

Schmidt, R. (1990). The role of consciousness in second language learning. *Applied Linguistics, 11*(2), 17–46.

Spada, N., & Lightbown, P. (1993). Instruction and the development of questions in the L2 classroom. *Studies in Second Language Acquisition, 15*(2), 205–221.

Todd, R. W. (2001). Induction from self-selected concordances and self-correction. *System, 29*(1), 91–102.

Tribble, C., & Jones, G. (1990). *Concordances in the Classroom.* Harlow: Longman.

Van Lier, T. (1995). *Introducing Language Awareness.* London: Penguin English Applied Linguistics.

VanPatten, B., & Cadierno, T. (1993a). Explicit instruction and input processing. *Studies in Second Language Acquisition, 15*(2), 225–243.

VanPatten, B., & Cadierno, T. (1993b). Input processing and second language acquisition. A role for instruction. *The Modern Language Journal, 77*, 45–57.

Westhoff, G. (1998). Een leraar met ondertitels. *Levende Talen, 530*, 266–269.

White, L., Spada, N., Lightbown, P., & Ranta, L. (1991). Input enhancement and L2 question formation. *Applied linguistics, 12*(4), 416–432.

Learner corpora and language testing

Smallwords as markers of learner fluency

Angela Hasselgren

University of Bergen, Norway

Chapter overview

In this chapter, Hasselgren tackles the difficult issue of how to evaluate fluency in a language testing situation, where judgements are frequently made by comparing learners' performance with some kind of descriptors of the way we perceive performance at different levels. Descriptors of 'fluency' have generally been drawn up intuitively or, more recently, by the analysis of transcripts, in terms of the symptoms of fluency – such as smoothness or speed. Hasselgren attempts to demonstrate how corpus analysis of learner and native speaker English can reveal evidence of both mechanical and linguistic markers of fluency, which in turn could lead to the establishment of descriptors of fluency which involve fairer judgements and enhanced washback effect in oral testing.

Hasselgren is one of only two contributors to this volume working with spoken data, which still presents many challenges for corpus analysts, both in terms of transcription and annotation (see Housen, this volume, for description of spoken corpus mark-up and annotation). Hasselgren demonstrates how use of smallwords, such as 'well' and 'sort of', can distinguish more from less fluent speech. Automatically retrieving a core group of these words and phrases from the speech of groups differentiated by mechanical fluency markers (such as frequency of filled pauses and mean length of turn) as well as test grade/nativeness, she provides evidence that greater fluency is accompanied by greater quantity and variety of smallwords. Adopting a relevance theory framework, she argues that smallwords work as a system of signals bringing about smoother communication, and her analysis of the signals apparently sent by the groups provides a basis for positing <u>how</u> fluency is brought about by smallword use. In conclusion she proposes a possible sequence for the acquisition of smallwords and a set of fluency descriptors based on the data studied.

1. Introduction

The primary aim of the study reported on in this chapter was to gain a clearer insight into the particular language that learners need to achieve fluency and thus pave the way for more objective evaluation of learner fluency in language testing. The research began with the belief that a limited set of common words and phrases, the 'smallwords' of speaking, are fundamental to successful communication. It had the advantage of access to an electronic corpus of spoken learner language, compiled from the transcripts of an oral speaking test for 14–15 year old pupils of English in Norway, supplemented with the language of native speaker pupils carrying out similar tasks. Access to this electronic corpus and the text retrieval software TACT for analysis made it possible to adopt a quantitative/qualitative approach which would have been impossible by manual means alone. Using TACT to retrieve all occurrences of potential smallwords in context, I was able to verify their 'smallwordness' and go on to compare the frequencies and ranges of the smallwords used in different turn positions by the native speakers and the two learner groups. I was able to further analyse these smallwords for evidence that they were being used by the various groups to send signals fundamental to verbal communication as interpreted from *Relevance Theory* (Sperber & Wilson 1995).

The research sets out to test certain hypotheses about the role of smallwords in contributing to learner fluency. While these hypotheses are, to some extent, corroborated, the size of the dataset does not allow stringent claims to be made, particularly in the case of the signalling function of smallwords. However, the evidence appears strong enough to propose a tentative description of the actual learner language which goes hand in hand with fluency at a range of levels. This is, at least, a start. It has the practical implication that those wishing to assess the fluency of their pupils' oral performance are presented with a yardstick which they can try out (and improve on), based on a considerably wider language base than has normally been used in putting together such descriptors. It has the particular value of providing feedback in terms of what speakers are actually doing with their language, in communication, and not simply in terms of how far they are succeeding.

As this chapter proceeds, the link which is pivotal to the research, i.e. between smallwords and fluency, is made more explicit, both theoretically and through the findings of the corpus analysis of the pupils' speech data. Before embarking on this discussion however, let us first turn to the data itself and the way it was compiled and used as an electronic corpus.

2. The corpus

2.1 The data

The data, collected at the University of Bergen English Department, EVA Project (Evaluation of school English) in 1995–1996, contains the speech of 14–15 year old pupils taking the EVA test of spoken interaction. 62 Norwegian pupils (35,544 words) and 26 British pupils (17,629 words) are represented in the whole dataset. The test was carried out by pupils in pairs, and the tasks were picture-based and involved describing, narrating and discussing (task 1), giving instructions (task 2), as well as semi-role play tasks involving a range of transactions, conducted face-to-face or by telephone (task 3). There were three parallel versions of the test, each containing the three corresponding task types.

The data was recorded on audio cassette, originally in order to facilitate grading by the tester and a second rater. This recorded material was transcribed and proof-read twice by a team of students with native speaker competence who were also familiar with Norwegian pronunciation.

2.2 Compiling the electronic corpus

The transcripts were put into electronic form as *The EVA Corpus* with the help of the HIT (Information Technology for the Humanities) Centre at Bergen University. Two subcorpora of spoken language were established, one containing the learner English and one containing the native speaker English.

During the compilation process, a certain number of decisions had to be made relating to who the corpus would be likely to be used by and for what purposes, and the level of detail in the information most likely to be needed. It was intended from the outset that this corpus would be released on the internet (accessed by password) for ESL speech researchers, generally with pedagogical interests, mainly in Norway. With these researchers in mind, it was decided to index the corpus for school and ID (both coded), as well as for gender and test grade awarded for each speaker. Test version and task number were also indexed for. This meant that when searching for speech items (words or phrases) in the corpus, the search could be restricted (e.g. among boys only, or for pupils within a certain range of grades). Moreover, this indexing made it possible for optional additional information (such as the task where the item occurred or the speaker's gender) to be accessed for any item that was searched for. The speaker ID and line number are provided by default when searching in context.

Certain decisions were made prior to transcribing, such as the convention for representing filled pauses and the length of silent pauses. It was also necessary to define what should be omitted from the search and analysis of language – in this case all teachers' speech which took place during the test, as well as any occurrences of Norwegian and non-verbal sounds.

It was decided not to include detailed linguistic coding, e.g. for word class or intonation. Tapes are available for loan to researchers within Norway, and further coding work can be carried out by any researcher wishing to conduct more detailed searching.

There were two further stages before the corpus was ready for analysis. The first, relatively simple stage involved using TACT, a DOS program offering indexing and text search facilities, to process the corpus text. The next, slightly more complicated stage, involved using a Web browser, TACTWeb, to make the text searchable by end users.

2.3 Using the corpus

Using the corpus to search for speech items is a relatively simple process. The query form is automatically presented on screen to initiate the process. A word or phase is entered in the *submit query* box, together with any restrictions to be imposed on the search. The type of display is then selected, allowing the user either to see the actual items listed in context, or as a set of statistics. Appendix A shows part of a variable context display of the occurrences of *well*, for pupils with grades above 09. Appendix C shows the normalised distribution of *well* for these same pupils, distributed across gender.

For practical purposes, the value of the statistical listings is limited to those cases where there is no need to consult the context to check whether an item qualifies as a true example of what is being studied. This can be the case, for example, if one wants to calculate the frequency of filled pauses relative to the number of words spoken. In the case of investigating *well*, used as a smallword, however, it is necessary to see each occurrence in context before deciding whether it qualifies as a smallword or not. In the utterance of B59, shown in Appendix A, this is clearly not the case.

3.   Fluency and smallwords

3.1   The need to identify a language of fluency

The notion of fluency is one that haunts language testers. We have a feeling that we know what it is, and that it is too significant to be left out when assessing spoken interaction. What is more, the people we test for – learners and teachers, and the public at large – seem to share this view. Yet pinning down and describing fluency with a degree of consensus is notoriously difficult, as researchers such as Esser (1996) testify, in studies of raters' perceptions of how they recognise and judge fluency in learners' speech.

However, studies of actual transcripts of learner speech perceived as being at different fluency levels, e.g. by Freed (1995) and Lennon (1990), reveal that certain features, when measured, do indeed seem to correlate with fluency ratings. These typically include higher speech rate and quantity, accompanied by fewer disruptive pauses. Towell et al. (1996) lend further support to such a characterisation of fluent speech, ascribing the longer and faster speech runs of fluent speakers to their heightened access to ready made chunks of speech. Fulcher (1996), in his detailed analysis of transcripts, draws up descriptors of fluency making reference to both the quantity and type of pauses which occur, and the length and quality (e.g. in terms of confidence or relevance) of utterances, as well as alluding to such features as reformulations, backchannels and clarifications.

It seems then that by studying enough learner language, it is possible to make reasonable assertions of what distinguishes more and less fluent speech. This has clear value for the language tester whose task it is to make this distinction, and the importance of data-driven testing scales is acknowledged and appealed for, e.g. by Fulcher (1996). However, the current tendency towards alternative 'non exam' assessment, typically characterised by diagnostic testing, self assessment and classroom observation, put together in portfolios, puts into question the value of fluency descriptors in terms of such features as speech rate and the distribution of pausing, clarification or reformulation. While these may inspire worthwhile strategies, they have limited didactic value for the learner, who probably already realises that his speech should be smoother, faster and clearer, and that reformulating and clarifying are a good idea. Is there, then, any point in troubling the learner with statements about fluency? Would it not suffice to make concrete statements about 'language', assuming that an improvement in language would automatically lead to smoother execution?

The contention of this study is that, in the case of spoken interaction, the picture of performance would be incomplete without reference to something over and above an understanding of the 'system' of language. Bygate (1987) makes this clear when summing up "the job we do when we speak":

> We do not merely *know* how to assemble sentences in the abstract: we have to produce them and adapt them to the circumstances. This means making decisions rapidly, implementing them smoothly, and adjusting our conversation as unexpected problems appear in our path. (1987:3)

What Bygate is referring to here seems to be what conventional wisdom has labelled 'fluency'. The following working definition of fluency, perceived through the ear of the listener, is adopted in this study:

> *Fluency: the ability to contribute to what a listener, proficient in the language, would normally perceive as coherent speech, which can be understood without undue strain, and is carried out at a comfortable pace, not being disjointed, or disrupted by excessive hesitation.*

The quest in this research is to identify some sort of language that learners can equip themselves with to assist them to do the very things Bygate is referring to, thus improving their fluency. Allocating this role to smallwords is the result of several factors. Studies such as Towell et al. (1996) have already demonstrated empirically that the use of formulaic language contributes to fluency, and the study of individual smallwords, e.g. by Schiffrin (1987), have shown how each one plays one or several tasks in bringing about coherence in conversation. Moreover, teachers, confronted in test training sessions with transcripts of Norwegian and native speaker pupils, have been in total accord in identifying the sparsity of smallwords as the clearest indicator of 'Norwegianness', even among pupils with an otherwise impressive vocabulary and control of syntax. The general feeling is that the acquisition of these words and phrases would make the pupils' conversation run more smoothly; clearly the omission of their mention in the descriptors of a test such as EVA would detract considerably from its washback effect.

3.2 The role of smallwords

Formulaic language or recurring 'chunks' of speech have been widely cited as being associated with fluent speech, e.g. in Nattinger & De Carrico (1992), and empirical research such as that of Raupach (1984) and Towell et al. (1996) has backed this up. Furthermore, a particular category of formulaic language, corresponding to what has been called smallwords here, has been identified by these authors as playing a key role in indicating fluency.

In her study of discourse markers, Schiffrin's (1987) basic contention is that these markers make a crucial contribution to coherence by "locating utterances on particular planes of talk" (1987:326). Schiffrin's conception of coherence, besides involving several planes of discourse, may be interpreted as involving the comprehensibility of discourse. She maintains:

> Coherence then, would depend on a speaker's successful integration of different verbal and non-verbal devices, to situate a message in an interpretive frame, and a hearer's corresponding synthetic ability to respond to such cues as a totality in order to interpret that message. (1987:22)

The ability to create coherence in Schiffrin's terms is compatible with the way fluency is defined in this article. Schiffrin's basic contention, therefore, supports the claim here that smallwords play a major part in contributing to fluency.

Further support is offered by Stenström (1994), who, in her account of spoken interaction, illustrates the way that coherence is brought about by smallwords, both in connecting and organising text in its narrowest sense – i.e. what is said – and in its broader aspects, such as whose turn it is, what ideas are being put across and which acts the speakers are performing through speaking. The role of smallwords in making speech understandable without undue strain is also reflected in Stenström's account.

4.   The empirical investigations

From the above discussion there appears to be a broad theoretical basis for maintaining that smallwords contribute to fluency as it is defined above. In order to empirically investigate this claim, two major lines of enquiry were pursued. Firstly, a study was carried out in order to establish that more fluent speakers appear to use more smallwords, in terms of both types and tokens. Secondly, in a more qualitative study, an attempt was made to analyse the way smallwords were used by speakers with differing degrees of fluency to send signals fundamental to communication.

Prior to carrying out the study, three pupil groups were identified: a native English speaking group (NS) and two Norwegian groups, defined as *more fluent* (NoA) and *less fluent* (NoB) and which comprised the top and bottom sets judged on the basis of the global grade awarded for performance in the

EVA oral test by consensus between two raters. The NoA group consisted of 19 pupils, who produced a total of 14,066 words. The NoB group consisted of 24 pupils, who produced a total of 10,467 words. The gender split was 22 boys and 21 girls (NoA 9:10, NoB 13:11). The NS group consisted of 18 pupils who produced a total of 12,349 words. This group, which contained all eight boys in the dataset and the first ten girls on the list (sorted by ID coding), was constituted primarily with the gender balance in mind.

4.1 Investigating the link between smallword quantities and fluency

4.1.1 *Which smallwords?*

A crucial first step was to identify the group of smallwords deemed relevant to the study, based on the following working definition:

> *Smallwords: small words and phrases, occurring with high frequency in the spoken language, that help to keep our speech flowing, yet do not contribute essentially to the message itself.*

The process of selecting the smallwords was as follows: firstly, a large section of the data (that of eight Norwegian and eight native speaker pupils) was scanned manually for any word or phrase which was judged to qualify as a smallword according to the working definition. The smallwords used by the Norwegians were given equal status to those used by the native speakers at this stage, implying that, in theory, any smallwords only used by Norwegians would also be included in the set. However, although certain preferences were evident, no smallwords were found that were peculiar to the Norwegian group. As a final check, any smallwords which might be expected, but had not been found, were searched for in the corpus. The words and phrases thus identified as relevant smallwords were then accessed from the whole dataset, and studied further, in context, to assess their absolute eligibility as smallwords, as well as their frequency.

As most words and expressions are polysemous and have senses that do not conform to the smallword definition, occurrences with these senses had to be eliminated. The following occurrences of words and phrases were <u>not</u> counted as smallwords: *all right* as in *she's all right*, and uses of *like* as in *she looks like she's worried*, and *I think*, as in *I think that it's her brother*. These words and expressions cannot be simply 'dropped' without fundamentally distorting the syntactic or semantic properties of the utterance. Occurrences of *just* which were clearly adverbial in function, e.g. *I'd just got there*, were also excluded.

Smallwords which occurred very infrequently, in the region of five times or fewer, were normally dropped from the study. However, there were a few low-frequency smallwords which were formally and functionally so similar that the selection of one or other of them was probably idiosyncratic and these were put together in groups. Two such groups were formed on this basis: *and everything/and that/and stuff/and things* and *sort of/kind of*. In total, the smallword identification process yielded the following 19 smallwords (or smallwords groups):

> *well, right, all right, okay, you know, you see, I know, I see, oh, ah, I think, I mean, like, sort of/kind of, a bit, just, or something, and everything/and that/and stuff/and things, not really*

Judgments as to what counted as a token of a smallword were initially made by myself. Where problems remained in deciding whether an occurrence constituted a smallword or not, the opinion of a second native speaker was sought and at times, the recordings were also consulted.

4.1.2   *Hypotheses and methods*
Two main hypotheses are tested in this part of the investigation:

- findings on temporal variables (such as pauses, length of utterance) will be found to support the grouping, based on ratings, of pupils into more and less fluent speakers
- the more fluent speakers will be found to have used smallwords in a more nativelike way than the less fluent, in terms of quantity, range and distribution across turns.

The method used in the investigation employed a combination of automatic retrieval of statistical information from the corpus and combing through printouts displaying items in context.

On the basis of the findings of the researchers cited in Section 3, as well as factors relating to the data itself, the study of temporal variables included the mean length of utterance and frequency of internal (regarded here as roughly corresponding to 'disruptive') filled pauses in the three pupil groups. Greater mean length of utterance and relatively fewer disruptive pauses are regarded here as indicators of greater fluency. Filled pauses, e.g. *erm, er, uh* were selected in preference to unfilled, as these were held to be more reliably transcribed in the original dataset.

The TACT search program provided numerical data on the quantity of turns and words produced by each pupil group. Printouts of individual filled pause types for each group were also produced and these were studied to find the total numbers of filled pauses (disregarding type) in different turn positions. The data from these computations are summed up in Tables 1 and 2.

Table 1. Group raw data on filled pauses, overall and with respect to position and number of words and turns

group	over -all	turn- initial	turn- internal	turn- final	sole	total words	turns	mean words/ turn	mean words/ filled pause	mean turn/ filled pause
NS	348	111	230	5	2	12349	707	17.5	35.5	2
NoA	842	134	674	17	17	14066	983	14.1	16.6	1.2
NoB	815	178	594	24	19	10467	1138	9.2	12.8	1.4

Table 2. Proportion of proper turns (i.e. not single word) initiated by filled pauses

group	turn-initial filled pauses	proper turns	ratio initial pauses : turns
NS	111	651	1 : 5.9
NoA	134	891	1 : 6.6
NoB	178	1089	1 : 6.1

A similar procedure was adopted for the investigation of smallwords. For each one, occurrences in context were printed out, groupwise (see Appendix A for a sample of occurrences of *well*), vetted for eligibility and the number of total occurrences and the number in different turn positions noted manually. The following turn-position categories were defined for smallwords: turn-initial, turn-internal, turn-final and 'loners' (i.e. where the turn is solely made up of one or more smallwords, alone or accompanied by *yes/no*). The mean number of occurrences of smallwords per pupil and the proportion of each group which actually used individual smallwords was also computed. The groups' uses of smallwords were compared as relative frequencies: turn-internal smallwords were considered relative to total words produced, while in other positions, frequencies were considered relative to number of turns. The total number of different types, i.e. the range of smallwords used by the groups, was also noted. This data is represented in Tables 3, 4 and 5.

Table 3. Group raw data on general smallword use with respect to overall use and turn-internal position

group	total	mean/pupil	mean user percentage	range	turn-initial	turn-internal	turn-final	loner
NS	551	31	53%	19	185	302	10	54
NoA	393	21	32%	17	133	155	29	76
NoB	242	10	24%	15	110	84	20	28

Table 4. Group data <u>per 10,000 words</u> on general smallword use with respect to overall use and distribution over turn positions

group	total	turn-internal
NS	445	245
NoA	279	110
NoB	235	80

Table 5. Group data per <u>1,000 turns</u> on general smallword use with respect to non-internal turn positions

group	turn-initial	turn-final	loner
NS	261	14	76
NoA	135	29	77
NoB	97	18	25

4.1.3   Summary of findings

TEMPORAL VARIABLES

The measures of the two variables studied – disruptive pausing and mean length of turn – indicate that the NoB pupils were less fluent than the NoA pupils, who, in turn, were (not surprisingly) less fluent than the NS pupils. Moreover, certain other facts emerged from the analysis which should be borne in mind when making statements about fluent performance at different levels. The first is that, in line with what Fulcher (1996) maintains, pausing did not appear to work universally as a marker of pupil fluency; at the beginning of turns, it did not appear to differentiate the groups (see Table 2), only doing so when it occurred in running speech. The second is that even the more fluent Norwegian pupils paused considerably more than native speakers. (NS:NoA:NoB = 35:17:13 words between filled pauses). However, these more fluent pupils managed to produce turns which, while rather shorter than the native speakers', were much longer than the less fluent pupils' (NS:NoA:NoB = 17:14:9 words per turn) (see Table 1).

Although there is no straightforward way of measuring the mean length of unbroken speech run, the joint findings of the decreased ratio of pausing to total words and the increased mean length of utterances of the NoA pupils suggest that their mean length of run – bounded either by pausing or turn boundaries – was longer than that of the NoB pupils. And following the reasoning of Towell et al. (1996), who found that the mean length of run was the greatest single contributor to a faster speech rate, it can be hypothesized that the NoA pupils also produced speech faster than the NoB pupils.

To sum up, the NoA pupils were found to be more fluent than the NoB pupils. They used relatively fewer pauses in mid turn and were able to sustain longer turns in the dialogue, and hence can be argued to have produced longer stretches of unbroken speech and to have spoken at a faster overall rate.

SMALLWORDS

The findings from this analysis of smallword use seem to support the hypothesis that the more fluent pupils used smallwords in a more nativelike way than the less fluent, as far as quantity and distribution across turns are concerned. Overall, the use of turn-internal position and the ratios of smallwords to words show that the NoA group used significantly fewer smallwords than the NS group, yet significantly more than the NoB group (see Tables 3 and 4). This pattern was repeated when the ratios of turn-initial smallwords to turns were compared for the groups. Both Norwegian groups actually used more smallwords in turn-final position than the native speakers. However, the NoA group showed themselves to use smallwords in loner position to the same degree as the NS group, while the NoB group seemed very little inclined to do this (see Table 5).

Further striking differences were revealed between both Norwegian groups and the native speakers in the range of smallwords used. While the more fluent Norwegian pupils had a somewhat wider range of smallwords in regular use than the less fluent, they generally used a narrower range than the native speakers and were more inclined to let certain smallwords dominate in a turn position. The smallwords used by the Norwegian groups were, however, among those generally used by the native speakers, but with some exceptions. The NS favourite, *right,* in non-internal position was not used by the Norwegians, who depended heavily on *okay.* In turn-internal positions the Norwegians used *I think* to an extent that was atypical of the native speakers.

The findings on the ranges of smallwords used by the groups echo those of other researchers. Raupach (1984) found that even after a stay abroad and acquiring extended vocabularies, students, as a group, stuck to a very similar and restricted repertoire of organising formulae. And Nikula (1996), in her study of 'hedge-like' modifiers among Finnish speakers of English, says: "As far as the types of expression used are concerned, the non-native speakers had a narrower range at their disposal even though they used most of the modifiers that ranked highest in the native speakers' performance." (1996:90).

In short, the more fluent pupils seem to have been more nativelike than the less fluent pupils in the extent to which they used smallwords in getting started and in keeping themselves going in their turns. Moreover, they appear to have used loner smallwords to the same extent as the native speakers in keeping their partner's side of the conversation going. However, even in this last respect, they fell short of the native speakers in the size of the pool of smallwords they drew on. It seems, in other words, that smallwords may be an area of vocabulary where learners like to draw on a stock of familiar words and phrases – the 'lexical teddy bears' of speaking (see Hasselgren 1994).

4.2 Investigating the link between smallword signals and fluency

4.2.1 *Bringing in* relevance theory

The discussion so far has suggested that there is empirical and theoretical support for the notion that smallwords and fluency go hand in hand. However, no explanation has been offered for <u>how</u> smallwords, as a body, contribute to fluency. The following qualitative investigation attempts to provide a hypothesis for such an explanation, by an analysis of the functions performed by smallwords based on Sperber & Wilson's (1995) *Relevance Theory* account of verbal communication.

According to relevance theory, we communicate a message to someone by making sure s/he realises roughly what we want to communicate, and gets just enough cues to effortlessly draw the inferences we (more or less) hope s/he will draw. We may not actually need to say anything, but when we do resort to verbal communication, our listener will assume that what we are saying makes sense, and s/he will provide the most obvious context to make it coherent. If we are normally able to give our listener the right cues, so that s/he can catch what we are saying with little effort, then clearly we have come a long way towards speaking fluently as it has been defined here.

Five factors fundamental to successful communication can be identified in Sperber & Wilson's account, and each of these can be associated with a particular type of cue, or signal. Firstly, we can signal our <u>communicative intention</u> which, at its most basic, involves whether we intend to communicate anything at all, and if so , what we want to 'do' through the communication. Secondly, we can signal the context for interpretation, e.g. from what has just been said, either within our own turn or earlier in the exchange, or from some external source. Thirdly, since this context may be partly derived from the previous speaker's utterance, we can signal how we react to the information or ideas expressed in that utterance, i.e. the cognitive effect of what was said. Fourthly, we can signal the enrichment of the explicature , interpreted here as how literally or vaguely a proposition is intended to be understood. And finally, we can signal the state of success of the communication, so that we can help ensure that the message is getting across as it should.

The use of 'can' rather than 'must' is intentional. Frequently there is no need for a signal. For example, the communicative intention may be predictable – after a request, it is normally expected that we will comply. And the context for interpretation may be obvious from what has just been said. In such default situations, the listener needs no cues. However, we frequently veer from the default situation, and need to help the listener to make sense of what we are saying. If we cannot comply with a request, we may signal our intention with *well*. If we are about to transgress so that what we say cannot be interpreted in the context of what has just been said, we may signal this with *by the way*. Smallwords, I believe, constitute prototypical linguistic cues in keeping with the relevance theory account of verbal communication, since they are short and familiar, thus putting a minimum of strain on the listener, and since, as I will demonstrate, between them they send all five types of signal outlined in the previous paragraph.

There are many precedents for using relevance theory to explain the way smallwords, under various names, work, such as Jucker (1993), Aijmer (1996) and Andersen (1998). Jucker, in his study of *well*, which he refers to as a 'signalling signpost' (1993:440), states "Relevance theory, I believe, is the only theory that can account for all the uses of *well* on the basis of a general theory of human communication based on cognitive principles." (1993:438). What is perhaps new in this research is that smallwords, *as a body*, are shown to send a *system* of cues fundamental to verbal communication as explained through relevance theory. The system, or framework of signals sent by smallwords is shown in Figure 1, where the five 'macrosignals', corresponding to the cues outlined above, are broken down into a series of microsignals, which can be sent by individual smallwords.

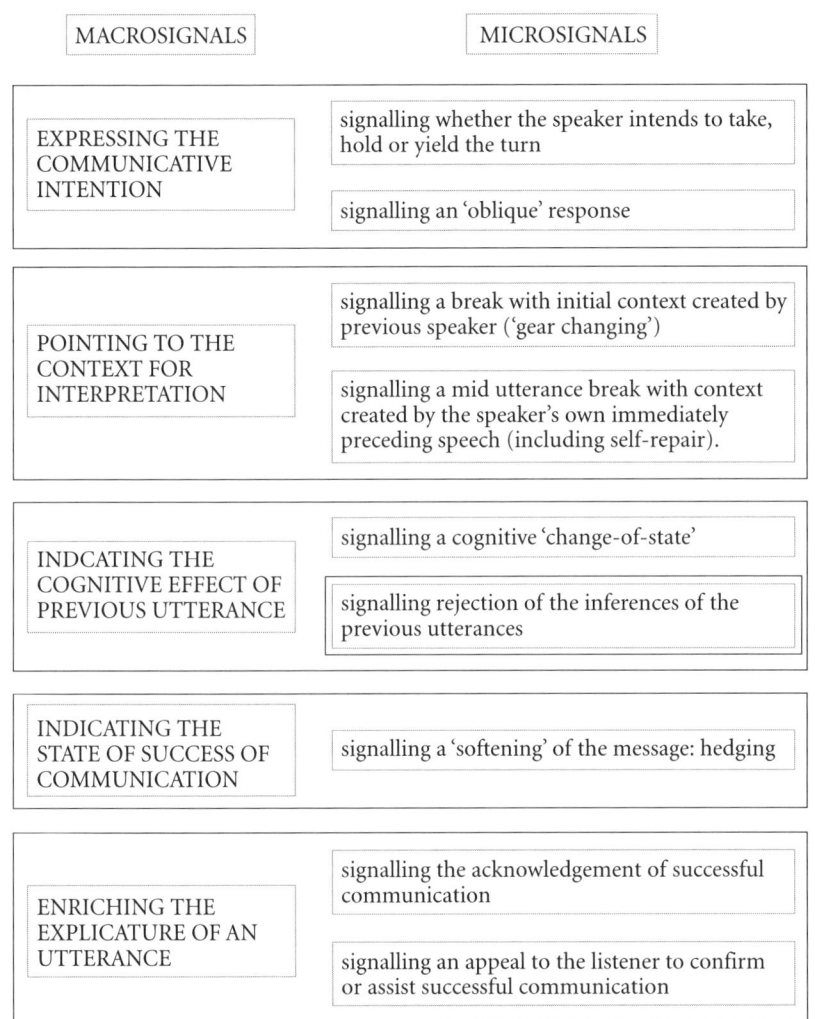

Figure 1. Framework for analysing smallwords in terms of the macro- and microsignals they send, based on the *relevance theory* account of verbal communication

4.2.2 *Hypotheses and methods*

Two main hypotheses are tested in this investigation:

- the more fluent pupils will be found to have used smallwords to send a greater <u>range of signals</u> than the less fluent pupils, and to have sent these signals with a more nativelike <u>range of smallwords</u>.

–   both Norwegian groups will be found to have had gaps and limitations in the signals they sent with smallwords.

The method used in this investigation was, as may be expected in a more qualitative study, less dependent on automatic retrieval of numbers, and more on close study of the printouts of smallwords retrieved in context for the three pupil groups, as illustrated in Appendix A.

In order to compare the smallword signalling between the groups, it was necessary, for each signal, to define evidence in the data which indicated that a group appeared to be using a smallword to send the signal. In the case of some signals (i.e. hedges and, to some extent, acknowledgers and appealers), where the signal is most easily identified by the smallword itself, this involved deciding which smallwords may be inherently regarded as sending the signal (e.g. *sort of* and *you know*). However, in all other cases, it meant defining the contextual slot(s) for the signal.

Defining contextual slots was a painstaking process, involving many rounds of trial coding by myself and a second native speaker, who was paid to do the task. The definitions had to be narrow enough for us to agree on codes, and broad enough so as not to exclude many cases which we both felt intuitively should be included. The procedure adopted was as follows:

–   define signals – this was done by myself, allocating a code to each signal
–   code separately – both coders going through the entire dataset
–   compare codings – trying to reach consensus, and altering the wording of the definitions when this was difficult
–   redefine signals where necessary
–   repeat process.

The procedure was gone through from start to finish about three times, in the course of two or three months, and was completed with the help of listening to cassettes for problem items. The nature of the way this process was carried out excluded the possibility of gathering hard data on reliability; finally we were able to agree on all cases. The reliability of the method was very dependent on both parties being assertive, yet at the same time open to discussion, which was, on the whole, the case.

To clarify what is meant by a contextual slot, and how tokens occurring in such a slot are classed as evidence, the example of signalling a mid-utterance break is considered. It suffices here to say that mid-utterance breaks occur when a speaker breaks into his/her flow with some sort of comment or repair, or to return to a previous theme. This occurs in examples (1) and (2):

(1)   T   ... just say what's happening

A   well , I think they are , these two are , they're going to see a match and , **well** , eh , they are now in the , in a station café and, eh, (NS)

(2)   A   all right . well , they've gone to the café , and then they go to buy tickets . **oh** no , he asks her where the tickets are , and she says ... (NS)

(In all examples, 'T' stands for tester and pupils are referred to as 'A' or 'B' according to their role as partners in the test. The testers' language is not analysed.)

The typical contextual slot for a mid-utterance break signal occurs between what is first said and the new or 'repaired' part of the utterance. As exemplified in examples (1) and (2), taken from the NS data, both *well* and *oh* recurred in this slot (5 *well*s and 7 *oh*s out of a total of 15 smallwords). This evidence suggests that the NS pupils used both *well* and *oh* to give this signal.

The main task prior to analysis involved the final coding of each smallword, principally according to the contextual slot it occurred in. Since smallwords can send several signals simultaneously, occurrences in the dataset were frequently assigned more than one code.

The analysis itself consisted of assessing which signals the Norwegian pupils seemed to be sending through smallwords, and whether this apparent signalling was done using some or all of the range of smallwords normally used by native speakers. Conclusions were drawn on the assumption that, all things being equal, the Norwegian groups should have had a roughly similar number of occasions for sending a signal as the NS pupils. Whenever the evidence suggested that the NS pupils were using a smallword to send a signal, the literature on native speaker (British and US) usage of the particular smallword was consulted in order to exclude the possibility that the NS pupils were using the smallword in an idiosyncratic way. Moreover, the number of pupils in any group using a smallword was also consulted before drawing conclusions, to eliminate the chance that a judgement was being made on the strength of a smallword's usage by a disproportionately small set of a group's members. It must be emphasised at this point that, in many cases, the tallies are very low, and cannot be regarded as more than evidence that a signal <u>may</u> be being sent by a group. This part of the study should be seen as hypothesis building rather than corroborating.

4.2.3   *Evidence and findings*

EXPRESSING THE COMMUNICATIVE INTENTION

Two signals are identified as expressing the communicative intention of an utterance. The first involves signalling whether the speaker intends to take, hold or yield the turn, and the second involves what s/he intends to communicate.

Signalling whether the speaker intends to take, hold or yield the turn

This signal is defined very simply on the basis of whether a smallword occurred at the beginning or end of a turn, or during it. As no group habitually ended turns with smallwords, the evidence is restricted to that of taking and holding the turn. Table 6 shows the smallwords that the three groups seemed to favour for sending these signals.

In signalling whether the speaker intended to take or hold the turn, the NoA group used smallwords much more often than the NoB group. However, both Norwegian groups heavily favoured *okay*, while the natives were more inclined to use *right*, or *all right* (borne out by Stenström (1990)). The NoA group showed some nativelike tendency to use *well*.

Signalling an oblique response

To put it very concisely, an oblique response is one which does not entirely comply with what the previous speaker was suggesting or might expect or hope for, as in example (3) below:

(3)   T   what about the first one . it says there the parents should decide when
          a teenager or a fifteen-year-old comes home at night . do you agree
          with that or
       A   **well** , yeah , I agree if it's not unreasonable
       T   mhm , what what would you say was reasonable
       A   em , **well** , it depends where she was going … (NS)

In giving this signal, the evidence suggested that the NoA group were remarkably similar to the native speakers in using *well*, conforming to conclusions by

Table 6. Signalling whether the speaker intends to take or hold the turn

smallword	turn-taking			turn-holding		
	NS	NoA	NoB	NS	NoA	NoB
right	55	–	–	14	1	–
all right	18	2	4	1	2	–
okay	22	52	51	11	14	9
well	48	32	12	24	15	4
total	143	86	67	50	32	13

R. Lakoff (1973) and Jucker (1993). The NoB group showed no tendency to
give this signal.

POINTING TO THE CONTEXT FOR INTERPRETATION

Two signals are identified here as pointing to a context for interpretation which
makes a break with the context resulting from previous utterance. The first is
when the break is made with the context created by another speaker and the
second is when the break occurs within the speaker's own speech.

*Signalling a break with the initial context created by the previous speaker
('gear changing')*

'Gear changing' occurs when a pupil embarks on a task after 'just talking' to the tester. Both Norwegian groups signalled this in a limited way, normally using *okay*, while the native speakers signalled it heavily with *well* or *right*
(normally preceding an instruction) as shown in example (4):

(4)   T   and also if there's anything you're not clear about
      A   **right** , you go in me front door , and the , the stairs going straight up
          (NS)

*Signalling a mid-utterance break with context created by the speaker's own imme-
diately preceding speech*

Both the NS and the NoA group signalled a mid-utterance break, i.e. a discontinuity in their own speech, normally using *well* or *oh*, as seen in examples
(5) and (6). The NoB pupils did not signal this.

(5)   B   it's very safe it never happens anything here , **well** I don't know about
          <name> , I think it's quite safe there too (NoA)

(6)   A   in a club , and a bloke comes over and he says . can I get
          you a drink . and it's a general sort , **oh** he's just come
          from a table that's empty now , and it's a general sort of (NS)

INDICATING THE COGNITIVE EFFECT OF THE PREVIOUS UTTERANCE

The default effect of the previous utterance is considered to be that of 'lack
of surprise', i.e. when any assumptions inferred from the utterance are either
anticipated by the listener or simply reinforce with what s/he already thought.
Only one type of non-default effect was found in the dataset, viz that the listener has formed new, unanticipated assumptions on the basis of what s/he has
just heard. The NoA group signalled this 'cognitive change of state' as often as
the NS group, both groups using *oh*, in line with what has been maintained by
Heritage (1984) and Schiffrin (1987). However, there was one essential difference: the native speakers in certain circumstances adhered to *ah*, to show that

Table 7. Smallwords used in *hedging*

smallword	NS	NoA	NoB
I think	29	71	56
just	102	42	31
sort/kind of	24	5	–
like	46	3	1
a bit	17	9	6
or something	17	24	14
not really	4	5	2
and things ..	14	2	2
total	253	161	112

they were somehow pleased with what they had learnt (see also Aijmer 1987), while the NoA pupils always used *oh* under these circumstances. Examples (7) and (8) illustrate this contrast and the resulting negative pragmatic effect due to the 'oh' rather than 'ah' used by the NNS in (8).

(7) B   er <reads> well , my name's Stephen White , I'm on my way to visit you</>

A   **ah** yes er my father said you should be we're expecting you soon (NS)

(8) B   <reads> well , my name's Stephen White . I'm on my way to visit you</>)

A   **oh** , you are (NoA)

ENRICHING THE EXPLICATURE OF AN UTTERANCE (hedging)

Hedging, or softening the force of an utterance, can be motivated by a 'genuine' need to disclaim total responsibility for what we are saying, or for pragmatic reasons, to empathise, or to preserve our listener's face in some way (see Brown & Levinson 1987; Stenström 1994). Table 7 shows the hedges used by the three groups.

The three groups displayed very different behaviour in both the quantities and ranges of hedges they used. Since the Norwegians hedged in a more unvaried way (in line with the findings of Nikula (1996) on Finnish students of English), they were deprived of the pragmatic effect which some hedges lend. Examples (9) and (10) illustrate how the Norwegian lack of *a bit* (which virtually all the NS group used in the role-play from which the examples are taken) made the statement that "the shoes are too small" sound like a complaint.

(9) B   er yeah sure , you can just try them on now

A   er , these are **a bit** small can I try a larger pair (NS)

(10) B   yeah, just try them on

     A   um , they are too small, um can you find a bigger uh pair (NoA)

In another task, pupils were required to ask their partners to do them a favour by taking a puppy for a walk, explaining the procedure involved. The contrasting effect of (11) and (12) shows how the typical Norwegian lack of *and everything* makes the request sound like an order!

(11) B   him for a walk , maybe in the park or somewhere , and you
         come home again , and you em , you wipe your feet
         and everything (NS)

(12) B   eh wipe his feet when he comes home
         and make sure he's got enough water (NoA)

INDICATING THE STATE OF SUCCESS OF COMMUNICATION

Two signals are identified as indicating the state of success of communication. The first is when we signal acknowledgement that the communication is running smoothly, as in example (13):

(13) A   … and then when you're finished you can go to the station and catch
         the train , which'll take you to Birmingham

     B   **right** (NS)

The second signal is that of appealing to the other speaker, either for confirmation that our message is getting across, as in (14), or to help us over a problem in getting it across, as in (15):

(14) A   she don't know my where my room [/**okay**]

     T   [no] no she doesn't know where that is she doesn't … (NoA)

(15) T   you wash clothes

     B   no wash, **you know**

     T   cleaning yeah (NS)

Once again the main difference in Norwegian and native speaker use of both of these signals was that the NS group used a variety of smallwords such as *all right* and *right* while the Norwegians largely stuck to *okay*.

4.2.4   *Summary of findings and further hypotheses*

FINDINGS

This necessarily sketchy account of the way smallwords were used to send signals that help make communication coherent, or fluent, has hopefully shown that neither Norwegian group was as adept at using them as the native speakers. However, the evidence suggested that the more fluent Norwegian group used smallwords in a more nativelike way than their less fluent counterparts. A major difference between the natives and more fluent non-natives was the relative lack of variety in the latter group's choice of smallwords, which put them at a disadvantage in terms of creating the right pragmatic effect. The findings of the study are summarised in Table 8, which gives an overview of the extent of the evidence found to support the nativelike use of smallwords by the NoA and NoB groups respectively.

Two types of evidence of smallword use are presented in Table 8. Firstly, there is evidence which indicates whether at all pupils used smallwords to send a particular signal. This evidence is based simply on the quantity of smallwords used in sending a particular signal, disregarding *which* smallwords were used or how appropriate they were. Secondly there is evidence which indicates whether pupils were using the same *specific* smallwords as native speakers to send signals. This evidence is also based on numbers of occurrences, but is more qualitative than the first, taking into account the range and appropriateness of the smallwords used.

A quantity of evidence for general smallword use in the Norwegian data is described in Table 8 as 'comparable with NS' when the number of tokens, relative to total words, was roughly similar to that of the NS group. As a rule of thumb, when this relative number dropped to between roughly one and two

Table 8. Summary of evidence of native-speakerlike use of smallwords, generally and specifically, to send signals

signal	evidence of NS-like use of smallwords generally		evidence of NS-like use of specific smallwords	
	NoA	NoB	NoA	NoB
turn-taking/holding	less than NS	less than NS	limited	very limited
oblique response	comparable with NS	–	comparable with NS	–
gear changing	less than NS	less than NS	limited	–
mid-utterance break	less than NS (mainly self-repair)	–	limited	–
cognitive change-of state	comparable with NS	–	limited	–
hedging	less than NS	less than NS	limited	very limited
acknowledgement	comparable with NS	less than NS	limited	limited
appeal	less than NS	less than NS	limited	limited

thirds of that for the NS group, the evidence is described as 'less than NS'. Below this level, evidence is regarded as non-existent. The evidence for specific smallword use is described as 'limited' when the range of smallwords typically used by native speakers was not fully utilised. It is regarded as 'very limited' when there is such heavy dependence on one or two smallwords that the NS range was hardly reflected at all.

As Table 8 shows, there is evidence that the NoA pupils used smallwords generally to a degree comparable with the NS pupils to send three of the eight signals investigated: *oblique responses, cognitive change-of-state,* and *acknowledgement of smooth communication.* Of these, only *oblique responses,* were signalled in an entirely nativelike way, by the use of *well.* The NoA group were found to use smallwords to send the remaining five signals, but to a lesser extent than the NS pupils, and again, through the use of a relatively limited range of smallwords.

The NoB group did not seem to send any signals to a nativelike degree, and only five of the signals seemed to be sent at all, with no evidence of the remaining three: *oblique response, mid-utterance breaks* and *cognitive change-of-state.* The range of smallwords selected by this group was always limited, usually to a favourite 'teddy bear' smallword (see Hasselgren 1994).

FURTHER HYPOTHESES

On the basis of what has been uncovered here, while bearing in mind the relatively small size of the corpus, it is tempting to posit stages in the acquisition of smallword use. It seems reasonable to assume that the NoA pupils were at a later stage of acquisition of smallword use than the NoB pupils. This theory is backed up by the fact that all smallwords used regularly by the NoB pupils were also used by the NoA pupils, while the reverse was not the case.

Table 9 shows three hypothetical stages at which the signalling functions of smallwords appear to be acquired, on the basis of what has been revealed in the research. Stage 1 represents the stage reached by a 'typical' NoB pupil. Stage 2 is that reached by a typical NoA pupil. Stage 3 is that (ideally) reached by a pupil with nativelike fluency. A smallword's being acquired is loosely equated with its being used regularly, i.e. (at least) in quantities comparable with those of the native speaker pupils. Smallwords are only entered in columns corresponding to the stage at which they are <u>first</u> used regularly.

The hypothesised order of acquisition of smallwords, at least for the groups under investigation, can be summed up as follows: *okay, just, I think, or something, you know* and most uses of *oh* are acquired early, by stage 1. Most uses of *well* are acquired by stage 2. Eventually, at stage 3, *right, all right, ah, you see* and

Table 9. Hypothetical stages at which the signalling functions of smallwords appear to be acquired

	stage 1 (as exemplified by NoB group)	stage 2 (as exemplified by NoA group)	stage 3 (as exemplified by NS group)
turn-taking	*okay, oh, I think*	*well*	*right, ah, all right*
turn-holding	*just, I think, okay, or something*	–	*right* (and a variety of hedges: see below)
oblique response	–	*well*	
gear changing	*okay*	–	*well, right*
mid-utterance break	–	*well*	*oh*
cognitive change-of state	*oh*	–	*ah* (with positive overtone)
hedging	*just, I think, or something a bit* (minus politeness overtones)	–	*sort/kind of, like, and things/that/ everything/stuff, a bit* (plus politeness overtones)
acknowledge-ment	*okay*	–	*right, ah*
appeal	*you know*	–	*you see*

the remaining uses of *well* are acquired, as well as the hedges: *sort/kind of, like, and things/that/everything/stuff* and *a bit*. It is important to note however, given the size of the dataset and the fact that only one mother tongue background was investigated, that there is a need to test this hypothesis on larger spoken corpora and on other mother tongue backgrounds before it can be taken as anything other than a hypothesis. Many different factors may come into play in the acquisition of smallwords, amongst which must certainly figure the extent of exposure to native speakers and the situation of learning/acquisition.

5.   Conclusion

I stated in the introduction to this article that the twofold aim of this research was to gain a clearer insight into the particular language learners need to achieve fluency and thus to pave the way for more objective evaluation of learner fluency in language testing. As regards the latter aim, the qualitative study of smallword signalling and the study of the correspondence between quantities of smallwords used and fluency, have made it possible to hypothesise a three level set of descriptors of fluency in performance for pupils of this age carrying out tasks of the type used in the EVA oral test. This set of descriptors is presented as Appendix C, and has clear advantages over traditional fluency descriptors: firstly it is based on actual language produced by sizeable groups of speakers taking a test in spoken interaction which shares many features typically found in currently used oral tests; secondly, it combines a description of fluency in terms of recognisable and familiar temporal markers, such as rate and smoothness, with didactically valuable statements about the actual language which goes into bringing fluency about. Of course this hypothetical three level set of descriptors needs much greater empirical testing before the acquisitional stages can be fully verified and it will be important to study a range of mother tongue backgrounds if the approach is ever to be widely implemented in a testing situation. However, the corpus analysis has already provided a starting point which can be built on in the search for a deeper understanding of how to research, teach and test fluency in learners.

As regards the first aim, I hope at least to have persuaded the reader that the acquisition of smallwords is a crucial step in the attainment of nativelike fluency. Although the amount of evidence in the case of certain signals is too low to draw absolute conclusions from, there appears to be some pattern in the way learners acquire the ability to use smallwords to send the signals necessary for fluent speaking, with a progressive increase in the range of smallwords used and the functions they perform.

I also hope to have demonstrated the interest of using a common framework such as *Relevance Theory* to establish a reproducible methodology for investigating smallwords collectively, using a common framework. Smallwords can overlap in their functions, and can perform multiple functions simultaneously. The functional framework used here accommodates these qualities alongside those ascribed to individual smallwords by writers such as Schiffrin (1987). Corpus linguistics has already revealed a wealth of information on individual smallwords, generally based on both their location and researchers' intuitions about how they are used by native speakers. By identifying a limited number of central signalling functions and defining evidence largely on the basis of contextual slot for these functions, this research has made it possible to study how smallwords are used, or not used, by native speaker and learner groups alike. Like the results it has produced, the framework is not 'final' – it is open to investigation and adaptation. However, it provides the basis of a model for further research into how this formidable body of small words and phrases works in the interest of fluent speaking.

Finally, I hope to have demonstrated the valuable contribution that learner corpora can make to language testing, and ultimately language teaching. The claims made in this research may potentially have consequences for the way spoken language is not only tested but taught, having put the spotlight on an essential but hitherto largely neglected body of language. Yet these claims could never have been made with any conviction without the use of the corpus at my disposal. Although the 35,544 word learner subcorpus was not large by corpus standards, it was sufficiently large to section off two distinct groups in terms of fluency, and to verify by independent measures that these groups were indeed distinct. It gave me 639 learner smallwords to look at, with another 550 from the rather smaller native speaker subcorpus. Without the aid of the searching program, the data would have simply been too unwieldy for me to cope with. By providing numbers where these were relevant and by sorting and listing items in context, it took away the donkey work and left my mind free to do the things which required real thinking.

This research is hopefully only a start. Other aspects of language use will be of interest to other teachers and testers. There remains unexplored information in the corpus, waiting to be tapped. The indexing for grade, gender and task create many research opportunities for language testers, who may wish to study the effect of gender and partner characteristics on performance, or the increasingly acknowledged effect of task, as put forward by such researchers as Foster and Skehan (1996). It is hoped that this chapter will inspire others to take advantage of the opportunities offered by the growing amount of spoken and written learner language being made available electronically to increase their own and ultimately their learners' awareness of what actually goes into the language they are trying to master.

Acknowledgement

I would like to acknowledge the invaluable assistance given in compiling the corpus by Knut Hofland at the HIT Centre, University of Bergen. Without his time and expertise, it would not have been impossible to put the corpus together, but it would most probably never have been done!

References

Aijmer, K. (1987). Oh and Ah in English Conversation. In W. Meijs (Ed.), *Corpus Linguistics and Beyond* (pp. 87–120). Amsterdam: Rodopi.

Aijmer, K. (1996). *Conversational Routines in English*. London: Longman.

Andersen, G. (1998). The pragmatic marker *like* from a relevance-theoretical perspective. In A. Jucker & Y. Ziv (Eds.), *Discourse Markers: Descriptions and Theory* (pp. 147–170). Amsterdam: John Benjamins.

Atkinson, J. M., & Heritage, J. (Eds.). (1984). *Structures of Social Interaction*. Cambridge: Cambridge University Press.

Brown, P., & Levinson, S. (1987). *Politeness*. Cambridge: Cambridge University Press.

Bygate, M. (1987). *Speaking*. Oxford: Oxford University Press.

Dechert, H. W., Möhle, D., & Raupach, M. (Eds.). (1984). *Second Language Productions*. Tübingen: Narr.

Esser, U. (1996). *Oral Language Testing: The Concept of Fluency Revisited*. Lancaster University: unpublished MA dissertation.

Foster, P., & Skehan, P. (1996). The influence of planning and task type. *Studies In Second Language Acquisition, 18*(3), 299–324.

Freed, B. (1995). What makes us think that students who study abroad become fluent?. In B. Freed (Ed.), *Second Language Acquisition In A Study Abroad Context* (pp. 123–148). Amsterdam: John Benjamins.

Freed, B. (Ed.). (1995). *Second Language Acquisition*. In A Study Abroad Context. Amsterdam: John Benjamins.

Fulcher, G. (1996). Does thick description lead to smart tests? A data based approach to rating scale construction. *Language Testing, 13*(2), 208–238.

Hasselgren, A. (1994). Lexical teddy bears and advanced learners: a study into the way Norwegian students cope with English vocabulary. *International Journal of Applied Linguistics, 4(2)*, 237–260.

Heritage, J. (1984). A change-of-state token and aspects of its sequential placement. In J. M. Atkinson & J. Heritage (Eds.), *Structures of Social Interaction* (pp. 299–345). Cambridge: Cambridge University Press.

Jucker, A. (1993). The discourse marker *well*: a relevance theory account. *Journal of pragmatics, 19*, 435–452.

Jucker, A., Ziv, Y. (Eds.). (1998). *Discourse Markers: Descriptions and Theory*. Amsterdam: John Benjamins.

Koponen, M. (1995). Let your language and speech flow! Is there a case for the construct of fluency in perception of oral performance. In *Language Testing Forum*, unpublished paper presented at Newcastle University, November 24–26, 1995.

Lakoff, R. (1973). Questionable answers and answerable questions. *Issues in Linguistics. Papers in Honour of Henry and Renee Kahane*: 453–467.

Lennon, P. (1990). Investigating Fluency in EFL: a Quantitative Approach. *Language Learning, 40*(3), 387–417.

Meijs, W. (Ed.). (1987). *Corpus Linguistics and Beyond*. Amsterdam: Rodopi.

Nattinger, J. R., & DeCarrico, J. S. (1992). *Lexical Phrases and Language Teaching*. Oxford: Oxford University Press.

Nikula, T. (1996). *Pragmatic Force Modifiers.* Jyväskylä: University of Jyväskylä.

Raupach, M. (1984). Formulae in second language speech production. In H. W. Dechert, D. Möhle & M. Raupach (Eds.), *Second Language Productions* (pp. 114–137). Tübingen: Narr.

Schiffrin, D. (1987). *Discourse Markers.* Cambridge: Cambridge University Press.

Sperber, D., & Wilson, D. (1995). *Relevance.* Oxford: Blackwell.

Stenström, A.-B. (1990). Lexical items peculiar to spoken discourse. In J. Svartvik (Ed.), *The London-Lund corpus of Spoken English* (pp. 137–176). Lund: Lund University Press.

Stenström, A.-B. (1994). *Introduction to Spoken Interaction.* London: Longman.

Svartvik, J. (Ed.). (1990). *The London-Lund Corpus of Spoken English.* Lund: Lund University Press.

Towell, R., Hawkins, R., & Bazergui, N. (1996). The development of fluency in advanced learners of French. *Applied Linguistics, 17*(1), 84–115.

URLs

TACT	http://www.chass.utoronto.ca/cch/tact.html
TACTweb	http://tactweb.humanties.mcmaster.ca/
COCOA	http://etext.lib.virginia.edu/helpsheets/cocoa.html
EVA corpus	http://kh.hd.uib.no/eva
	(for password/user name contact angela.hasselgren@eng.uib.no)

Appendix A. Extract from variable context display for *well*

TACTweb (1.0 (Beta A)) Results
Database Title:
Query: well; when grade > '09'

B03 138
<137><A03> <reads> ((yes, can I help you</>))
<138><B03> my er well I'm came from Oslo now and
   erm my baggage haven't arrived and I wonder if it could be

B03 144
   the luggage</>))
<144><B03> well I had a , red rucksack and black
   er , er ... and black suitcase , and that was all I had

A03 161
   not sure exactly how to get to your house</>))

<161><A03> <u>well</u> er you take the main road towards
the town and take take the third , um left and , the then the

B59 107
are very popular , and um very good to play with . er when
you are playing tennis very <u>well</u>
<108><A59> yeah , but they they're too small can

A61 9
<9><A61> they get to the football game and all
is <u>well</u> they someone comes to pick them up on the road
<10><T> ((okay that was the story <hidden> told us and <hidden>

B64 20
<19><T> ((yes and er what about <hidden>))
<20><B64> <u>well</u> yes , but I'm the type that don't
like it it's become too loud the music as if you are sitting

B64 62
people are they are feeling))
<62><B64> <u>well</u> I really don't know but . I don't
like happy endings so I don't choose number one . er so I

[About TACTweb] (Ver. 1.0 (Beta A))

Appendix B. Normalised distribution by gender of *well*, for pupils with grade > 09

TACTweb (1.0 (Beta A)) **Results**

Database Title:

Query: well; when grade > '09'

GENDER	#	Size	# / Size	Z-Score
F	34	16373	2.0766E-3	3.44091
M	37	18531	1.9967E-3	−0.04285

Total: 71, Total in Database: 35544.

Appendix C. Hypothesised descriptors of performance at three levels of fluency in 14–15 year old students of English in Norwegian schools

Native-speakerlike

Pupils are able to freely connect their utterances unrestrained by language difficulties and at a natural speed. Although they use filled pauses (e.g. *erm*), particularly when starting turns (roughly every sixth turn on average), this is not disruptive, and pupils are more likely to use smallwords, such as *right* and *well* to get started and *just, sort of* and *like* to keep going. They begin about a quarter of their turns with a smallword. They also regularly use backchannels such as *right* and *okay* to help keep the other speaker going. They are able to counteract possible breakdowns in communication by appealing to the other speaker, e.g. with *you see?*, and by acknowledging that they have understood, e.g. with *ah* and *right*. They correct or adjust their own speech with *oh* and *well*. They use *well* to signal some kind of discontinuity or doubt, and a wide range of vagueness terms, either to soften the force of what they say, e.g. *a bit*, to show that they mean something approximately, e.g. by *like* or *sort of*, or to show that they want to extend an idea, e.g. by *and things*. They vary their smallwords in all positions, expressing nuances of meaning and positive overtones, e.g. through *ah* on receipt of new information.

Grade 5–6 (as represented by NoA pupils)

Speakers are able to fairly freely connect their utterances, producing turns that seem only occasionally curtailed by language difficulties. Their running speech is rather broken up by filled pauses – about twice as often as native speakers – which slows down their speech rate somewhat. They use smallwords as backchannels (usually *okay*) as frequently as native speakers, but in getting started and keeping going, the frequency is about half that of native speakers'. They show much less variety in their choices of smallwords, usually depending on one or two, such as *okay* and *well* in getting started and *okay* and *I think* in keeping going. They are as likely as native speakers to acknowledge when they have understood, using *okay*, and to appeal somewhat less, typically using *you know*. They signal self-repair readily, using *well*. Their range of vagueness markers is mainly limited to *I think, just,* and *or something*. They are aware of the functions of *well* to signal some kind of discontinuity or doubt, and of *oh* to show receipt of new information, but seem unaware of the overtones of pleasure and politeness lent by smallwords such as *ah* and *a bit*.

Grade 3–4 (as represented by NoB pupils)

Speakers are not able to freely connect their utterances, producing turns that are distinctly curtailed by language difficulties, being on average about half the length of a native speaker's, in a corresponding situation. In beginning turns, they are no more likely to use filled pauses than native speakers. However, their running speech is broken up by filled pauses – about three times as often as native speakers – which slows down their speech rate considerably. They rarely use smallwords as backchannels, but compensate somewhat with non-verbal backchannels, such as *mm*. In getting started and keeping going, their small-word frequency is about one third of that of native speakers'. They are very limited in their choice, depending heavily on *okay* in getting started and *okay* and *I think* in keeping going. They do not use smallwords to signal self-repair but signal both acknowledgement and appeal to the other speaker to a limited degree, using *okay* and *you know* respectively. They are apparently not aware of the functions of *well*, but are able to use *oh* to express receipt of new information. Their range of vagueness markers is mainly limited to *I think*, *just*, and *or something*.

Business English
Learner data from Belgium, Finland and the U. S.

Ulla Connor, Kristen Precht and Thomas Upton
Indiana University Purdue University Indianapolis and Kent State
University

Chapter overview

In this chapter, Connor et al. seek to demonstrate the value of combining the traditional textlinguistic tools of genre analysis, such as the identification of rhetorical moves, with a genre-specific corpus to make broader statements about how different writers approach writing for a specific purpose. Accordingly, the chapter also highlights the value of developing genre-specific learner corpora to facilitate the analysis of student writing for specific purposes.

The learner corpus used in this study is an intercultural collection of letters of job application from native and non-native speakers of English studying in three different undergraduate business classes in Belgium, Finland, and the United States. While the rhetorical moves that define the genre of application letters had to be identified and tagged manually, the text retrieval program *Wordsmith*, was used to automate part of the analysis. Their analysis revealed that while some rhetorical moves were used by all three groups in their letters of application, others were more group-specific, suggesting that different cultural norms might exist for the genre. Connor et al. highlight the sometimes unexpected impact that such differences may have for people attempting to apply for jobs across languages and cultures.

1. Introduction

The past decade has witnessed the rise of computer learner corpora. The most notable corpora include the International Corpus of Learner English (ICLE), a corpus of learner English containing argumentative writing by students from many L1 backgrounds (Granger 1998), and the Hong Kong University of Science and Technology (HKUST) Learner Corpus, a corpus of undergraduate assignments and "A" level Use of English exam essays from the Hong Kong Examination Authority (Hyland & Milton 1997). The focus in learner corpora such as these in collecting data is on argumentative essays, other timed writing exercises, or school assignments.

The learner corpora described above represent an important new development in corpus linguistics. They provide significant data of general written English proficiency for interlanguage contrasts, which is beneficial for research in L2 acquisition as well as L2 teaching. The data describe general EFL proficiency of a significant number of EFL learners in their first few years after high school.

Most of the learner corpus based analyses conducted to date have centered on the lexico-grammatical patterning of texts with less regard for functional and rhetorical, textlinguistic aspects (Flowerdew 1998). However, there is no reason corpus-based analyses cannot also be used to investigate how writers use discourse structures to accomplish the aim or purpose of a writing task (Kinneavy 1971).

Recent research in two related fields – namely contrastive rhetoric and genre analysis – provides new evidence about learner English with direct relevance to the corpus work. There is convincing evidence about systematic variation in learners' performance depending on the specific language task. Contrastive rhetoricians, following Kinneavy's (1971) classification of discourse, describe task-induced discourse structures and other language use. Kinneavy (1971) categorizes discourse according to the aim or purpose of writing and identifies four discourse aims, namely, persuasive, informative, expressive, and literary. According to Kinneavy, the purpose is a key element in shaping text and thus cross-cultural differences in the writer's purpose would have significant effects on the final text. Although contrastive rhetoric points to some universal features of argumentation and narration, language subtleties, such as the expression of purpose through the interweaving of discourse, syntax and lexicon, have been overlooked by most previous research. In order to investigate the cross-cultural expression of purpose, a very carefully controlled purpose – such as applying for a job – in a corpus would be essential.

Genre analysts, such as Swales (1981) and Martin (1993), situate purpose within other genre features such as content, style, discourse community, structure and audience. All of these features are understood implicitly in the process of acquiring a new genre. Traditional genre analysis proposes 'moves' or functional components as basic to each genre; such moves can be taught to a novice writer of a particular genre (Dudley-Evans 1995; Bhatia 1993, 1995). Genres must then consequently have cultural expectations – disciplinary as well as national or ethnic – and crossing cultural boundaries within the same genre requires re-learning part of the genre. Negotiating cultural differences in the translation of genres would then be an expected part of writing for a new cultural group.

The above discussion suggests that attention to ESP writing is crucial for language learners since writers of different L2s may acquire genres differently based on cultural assumptions. The implication for the development of learner corpora is that situation, context, and stimulus need to be identified, since variation in each of these may elicit different types of language. Indeed, a corpus study in ESP may have interesting implications both for SLA and ESP pedagogy. Consequently, we see a need for corpora that are specific to ESP situations and include the writing requirements appearing in them. The subtleties of accommodating one's writing for another culture may well become apparent in tightly controlling for genre and purpose in a learner corpus. The Indiana Business Learner Corpus (IBLC), used in this study and described below, is one example of the type of genre-specific learner corpus that can be collected and used to investigate cross-cultural variations in a genre.

2.   Textlinguistic approaches to corpus linguistics

In addition to arguing for more specificity in applied learner corpus development with regard to situation, context, and stimulus, we will also show how a textlinguistic approach is useful in analyzing the corpus data. As Flowerdew (1998) points out, a great deal of the corpus-based, more applied work has focused on the lexico-grammatical patterning of text, producing collocations and lists of fixed phrases; much of this work has centered on the propositional level of texts with less regard to functional and rhetorical aspects.

For pedagogical purposes, instead of producing lists of modals and hedges, for example, it would be beneficial to show how modals are used persuasively in specific sections of an application letter, as in politely indicating a desire for an interview. A promising direction, according to Flowerdew, will be tagging not only lexicon and syntax, but also discourse features such as 'moves'. In Flowerdew's words:

> Another suggestion, which I believe would have wide pedagogical applica-
> tions, is more exploitation of the tagging function of existing software on the
> market. As Leech (1991) remarks, most of the work on text annotation (tag-
> ging) has been done at the grammatical (word class) or syntactic (parsing)
> level. Very little has been done on the semantic or pragmatic discourse level to
> date. For example, text could be tagged manually to indicate the generic 'move
> structures' such as background, scope, purpose in the introductory sections of
> a report. (p. 549)

In this study we tagged the rhetorical moves – explained below – in letters of application and begin to investigate differences and similarities in letters of application from different cultures.

3. Letters of application as a genre

Letters of application would fit a genre definition such as Swales': "a class of communicative events, the members of which share some set of communica-tive purposes" (1990: 58). According to Swales, genres have certain structural characteristics: they have a beginning, middle and end. Letters of application also conform to traditional definitions of genre in that they have a well-defined purpose. In addition, the readers of the discourse have certain expectations of the content and format of such letters. As such, the prototypical forms of application letters can be studied in terms of content and structure.

Bhatia (1993) has the most complete discussion of letters of application as a genre, drawing up a six-part structure: establishing credentials, offering incentives, enclosing documents, using pressure tactics, soliciting response, and ending politely.

In a cross-cultural comparison of application letters, based on some 200 applications for jobs and scholarships from India, Pakistan, Sri Lanka, and Bangladesh, Bhatia found differences in the function of the job applications in South Asia and the West. The main function of a Western job application letter is to highlight and make relevant the qualifications and experience of the ap-plicant to the specifications of the job, thus to provide self-appraisal. In South Asia, on the other hand, the applicants typically used the cover letters to enclose the *curriculum vitae*, but did not take the opportunity to offer self-appraisal in order to persuade the readers about their strong credentials. Instead, many

applicants used 'emotional' strategies such as 'target glorification' (i.e. prais-
ing the prospective employer) and 'self-degradation'. The Western reader finds
these strategies too emotional and prefers 'logical' self-appraisal, according to
Bhatia's interpretation.

Although our research has benefited from Bhatia's model building of application letters, like Scollon (2000) we consider it important to begin a description of genre characteristics from the data sets in question, rather than super-
imposing a predefined prototype. Consequently, the development of the moves
analysis in our study began from the data at hand and will be described below.

4. Data

The Indiana Business Learner Corpus (IBLC) which was used in this study
comprises job application letters and résumés of business students from the
U.S., Belgium and Finland. The goal of the larger corpus project is to study
language use, accommodation, and genre acquisition of native and non-native
speaking students in an undergraduate business class. Specifically, the corpus
project plans:

1. to build an advanced EFL learner corpus of letters of job applications, with
    a native English speaker comparison group
2. to make interlanguage comparison possible among learners of different L2s
3. to identify the genre thoroughly, with simulated letters of application as
    a genre, to produce a prototype and then describe variation based on L2,
    business background, etc.

The corpus was initiated to help meet the need for situation-specific corpora.
The data consist of a cross-cultural job application simulation. Participants in
this simulation are undergraduate university students in courses which have
parallel components, including: "1) instruction in international business writing; 2) a simulation, in which students exchange business documents internationally; and 3) case studies of business people who communicate internationally in writing" (Connor, Davis, De Rycker, Phillips & Verckens 1997:65).
The IBLC is compiled from the learner material generated during the simulation project. Each year, the U.S.-Belgian-Finnish writing project involves three
simulated, but tailor-made and roughly identical job advertisements, describing a summer internship in an international business seminar to be held at the
respective institutions. Job advertisements are written by the project instructors. Each group of students writes cover letters and résumés for the foreign

internship and these letters and résumés are exchanged between the institutions. Students at each institution then go through the documents from their counterparts and, acting as simulated shortlisting committees, decide which candidates will get an invitation for a telephone interview. Students then indicate what the bases of their shortlisting decisions were. During all stages of this project, participants in each country discuss what they learned about the foreign students' textualizations and about their own textualizations in light of the foreign students' evaluations of their own letters.

The products from this simulation, which has been conducted since 1990, have been collected on a yearly basis from the various instructors and together comprise the IBLC. (For further description of the course outlines, students and assignments, see Connor et al. 1997).

For this study, we examined ninety-nine learner generated letters of application from Belgium, Finland and the U.S. from 1990, 1991, 1993, 1994, 1996, 1997 and 1998. The Belgian and Finnish participants were non-native speakers of English who had had at least six years of English instruction, though a good many participants had had considerably more English study than that. The Belgian students were majors in business administration, while the Finnish learners had a double major in business and English. The American learners had mixed majors: some were English majors, others business majors.

The Belgian and Finnish participants were, on average, younger and less experienced in business than the American participants and attended their schools as full-time students. The American university participating in the study is situated in a large Midwestern city; many of these students were returning to school after beginning their careers and were attending school part-time while working full-time.

5.   Data analysis

An analysis based on Swalesean genre moves was performed on initial data in Connor, Davis & De Rycker (1995). The notion that prototypical forms of genres can be generated and studied is key for our study. A moves analysis is a useful methodology, since moves are semantic/functional units of texts which can be identified first because of their communicative purposes, and second because of linguistic boundaries typical of the moves. The moves have been empirically developed from a corpus of application letters from Belgium, Finland and the US, and describe the majority of functions generally performed in an application letter.

The study reported here employs that coding scheme for genre moves, with slight modifications. Following is a description of the modified coding scheme:

Table 1. Meaning Components of a Letter of Application: a Coding Scheme (based on Connor, Davis & De Rycker 1995).

1.	Identify the source of information. (Explain how and where you learned of the position.)
2.	Apply for the position. (State desire for consideration.)
3.	Provide supporting arguments for the job application. a. neutral evidence or information about background and experience. b. arguments based on what would be good for the hiring company. ("My intercultural training will be an asset to your international negotiations team.") c. arguments based on what would be good for the applicant. ("This job will give me the opportunity to test my intercultural training.")
4.	Indicate desire for an interview or a desire for further contact, or specify means of further communication/how to be contacted.
5.	Express politeness (pleasantries) or appreciation at the end of the letter.
6.	Offer to provide more information.
7.	Reference attached résumé.

Note. Further explanation of the scheme is available in Connor, Davis & De Rycker 1995.

For examples of each of these coding categories from actual letters, see Appendix A.

The original data-coding scheme was modified for the current study to reflect the further analysis of the data and to remove ambiguities that surfaced in training raters. In order to reflect the types of arguments being made in Move 3 (arguments for the job application), subcategories of arguments were added: a) information that was not directly used in support of an argument of the benefits to the company or the individual, b) arguments and information used to support arguments which focused on the benefit to the hiring agency, and c) arguments and information used to support arguments which focused on the benefit to the applicant.

The original coding scheme had separate categories for requesting an interview and for specifying methods for further contact. Since specifying methods for contact presumes that such contact would be for the purpose of setting up an interview, we decided to collapse these two moves into one: Move 4 – "Indicate desire for an interview or a desire for further contact, or specify means of further communication/how to be contacted."

Lastly, based on analysis of the common elements in the 99 application letters in this study, it was determined that this genre clearly included two further rhetorical moves than were originally proposed. Consequently, Move 6, "the offer to provide more information", and Move 7, "reference to an attached résumé", were added.

The moves were coded by two trained raters, who had a .92 correlation in identifying and categorizing the moves. The occurrence of each move was coded in the data. Analyses were then performed on the occurrence of moves by country using a concordance software program (*WordSmith*).

6.   Results and discussion

To test for statistical significance in the rate of occurrence of moves across countries, a 2 × 3 chi-square test was run on each move. The chi-square test is used to determine whether categorical data has the same proportion of 'events' (in this case 'moves') across subjects; consequently, the null hypothesis is that there is no difference between the rate of use of any particular moves between the Belgian, Finnish and American subjects. With a level of significance set at $p < .05$, no significant difference in the rate of occurrence was discovered in five of the seven moves: Move 1 (source of information), Move 2 (application for the position), Move 3 (supporting arguments for the application) with the sub-moves a, b, and c combined, Move 4 (desire for interview/further contact) and Move 7 (reference to attached résumé). Based on this evidence, there seems to be a general consensus cross-culturally on the moves that should be included in a letter of application, but clearly there is also some variation across cultures.

Significant differences did occur in three areas. These will be discussed below.

6.1 Move 3 (arguments for the application)

Although there was no significant difference across countries in the use of Move 3 with sub-moves a, b, and c combined, there was a significant difference in the types of arguments used in Move 3 when sub-moves were analyzed separately. A chi-square test showed that there were significant differences between groups in the use of Move 3b (arguments of benefit to the hiring company) $(X^2(2) = 6.81, p < .05)$. A post-hoc Fisher Exact Test indicated that the Finns ($p < .05$) and the Americans ($p < .05$) used this move significantly more frequently than the Belgians did. In terms of percentages, Move 3b was found in only 76% of the Belgian letters, compared with 96% and 91% for the Finnish and U.S. letters respectively. Below are two examples of American application letters using Move 3b:

(1)   Currently enrolled at Indiana University at Indianapolis, Business and Communications are my double majors. By working for such established companies as Malone Communications, I have acquired quite a bit of business experience. Through my determination and hard work ethic, I have been awarded a law scholarship from The Ohio State University for the fall of school session in 1994.

(2)   I have a strong desire to work in some way with an international system, and although I am sure that positions with your institution are very competitive, I am sure I can be of benefit.

Although the first paragraph above does not specifically mention benefit to the company, the information given (business experience, personal qualities, achievements) is clearly intended to highlight qualities which the company would presumably value. The second paragraph specifically argues that the applicant can be of benefit to the hiring company.

Move 3c (arguments of benefit to the applicant) also showed significant differences $(X^2(2) = 13.68, p < .001)$, with post-hoc Fisher Exact Tests showing the Belgian application letters using this move more frequently than either the American $(p < .001)$ or Finnish $(p < .05)$ letters. In terms of percentages, 56% of the Belgian application letters contained Move 3c, compared with only 26% and 17% respectively of the Finnish and U.S. letters. Below is a Belgian letter showing a typical Move 3c:

(3)   I feel good in my current position. However, the young age of the management will significantly reduce my career opportunities on a short-term basis. I am an engineer in electronics and I have 8 years of experience in R&D projects and project management. With my current university studies in economics I would like to focus my career on marketing projects where I can further build on my organizational skills and experience in working with subcontractors both nationally and internationally. Developing and implementing creative solutions is one of my strongest assets.

The above example contains information that could also address the benefit of the applicant to the hiring company (experience, university courses), but the thrust of the arguments in this paragraph is focused on how the internship could help the student achieve her goals. The entire paragraph, then, is characterized as Move 3c.

The more frequent use of Move 3b by the Americans and Finns and the more frequent use of Move 3c by the Belgians may suggest a cultural difference in what are considered to be effective arguments when applying for jobs.

6.2 Move 5 (expression of appreciation)

The chi-square test also showed significant differences in the use of Move 5 across countries ($X^2(2) = 9.72, p < .01$). Post-hoc Fisher Exact Tests showed that both the Belgians ($p < .05$) and the Americans ($p < .01$) used this move more frequently than the Finns, with 43% of the U.S. letters and 35% of the Belgian letters containing expressions of appreciation, compared with only 7% of the Finnish letters.

While Move 3 (arguments for the application) is highly individualized, Move 5 is very formulaic. Nearly all of the expressions were either "Thank you for your time" or "Thank you for your consideration." The formulaic nature of Move 5 is in compliance with the expectations of the genre (Bhatia 1993; Atkinson 1999). A formulaic expression of gratitude (Move 5) seems to be expected in the US and Belgian contexts, while it does not seem to be expected in the Finnish context. Thus, the presence or absence of Move 5 is probably more related to audience awareness and expectations of politeness markers than to the relative politeness/impoliteness of any of the groups. The expression of gratitude itself is not the issue here: rather, what is key is the difference in the writers' concept of whether their audience expected to be thanked or not.

The reasons for the differences in the use of Move 5 across countries are likely due to differences in audience expectations and writer concepts of how politeness is expressed. In order to investigate this, further research is needed into expressions of politeness beyond the overt use of Move 5.

6.3 Move 6 (offer to provide further information).

There were also significant cross-cultural differences in the use of Move 6 ($X^2(2) = 7.55, p < .05$). Post-hoc Fisher Exact Tests showed that the Belgians used this move more frequently than the Americans ($p < .01$). Thirty-five percent of the Belgian letters offered further information, while only 9% of the US letters did so. Move 6 also tended to be quite formulaic, with Move 6 often combined with Move 4 (requesting information/indicating method of communication), as in:

(4)   Please contact me at [phone number] if you need any further information.

(5)   I can be reached at the above address should you need any further information.

As with Move 5 (expressions of gratitude), the formulaic nature of Move 6 suggests that its presence indicates a cultural expectation of offering more information. In fact, a formulaic expression nearly identical to (5) above appeared in 25% of the Belgian letters. This formulaic phrase is likely to be more standard in the Belgian manifestation of the application letter genre than the American one. The use of a formulaic phrase, as in Move 5 above, is more likely to fulfill a reader expectation of such an offer than to express an expectation that the reader needs more information. Had the applicant genuinely thought that more information was required or expected, it would certainly have been provided in the application package. The type of information being offered is not specified, and perhaps the assumption is that further information would only be required if the applicant were invited for an interview. Move 6, then, may be functioning as a politeness marker in that the writer feels that it is polite to offer further information.

In examining the words used in Move 6, there is a clear difference between the Belgian and the American letters, which would tend to support the purpose of Move 6 for the Belgians as a politeness marker. In fact, in the eleven Belgian letters that contained Move 6, 15% of the total number of words in the move (19 out of 128 total words) were modals. Four of the eleven letters included a hypothetical (e.g., an if-clause or a phrase such as "should you need...."). The use of modals and hypothetical structures is much higher in the Belgian letters than in the Finnish or US letters, which have no modals or hypothetical structures in the move. Such modals and hypothetical structures add an air of politeness to the Belgian letters.

7.   Summary of findings related to the moves analysis

This study examined the ways in which application letters differ cross-culturally. Using a corpus of 99 application letters written by business students in a business simulation project in Belgium, Finland and the US, a moves analysis was conducted based on the moves description from Connor et al. (1995). Statistical analyses were performed on the cultural differences in the use of moves. No statistical difference was found in the frequency of five of the seven moves, suggesting a cross-cultural consensus on the use of the majority of moves.

These results suggest a remarkable consensus on the moves which are central and which are optional in the genre. Move 1 (indicating source of information), Move 2 (applying for the position), Move 3 (arguments for the position) and Move 4 (requesting contact or an interview) seemed to be obligatory in all countries, with all three countries using these moves on average 91% of the time. Move 5 (expression of appreciation), Move 6 (offering further information) and Move 7 (reference to attached resume) were clearly optional moves as they were used on average only 33% of the time. Although Moves 5 and 6 differed significantly cross-culturally, in both of these moves, the frequency of use of each move was low to begin with. These results show not only that the frequencies are similar, but that the cultures share a similar concept of which moves are central and which are optional to the genre. This suggests that the overall genre of letters of application does not differ significantly cross-culturally, at least for the Western cultures included in this investigation, even though there is clearly variability in the use of optional moves within the genre.

Although Move 3 (arguments for the application) showed no significant difference cross-culturally, this move was comprised of three sub-moves, two of which did show significant differences. These sub-moves were intended to show differences in argumentation strategies: neutral evidence for the application (3a), arguments based on what would be beneficial to the hiring company (3b), and arguments based on what would be beneficial to the applicant (3c). Moves 3b and 3c differed significantly across the cultures. Move 3, in which arguments are made and reasons are given for being chosen for the position, is the most overtly persuasive move in the text. In this move, the Finnish and US students used arguments based on what was good for the hiring company significantly more often than the Belgian students did. The Belgian students used arguments based on what was good for the student significantly more often than the Finnish or US students. It seems that what is considered persuasive evidence differs significantly, and we suspect that such differences may result in applicants not being chosen due to their choice of an argumentation strategy that conflicts with reader expectations.

This study further found significant differences in the use of formulaic expressions, as in Move 5 (expressions of gratitude) and Move 6 (offering more information). Although there were significant cross-cultural differences in the use of these moves, neither Move 5 nor Move 6 was obligatory, and so the absence of the move may not be a significant factor to the reader. That is, in the groups that most frequently used Move 5 (US) and Move 6 (Belgium), the move was still used in less than half of the letters (43% for Move 5 in the US letters and 35% for Move 6 in the Belgian letters).

8.   Implications for future research and teaching

8.1   Contributions of the study

One major contribution that this study makes is to show that genre-specific corpora can play an important role in understanding and evaluating language use by language learners. Most current language corpora are eclectic collections of spoken and written text from a wide variety of native-language contexts. Although many of these corpora are quite large and much can be discerned about the general lexical and grammatical features of a language from them, they offer little insight into the moves or cultural expectations of individual genres that may make up the larger corpus. Further, the typical, large generic corpus does not reveal how learners of a specific genre may struggle with acquiring expected characteristics of the genre. We argue that teachers will find genre-specific learner corpora much more useful in evaluating student needs.

This study also shows that a textlinguistic approach is not only feasible but also very informative when analyzing learner corpus data. Although individual rhetorical features in a genre-specific corpus must still be hand-tagged if one is investigating such features as moves, any generic software concordance program dramatically facilitates the searching, selecting, and sorting of textlinguistic features in a way that is impossible to do by hand with large numbers of individual items. Rhetorical patterns and features that are not apparent in a manual analysis of a small number of texts become very evident when revealed through a computerized analysis with a concordance program on a larger sample of texts. Most generic software concordance programs (e.g., *Wordsmith*, *MonoConc*) are not only relatively inexpensive and easy to obtain, but are fairly easy to learn to use. The effort needed to learn these programs is more than offset by the speed, accuracy and complexity of analysis of large numbers of texts that they permit.

In short, we strongly advocate the collection of genre-specific learner corpora and the use of textlinguistic tools of genre analysis as a source of insight into the rhetorical decisions writers make when writing in a particular genre.

8.2   Implications for teaching

As to the question of the appropriateness and effectiveness of teaching genre moves, the current study suggests that there may in fact be a great deal of consensus among writers about the occurrence and sequencing of moves in a common genre such as an application letter. While Goby (1999) has suggested that teaching genre moves may not be necessary, we believe there is value in helping developing writers understand what types of moves are generally expected in a genre. Further, we believe that moves analysis on cross-cultural samples of a genre allows us to spot the type of subtle but important differences that we have found in this study, which also have instructional value.

The implications for teaching the genre of the letter of job application cross-culturally are also worth reflection. Naturally, students need to be made aware of the kinds of differences found in this study and about the possible negative impact of 'inappropriate' moves. However, informal observations throughout the nine-year history of the IBLC suggest that students who try to imitate the supposed writing style of the country to which they are sending their applications are not necessarily successful in obtaining the simulated jobs. An example of a Finnish student will suffice. Early on in the collection of the IBLC letters, it was noted that U.S. students' arguments about experience and background were much lengthier and more boastful than the Belgian and Finnish students' arguments. Trying to imitate the U.S. style, a Finnish student wrote a long application letter boastfully describing his accomplishments, using references to his "fun personality", "team spirit" and other characteristics he considered American and thought would appeal to the U.S. student "judges." His application was flatly rejected because he sounded "phony" and "non-Finnish," according to the Americans.

Furthermore, based on observations throughout the years, the letter writing styles of the three countries have converged toward a model with fewer extremes. For example, the U.S. students write shorter letters and the Belgian students write longer ones; the result is what appears to be a more homogenized form of letter writing due to the interaction between the writers from the different cultures. These observations concur with Crystal's (1997) notions about the rapidly changing English norms in which speakers of different varieties of English accommodate to each other's forms and styles. Yet the notion about the increasingly homogenized forms of letters in the sample needs to be put to empirical testing in future research studies.

8.3   Challenges in conducting this study

There are three significant hurdles inherent in conducting a study like this on a genre-specific corpus. Unlike corpus studies that look at lexico-grammatical patterning, having a computer produce frequency and collocation lists of words and structures to highlight patterns does not work when trying to analyze the discourse of a genre. The first challenge is to establish a rubric for identifying the rhetorical and functional features one is looking for within a text. As noted earlier, traditional genre analysis argues that there are functional components (moves) that are basic to each genre. There are sources available describing the application of moves analysis in ESP settings (e.g. Bhatia 1993, 1995; Connor 1996; Dudley-Evans 1995) that can be consulted to help facilitate a moves analysis of a genre. However, while work has been done to investigate the move structure of several genres (e.g. Bhatia 1993) or sections of specific genres (Swales 1981), one cannot rely on an *a priori* model without first mapping out the entire range of potential moves in one's data set.

After a rubric for identifying the genre moves has been established, the moves must then be tagged within each text. This presents the second challenge. While computers are excellent for locating specific words or letters within a corpus, there are no computer programs that can currently evaluate text for the rhetorical functions of moves; consequently, moves within a text must still be evaluated individually by hand. It is important to have detailed descriptions, i.e. rubrics, for each move with representative examples. The development of these descriptions is a crucial step and is often best done or reviewed by a team. After the rubrics have been tried on a sample of texts and necessary modifications made, a final set of rubrics can be produced to guide the raters. The next step is hand-coding, which takes time and must be checked – at least a statistically appropriate percentage of the time – by a second rater. This need not be considered a major burden however and the ultimate benefits of the tagging for future analysis is dramatic. Assuming the rubric established for identifying the moves for the genre of the texts being analyzed is well conceived, it usually only takes a few minutes to identify and tag in a specific text the six to twelve moves that typically make up a genre. Since most genre-specific corpora are made up of only a couple of hundred texts at the most, hand-tagging of the moves in all of the texts can easily be done and checked in a few hours.

Once all of the genre-specific texts are tagged for rhetorical moves, it then becomes possible, as in the study described in this paper, to use a computer to gain quantitative information about how the moves tend to be used across a genre. We believe it is this combination of textlinguistic and computer corpus analyses, facilitating the qualitative, functional analysis of quantitative patterns as called for by Biber, Conrad, & Reppen (1998), that will bring dramatic insights into how language is used by writers to accomplish specific goals within a text.

The third significant hurdle to a study like the one described in this paper is that it takes time to collect a genre-specific corpus that is large enough to permit reasonably reliable conclusions based on a corpus analysis. Because the data that are collected must match the specific features of the genre that is being targeted, there are fewer sources from which to draw upon when collecting material. Material for the IBLC, which is not a large corpus, has been collected over the course of nine years; the sources for the data were three relatively small classes of upper-division business students, one from each country (Finland, Belgium and the U.S.), which met only once a year. The major advantages of collecting data in such a teaching situation are two-fold: (1) no extra costs will be incurred since the data are part of the classroom assignments, and (2) teachers are able to exert control over learners so that they will adhere to the prompt. Costs and lack of control over the data are important factors and ones which often plague large-scale corpus projects.

None of the three hurdles outlined above are new or unusual concerns. While significant, with planning they can be fairly easily addressed. It is our opinion that the advantages afforded to both teachers and researchers by a textlinguistic analysis of genre-specific corpora more than outweigh the challenges posed by using this approach.

References

Atkinson, D. (1999). *Scientific discourse in sociohistorical context: The philosophical transactions of the Royal Society of London, 1675–1975*. Mahwah, NJ: Erlbaum.

Bhatia, V. (1993). *Analyzing genre: Language use in professional settings*. New York: Longman.

Bhatia, V. (1995). Applied genre analysis and ESP. *The Journal of TESOL-France, 2*(2), 161–179.

Biber, D., Conrad, S., & Reppen, R. (1998). *Corpus Linguistics: Investigating Language Structure and Use*. Cambridge: Cambridge University Press.

Connor, U. (1996). *Cross-cultural aspects of second-language writing*. New-York: Cambridge University Press.

Connor, U., Davis, K., & De Rycker, T. (1995). Correctness and clarity in applying for overseas jobs: A cross-cultural analysis of U.S. and Flemish applications. *Text, 15*(4), 457–476.

Connor, U., Davis, K., De Rycker, T., Phillips, E. M., & Verckens, J. P. (1997). An international course in international business writing: Belgium, Finland, the United States. *Business Communication Quarterly, 60*(4), 63–74.

Crystal, D. (1997). *English as a global language*. Cambridge: Cambridge University Press.

Dudley-Evans, T. (1995). Genre models for the teaching of academic writing to second language speakers: Advantages and disadvantages. *The Journal of TESOL-France, 1*, 181–192.

Flowerdew, L. (1998). Corpus linguistic techniques applied to textlinguistics. *System, 26*, 541–552.

Goby, P. (1999). All business students need to know the same things! The non-culture-specific nature of communication needs. *Journal of Business and Technical Communication, 13*(2), 179–189.

Granger, S. (1998). The computer learner corpus: A versatile new source of data for SLA research. In S. Granger (Ed.), *Learner English on Computer* (pp. 3–18). New York: Longman.

Hyland, K., & Milton, J. (1997). Qualification and certainty in L1 and L2 students' writing. *Journal of Second Language Writing, 6*(2), 183–205.

Kinneavy, J. (1971). *A theory of discourse*. Englewood Cliffs, NJ: Prentice-Hall.

Leech, G. (1991). The state of the art in corpus linguistics. In K. Aijmer & B. Altenberg (Eds.), *English Corpus Linguistics: Studies in Honour of Jan Svartvik* (pp. 8–29). London: Longman.

Martin, J. R. (1993). Genre and literacy-modeling context in educational linguistics. *Annual Review of Applied Linguistics, 13*, 141–172.

Scollon, R. (2000). Genre variablility in news stories in Chinese and English: A contrastive study of five days' newspapers. *Journal of Pragmatics, 32*, 761–791.

Swales, J. (1981). *Aspects of article introductions*. The University of Aston, Birmingham: Language Studies Unit.

Swales, J. (1990). *Genre analysis: English in academic and research settings*. New York: Cambridge University Press.

Appendix A. Move samples

1. Identify the source of information. (Explain how and where you learned of the position.)

"I was delighted to hear from Professor Ken Davis of your plans to create a team to investigate global business issues."
"I recently received word from Blockbuster Recruiting about a management position available at your company."
"After reading your advertisement,..." [only this part of the sentence is move 1].

2. Apply for the position. (State desire for consideration.)

"I am very interested in the vacancy of an intern."
"I am very interested in a temporary job working as a European business student intern in the U.S.A."
"This is why I am applying for the 13 June 1994 student internship."
"I hope that you will consider me for this position."

3. **Provide argument, including supporting information, for the job application.**

a.   Implicit argument based on neutral evidence or information about background and experience.

In providing supporting information or arguments, the writers sometimes simply listed their background experience. These descriptions seem to be putting information from the resume into prose:

> "I will be completing my degree of Business-Accounting in December of 1993. My current employment requires collecting, processing, and interpreting data every day. I summarize this data into a report which is sent to top executives of corporations for them to make decisions. I am very interested in the globalized economy, especially the US and EC business environment. My oral and written English are very fluent and my communication skills are excellent."
>
> "I received my Associates Degree in General Studies in May 1993. Previously I have received a degree in Office Management from Indiana Business College and I have obtained the Certified Professional Secretary (CPS) certification..."

b.   Arguments based on what would be good for the hiring company

In 3B, the writers argues explicitly that their experience or education will benefit the company that hires them. This includes the entire argument structure.

> "I feel I can offer my business experience which I have gained working as an Accountant."
>
> "I have a strong desire to work in some way with an international system, and although I am sure that positions with your institution are very competitive, I am sure I can be of benefit."
>
> "I also feel that my communication skills and employment experience would be beneficial to your research team."
>
> "I believe that my interest in the subject, as well as my background and work experience, will enable me to contribute to your project."

c.   Arguments based on what would be good for the applicant

Sometimes the writers directly stated how the experience would benefit them. The evidence in this argument is an aspect of the employment position which would be beneficial to the applicant, rather than discussing the applicants' background. This includes the entire argument structure.

"This Studentship will offer me good experience in International business."
"The opportunity to study abroad the globalised business environment would help me gain the knowledge and experience to grow in the changing business world of today."
"This would be a perfect opportunity to have foreign business experience."
"This is a unique opportunity to create an impartial view of the American way of life in general and the working of a foreign university in particular."

4. **Indicate desire for an interview or a desire for further contact, or specifying means of further communication/how to be contacted.**

"I hope I got you interested so that I will be selected for an interview."
"I'm always prepared to participate in an interview."
"Let us get together to discuss the position and the possible opportunity to work with you in Belgium."
"I will look forward to your call."
"My telephone number at work is <PH>, and at home is <PH>."
"Please feel free to contact me at <PH>."
"I can be reached at the above address."

5. **Express politeness (pleasantries) or appreciation at the end of the letter.**

"Thank you in advance for your consideration."
"I should be very grateful for a favorable consideration of my application..."
"If the position referred to is still vacant I would be grateful for the opportunity of an interview with one of your responsible colleagues." [underlined section only; the second half is move 4 ("request for interview")]
"Thank you for your time in reviewing this material."

6. **Offer to provide more information.**

"I can be reached at the above address should you need any further information."
[underlined section only]
"I'm prepared to send you more information."
"I will be happy to provide you with any additional information that you may need."

7.   **Reference attached resume.**

"I have enclosed my resume…"

"A resume is enclosed."

"Enclosed is a copy of my resume (CV) which will provide additional data."

"<u>As you will see from my enclosed curriculum vitae</u> I worked parallel to my studies for Lufthansa as Senior Flight Attendant." [underlined section only; the rest is 3A.]

The TELEC secondary learner corpus
A resource for teacher development

Quentin Grant Allan

Teachers of English Language Education Centre, University of Hong Kong

Chapter overview

In this chapter, Allan addresses some of the practical issues of Learner Corpus Research (LCR) within the domain of teacher training with a novel application: a resource which uses corpus data in systematic ways to raise the language awareness of secondary level English teachers in Hong Kong. This is done under the auspices of the Teachers of English Language Education Centre (TELEC), through an Internet network (*TeleNex*), which is designed to provide continuous professional Support for secondary level English teachers, many of whom lack a specialist knowledge of the English language.

The TELEC Secondary Learner Corpus (TSLC) has been developed over a number of years, and consists of over two million words of running text comprising written compositions from the secondary classroom (narratives, recounts, descriptions, explanations, arguments), as well as a smaller spoken component. The corpus is designed to be accessed with standard text retrieval software such as MicroConcord or WordSmith Tools. The chapter begins by describing the development of the TSLC, touching on some of the specific problems regarding the logistics of compilation. It then outlines the ways in which the corpus has been used in the *TeleNex* teacher development network, and concludes with a discussion of how teachers can benefit from accessing this corpus (and other corpora) via a self-access concordancing package.

1. Introduction

The TELEC Secondary Learner Corpus (TSLC) is a resource which is being developed and drawn on by a team of teacher educators and materials writers at TELEC (Teachers of English Education Centre), a teacher education facility based at Hong Kong University's Department of Curriculum Studies. TELEC fulfils three main functions: running periodic workshops for in-service teachers, conducting research into English language teaching, and administering *TeleNex*, which is a computer network designed to provide professional support for secondary level English teachers in Hong Kong, many of whom lack specialist knowledge of the English language.[1] The *TeleNex* network draws on the experience of developers and participants of asynchronous learning networks (ALNs), which are web-based learning venues that emphasize people-to-people communication in conjunction with traditional and/or multi-media learning tools. ALNs enable people to learn and develop professionally through self study, and in interaction with other interested parties through e-mail and/or threaded conferencing systems anywhere and at any time without traditional constraints of time and space. In a recent article, Bourne (1998) traces the development of such networks, noting their significant impact in many educational arenas including on-campus education, off-campus education, and continuing education. For further background relating specifically to the development of *TeleNex*, including a full discussion of TELEC's aims and objectives, see Wu and Tsui (1997).

The *TeleNex* network is then the most visible face of TELEC and is available over the internet, free of charge to all secondary level English teachers in Hong Kong. *TeleNex* comprises two hypertext[2] databases (*TeleGram* and *TeleTeach*), and a range of theme-based conference corners. *TeleGram* is a pedagogic grammar, a database of information about English grammar and usage, customised for the Hong Kong teaching context. For further information about the development and theoretical rationale for *TeleGram*, see Lock and Tsui (1999). *TeleTeach* is a database of graded teaching materials which are designed to be printed out and used in the classroom. These materials are tailored to the Hong Kong ESL teaching situation, and designed to supplement school coursebooks. For further information about the development of and theoretical rationale for *TeleTeach*, see Sengupta and Nicholson (1996). Access to *TeleNex* is restricted to registered English teachers in Hong Kong; however, a sampler of files from both databases, and sample messages from the conference corners can be accessed at http://www.*TeleNex*.hku.hk/

The TSLC impinges on all three components of *TeleNex*, and is used in two main ways: firstly, it is used for systematic linguistic analysis of areas of English in which Hong Kong secondary students experience difficulty. These analyses are used to inform the development of the *TeleNex* databases. The corpus is also invaluable as a resource for TELEC staff to draw on when answering teachers' questions about aspects of grammar and usage through the *TeleNex* conferencing corners.

The chapter begins by briefly outlining the development of the TSLC, touching on some of the specific problems regarding the logistics of compilation. The main body of the chapter explores the ways we have used the corpus (in conjunction with other native speaker corpora) in the process of producing grammar files and answering teachers' questions. The chapter concludes with an outline of our plans for future development.

2.   Development of the TSLC

Work on the TSLC began in 1994, and it currently contains some 2.2 million words of running text comprising Form 1–7 compositions written in class, Hong Kong school examinations and examination scripts from the Hong Kong Examinations Authority. More recently, we have included scripts at Form 7 level from the University of Hong Kong's extra mural department.[3] In order to ensure that the TSLC is representative of the sorts of writing being done in Hong Kong schools, it was decided, in the early stages of development, that rather than telling teachers what sorts of writing we wanted to collect, we should take everything and see what patterns emerged, as we were interested to see how teachers interpreted the syllabus guidelines, and what their emphases were in terms of composition type allocation. At present, the corpus contains student writing representative of the following text types: personal letters, formal/business letters, letters to the editor, newspaper or magazine editorials, feature articles, speeches, reports and free composition. Within these text types, the following genres are represented: narratives, recounts, descriptions, explanations and arguments. Each piece of writing is coded for the following parameters:

-   spoken or written
-   level
-   genre[4]
-   production conditions
-   banding[5]

The filename for each text is designed to reveal information about the text: the first alpha-numeric in the eight-character filename is either 's' or 'w', indicating spoken or written; the second alpha-numeric is either 'p' or 's', indicating primary or secondary; the third is 1–7, indicating Forms 1–7; the fourth is an initial indicating which genre the text exemplifies; the fifth is either 'c' or 'e', indicating whether the text was produced in class or under examination conditions; the sixth is 1–5, indicating the band label assigned to the author's school, (see note iv above). Using any of the standard, commercially available corpus access tools such as *MicroConcord* or *WordSmith Tools*, it is possible to run searches through the entire corpus or, with judicious use of wildcards, to specify a sub-corpus of, for example, argumentative writing only (???a*.*); or all Form 1 students (?s1*.*); or only Form 1 students from Band 5 schools (?s1??5*.*). When viewing a concordance in KWIC format, this coding system also allows a user to see at a glance a citation's provenance, for example, the filename 'ws4ne500.001' would indicate that the highlighted line is from the secondary written component (ws), and is a narrative composition (n), written under exam conditions (e), by a Form 4 student (4) studying in a Band 5 school (5). Because we have assured our teachers that individual writers will remain anonymous, the last five figures reflect confidential archive information about the school and date of composition.

3.   Ways in which the TSLC is used

Raw material from the TSLC is used in developing teaching files for *TeleTeach*. The corpus has proved to be particularly useful in developing files designed to equip students with skills for dealing with proof-reading and revision, as Figure 1 shows.

The TSLC is used in conjunction with a number of modern English corpora[6] to conduct investigations into Hong Kong secondary students' writing. These investigations reveal interesting and useful patterns of usage: overuse, underuse (or avoidance), errors (lexical, collocational and syntactic), and of course correct usage. Together, these corpora are invaluable as a resource for TELEC staff to draw on when answering teachers' questions about aspects of grammar and usage through the *TeleNex* conference corners. These questions sometimes originate from students, and sometimes from teachers themselves. As indicated previously, many English language teachers in Hong Kong are not subject trained, and in addition to their lack of explicit linguistic knowledge, many teachers harbour certain misconceptions about the language, as well as

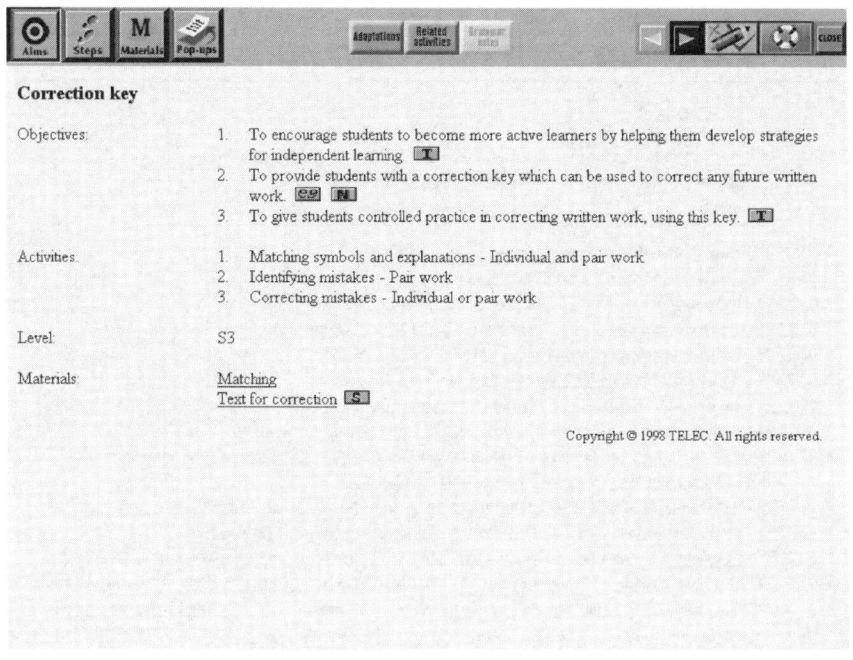

Figure 1. Example of a writing activity (from *TeleTeach*)

having their own problems with fluency and accuracy. The Language Corner is typically used by teachers to query aspects of usage which they (and/or their students) find puzzling or anomalous, and to raise questions about 'rules' which they had been taught themselves, but which for various reasons, they are now questioning. See, for example, Figure 2.

Most of the questions in this corner focus on micro aspects of language use such as the difference in meaning between two synonyms, complementation patterns with particular verbs, or the 'correct' use of connectives. For example, in response to a teacher's question about the use of 'besides', it was possible to point out that comparing Hong Kong student data with a corpus of modern English revealed an apparent overuse of 'besides' by Hong Kong students and that 'besides' in fact has a relatively low distribution in modern English. Moreover, whereas 90 % of all instances of Hong Kong student 'besides' were sentence-initial, when it *is* used by proficient native speakers and writers, its syntactic function is as likely to be intra-sentential as inter-sentential. In their messages, a number of teachers have indicated that they find conventional reference books such as grammars and dictionaries unhelpful, and from the feedback we have received, it is clear that teachers find corpus data useful in ex-

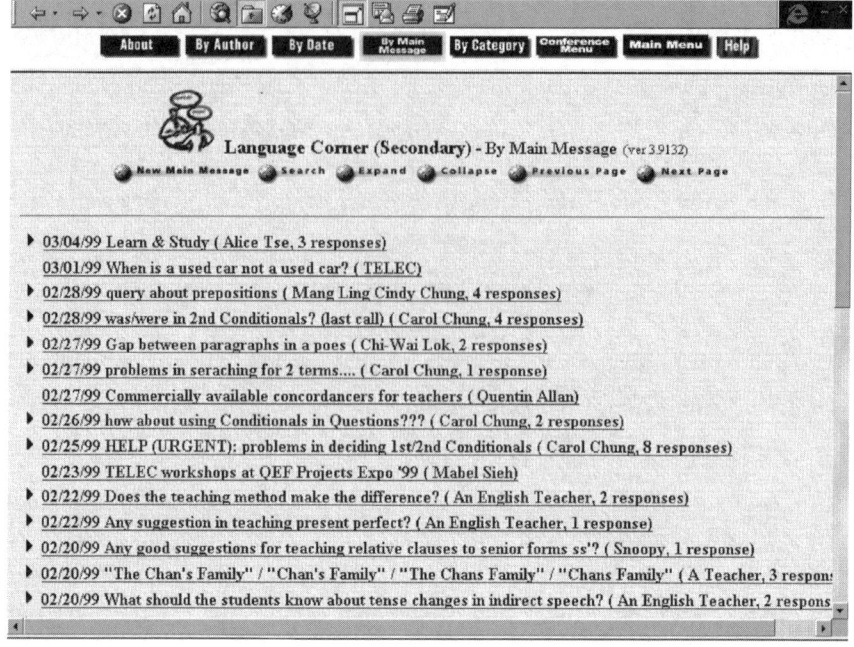

Figure 2. Directory of discussion topics (from secondary 'Language Corner')

plaining and illustrating points of grammar and usage. For further discussion of the ways in which corpus data are used in response to teachers' queries, see Allan (1999) and Tyrwhitt-Drake (1999).

Although used extensively in these domains, the TSLC is primarily used for systematic linguistic analysis of areas of English in which Hong Kong secondary students experience difficulty.[7] These analyses are used to inform the approach taken in compiling *Students' problems* files in *TeleGram,* focusing on problems in the following main functional areas:

1. Representing things (dealing with the nominal group: countability, qualitative and classifying adjectives, post-modification, and nominalisation)
2. Referring to people and things (general, indefinite and definite reference)
3. Indicating likelihood, obligation and willingness (epistemic and deontic modality)
4. Representing direct and indirect speech
5. Locating events in time (tense and time adverbials)
6. Offering and requesting information and services (speech function and mood: directives, offers, question types)

7. Representing actions and events (transitivity, ergativity, phase)
8. Representing thinking, perceiving, liking and desiring (complementation patterns with mental process verbs)
9. Representing when, where, how and why (adverbials)
10. Identifying and describing people and things (comparison, linking verbs, etc.)
11. Organising information in sentences (passive voice, cleft sentences)
12. Creating coherent texts (cohesion, coordination and subordination)

Because *TeleGram* is designed primarily for teachers, each main area is broken down into a number of sub areas, with each sub-area containing, in addition to the grammar descriptions, five pedagogically oriented core files. An *Overview* file provides a general introduction to the sub-area; a *Teachers' quiz* file aims to arouse teachers' interest and awareness of key points; a *Misconceptions* file aims to draw teachers' attention to common myths about aspects of the language and areas of misunderstanding shared by learners (and sometimes also by teachers); a *Students' problems* file focuses on the specific problems faced by Hong Kong secondary students and a *Teaching implications* file aims to show how the grammatical information relating to a particular area can best be dealt with in the classroom. Hyperlinks are made where appropriate to graded teaching activities in *TeleTeach*, as shown in Figure 3.

For productive problems, items are selected for inclusion in the *Students' problems* files following analyses of the TSLC, and comparisons made where necessary with native speaker corpora. The starting point is often intuition; for these files, a joint brainstorming exercise is conducted with a committee of materials writers, each of whom has experience teaching local students and either fluency in, or some familiarity with Cantonese, which is the mother tongue of the vast majority of Hong Kong students. To complement the brainstorming exercise, systematic searches are made in the Language Corner, for relevant messages containing explicit references to students' problems. This preliminary research provides the impetus for the initial corpus searches, which inevitably lead to further searches, and further discoveries, in keeping with Sinclair's observation that it is this heuristic power that is the exciting contribution of corpus linguistics, rather than 'the mirroring of intuitive categories of description' (1986: 202).

The data generated from this research are used as a basis for drafting files which are then passed around for colleagues' comments and suggestions. The completed files are to a large extent a collaborative effort, evolving through a process of multiple drafts based on the experience of the TELEC specialists,

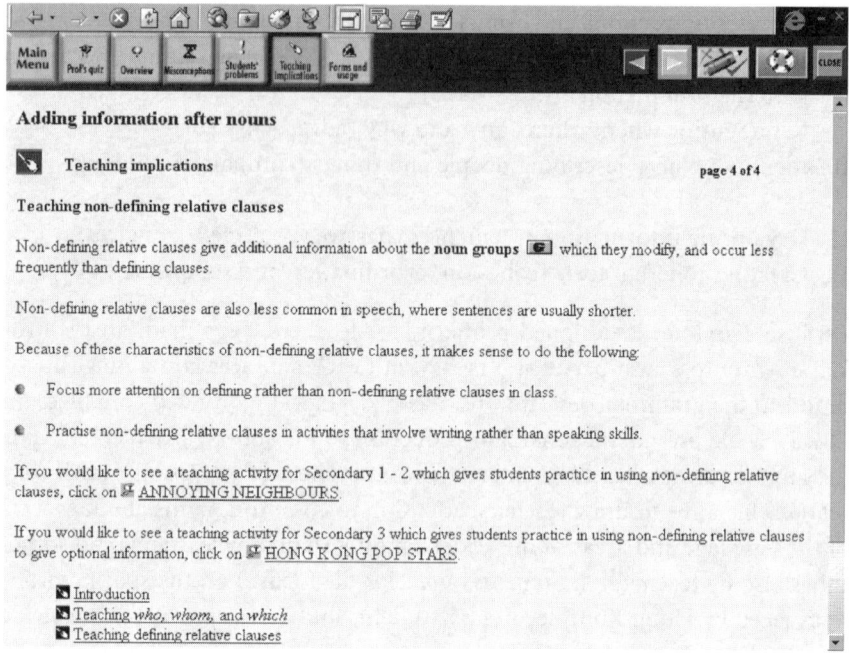

Figure 3. Teaching implications (from *TeleGram*)

extensive corpus analysis, input from the Language Corner and revision in response to peer review.[8] In addition, a Comment facility allows readers to send in messages about any of the completed files, so a teacher might choose to contribute further examples or observations related to a particular problem, and these comments are taken into account when the databases are periodically updated. Despite our best intentions, we nevertheless recognize that teachers and researchers are not always aware of all of their students' difficulties, and there may well be problem areas which have been inadvertently neglected. Systematic error tagging using an approach similar to that outlined in Dagneaux et al (1998) would be an ideal method of discerning additional problem areas, and would provide a useful supplement to intuition tapping and reference to the Language Corner.

The approach taken with each *Students' problems* file follows the same format, and our policy is that just one problem, or main type of problem is dealt with per page. This means that the same lexical item may be dealt with in a number of places, e.g. 'would' is covered in both modality files, and future time files, although with a different focus in each case. Each page opens with an outline of the problem, followed by an example, or examples from the TSLC. These examples are edited where necessary in order to remove other distracting errors. For example, 'more' would be removed from the following text if the focus is on confusion between adverbs and adjectives in attributive clauses, rather than problems with the form of comparatives: '... *it is certainly that the opportunities for education will be more greater.*' In addition to the use of red to indicate the presence of a problem, we have developed a number of conventions for highlighting different kinds of problems. For example, both underlining and strikethrough are used with morphological, syntactic, collocational and stylistic problems – underlining to indicate that the offending word(s) should be changed (as with *certainly* above), and strikethrough if the offending word should be deleted, e.g. when making general statements with plural nouns: *~~Those~~ rich people may not have love even though they have money.*' To indicate a missing word, a caret in square brackets is used, e.g. with failure to include a finite verb in relative clauses: '*When they see anybody who [^] wearing a fur coat...*'.

A correct version is provided, followed by explication of the text where appropriate, and discussion of possible reasons for the problem. For example, in the following sentence, the problem involves confusion between verb and noun: '*The resources are not evenly distribution especially in undeveloped countries.*' Here, two possible explanations are proffered. The first (pertaining to second language acquisition theory), is that students may have learned the noun form first, which is therefore more familiar to them; the second (suggesting first language interference), is that students may also be influenced by the fact that in Chinese no change is needed: a word like 'sìhnggùng' (succeed/success) can be used as either a verb or a noun. Each *Students' problems* file contains a link to a relevant file or files containing more in-depth information about that area. See, for example, Figure 4.

4. Types of problems covered

Brown (1987:171) notes that 'only *some* of the errors a learner makes are attributable to the mother tongue, that learners do not actually make all the errors that contrastive analysis predicted they should, and that learners from disparate language backgrounds tend to make similar errors in learning one target language. Errors – overt manifestations of learners' systems – arise from several possible general sources: interlingual errors of interference from the native language, intralingual errors within the target language, the sociolinguis-

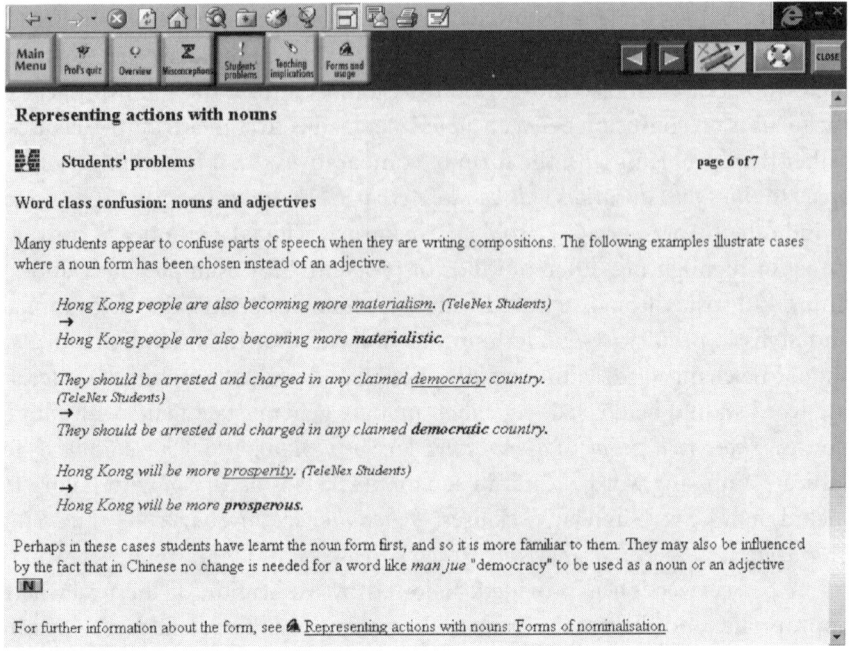

Figure 4. Students' problems (from *TeleGram*)

tic context of communication, psycholinguistic or cognitive strategies, and no doubt countless affective variables. In analyzing students' written English, we recognize that it is not always possible to distinguish between 'mistakes' (i.e. performance problems, which are correctable by the student) and 'errors' (i.e. idiosyncracies in the student's interlanguage). In a number of cases, it is possible to make judgements as to the likely cause of the problem, such as first language interference. For example, 'have' (instead of 'be') is often used incorrectly by students after 'there' to represent existence or location: '*If there has no electricity supply, a lot of things cannot work.*' This is likely to be a direct translation from Cantonese. However, it is not always clear from corpus data by itself whether this represents a mistake or an error. Therefore, without having recourse to the author of the text, we have to make a judgement as to whether, and how, the problem will be dealt with. The problems dealt with in *TeleGram* are mainly productive and include morphology, lexis, syntax, punctuation, ellipsis, style, register, collocation and coherence at both sentence and discourse level. A typical morphological problem for example, is outlined in the files dealing with post-modification with relative clauses, and involves confusion between *whose* and *who's*, possibly because both words are identical in pronunciation /hu:z/, as in the sentence, '*I found that the student was surrounded by three teenagers who's ages were around 18 to 20.*'

While recognising the fuzzy boundary between lexis and grammar (see for example, Sinclair 1991:81), it is nevertheless useful at times to narrow the focus to individual lexical items, especially as many of the problems experienced by Hong Kong students are at word level, and may involve morphological mix-ups and word class muddles as noted above, or confusion with countable and uncountable nouns for example, leading to instances where students use uncountable nouns as if they were countable: '*They can also revise their homeworks together.*'; or where students use countable nouns as if they were uncountable: '*Many companies and countries are using computer every day.*'; or where students are unaware that some nouns can be used with both countable and uncountable meanings in some situations, but not in all: '*... traffic jam is inevitable in modern cities.*'

The files dealing with transitivity offer insights into the sorts of syntactic problems students have, such as omitting the preposition after verbs like 'listen' (which in Chinese does not require a preposition): '*They can listen [^] music in this room ...*'. Sometimes, transitive verbs are used as if they were ergative: '*He found the heroin in my bag so I [^] arrested in the airport.*' In other cases, students use what looks like the passive voice with intransitive verbs: '*When the snake was escaped, the people were afraid.*', possibly taking 'was' and 'were' to be general markers of past tense. A related problem is overuse of the passive voice with ergative verbs, where the implication of a causer of the action is not always appropriate: '*English was developed from Latin, like many other languages in Europe, such as French and Italian.*'

One of the (many) problems that students have with ellipsis is lack of awareness that the subject should be omitted in certain circumstances, for example with negative imperatives (unless it is needed for contrastive or emphatic purposes): '*When your classmates ask you to play with them, you don't be shy. You should go with them.*' The problem of unintended emphasis also occurs with the formula 'It is because': '*Causeway Bay at 7:00 pm is very busy. If you want to go shopping, I think you will be very unhappy. It is because you can only see people and not any goods.*' The problem here can be traced back to the injunction that lower secondary students answer all comprehension questions using a complete sentence. The extent of the problem is suggested by the following figures: in 2.8 million words, 'it is because' occurs 1,025 times, while in the Bank of English corpus of 50 million words, 'it is because' occurs only 169 times, a ratio of 108:1. While the example above does reflect a problem with syntax (in that if a pronoun is used, it should be 'this' to refer to the preceding clause), many of the other 1,024 examples could more correctly be considered infelicitous, i.e. stylistic rather than syntactic problems. A number of stylistic problems are due to underuse of particular strategies such as a lack of hedging, particularly in argumentative writing, which has been documented by Milton and Hyland (1997). Another stylistic problem area concerns avoidance of 'have' in favour of the 'there be' structure, attributable to the widely-held misconception that 'have' cannot be used unless the subject is a person (or persons). This results in the following sort of prose: '*There are many fascinating historical sites in India which are worth visiting. For example, there are the Mogul Gardens which were built in the eighteenth century. Besides, there are also many famous museums in India, such as the Maharajah Palace, which is one of the most famous museums in the world.*' Students have all sorts of problems with collocation, including deciding which adjectives normally go with which nouns: '*I am the highest student in our class.*', and the appropriate verb in delexical verb structures: '*I hope we can make a discussion to try and solve the present problems.*'

Milton (1998: 190) refers to a 'a narrow range of words and phrases (which) have been elevated to the level of an academic catechism'. Connectives rank high on this list, and many of the problems which students have can be attributed to the way in which connectives are taught, i.e. students are given lists of 'useful' words to learn, with instructions to use them to link sentences, often followed up by decontextualised, mechanical exercises. Inevitably, sentential adverbs such as 'thus, moreover, besides, furthermore, however, therefore' are overused and even misused, typically only ever appearing in sentence initial position: '*The pressure of studies and examinations places a great load on young people as they grow up and develop. Thus, some people advise that romantic relationships between boys and girls should be important and advocate them during their school life. However, a coin has two sides.*' This has the undesired effect of drawing undue attention to the linking words themselves rather than to the ideas being expressed, and of course results in an unfortunately ponderous style. See Crewe (1990), for further discussion. Other problems have more serious consequences for the coherence of a piece of writing, and in some cases can be attributed to first language interference, for example, students' misuse of 'on the other hand' can probably be explained with reference to its Cantonese equivalent 'lihngyatfòngmihn' which does not generally mark contrast: '*You should try to make your premises unattractive to thieves and your staff should always be alert to deter the would-be thief. On the other hand, you should try to avoid 'hidden' areas.*'

Most of the problems outlined above are productive; however, the *Students' problems* files also cover receptive problems such as the difficulties students have in processing heavily nominalised text, students' unfamiliarity with the convention whereby present simple tense is used to indicate past time in newspaper headlines, and students' difficulty in understanding zero relative clauses.

5.   Future plans for the TSLC

The TSLC is still under development. In addition to exploring POS and error tagging, it is our intention to expand the secondary corpus to ensure a representative sample of student writing at all ability levels, across the major genres, and across production conditions, e.g. whether written in class under the direction of a teacher, or under examination conditions. In order to balance the writing with a spoken component, we intend to obtain and transcribe recordings of students engaged in presentations, role-plays and group discussions on a range of topics.[9] We are currently exploring the possibility of complementing the transcribed spoken corpus with digital audio files, which will allow users the option of hearing as well as seeing the data.

In December 1998, TELEC embarked on a three-year project to develop (along the same lines as *TeleNex*) a support network for primary level English teachers. Work has commenced on the development of a corpus of primary level student writing and transcribed speech which will be used as a resource to inform the development of the databases and conference corners in *PrimeGram*.

At present, corpus data (both English native-speaker and student corpora) are only available to teachers as filtered through TELEC staff. However, a number of teachers have expressed interest in using a corpus access program to discover for themselves how the English language operates, and to investigate recurrent patterns of student errors. TELEC is currently exploring the possibility of creating a concordancing program to allow teachers to conduct their own searches, accessing the TSLC and a Hong Kong focused English corpus through the *TeleNex* interface. This development, when implemented, will have a number of significant benefits, as outlined in Allan (1999: 71) and summarized here.

Firstly, it is felt that interacting with corpora should help teachers to improve their own command of the English language. It is becoming increasingly apparent that access to various corpora has a unique potential to raise teachers' awareness of patterning and usage within specific genres and texts, as well as across the language as a whole. Berry (1994: 107) notes that through the process of analyzing data in the form of concordance lines and frequency lists, teachers can develop confidence in their intuitions, as well as discover their limitations. Furthermore, the systematic analysis of concordance lines lends itself to an inductive approach and provides a focus for the development of analytical skills, with the *teacher* as researcher following Johns (1988), and in keeping with the current trend towards teacher-initiated action research. The data driven learning approach is, moreover, inherently motivating: teachers can conduct tailor-made searches relevant to their own interests and preoccupation. By using a discovery-learning approach, the teacher comes to 'own' the knowledge gained; and, as the findings from any given search will invariably suggest other avenues for exploration, the process of investigation and analysis will be never-ending.

For teaching purposes, corpus-based investigations can guide teachers in making decisions as to how much time should be devoted to a given lexical item or grammatical structure. Some teachers, especially those with responsibility for more advanced students, may wish to use the concordancer for the preparation of exercises which would be given to students as handouts in accordance with Johns' data-driven learning approach. Another major use of the concordancer would involve teachers conducting research into writing from specific classes in order to investigate patterns of usage, particularly recurrent errors, and avoidance strategies as well as identifying what students *do* get right. And for language awareness activities in the classroom, students could compare concordances from the student corpus with concordances of the same item taken from a suitably matched native speaker corpus. See Pickard (1994:218), and Granger and Tribble (1998:201) for a discussion.

In developing a self-access concordancing package for teachers, we are well aware of the potential pitfalls; the literature stresses the need for adequate preparation in the techniques of language analysis, and we intend to give high priority to training and provision of on-line help, bearing in mind that concordances in KWIC format appear quite alien to many people. For most *TeleNex* teachers, seeing concordance lines in the grammar files and conference corners has been a new experience, and not least of the problems reported by some of these newcomers is the initial shock of arbitrarily truncated lines, coupled with the limited context which can be a source of frustration for users who expect to but do not necessarily understand every line. It is to be hoped though, that when the TELEC concordancing package is available, *TeleNex* teachers will have benefited from the experience of having already been exposed to an extensive range of corpus data, including concordances, the majority accompanied by more or less detailed explication, with significant patterns and collocations highlighted. Through familiarization with the sorts of searches which they have seen conducted by TELEC staff, it is envisaged that they will have a head start when it comes to running searches of their own, and analyzing the resulting data.

Notes

1. The ELT situation in HK is perhaps unusual in that not all English language teachers are subject trained. A 1994 pilot survey of *TeleNex* teachers found that of 328 teachers, only one third had a degree which involved systematic language study. Of the total cohort, approximately one quarter were non-degree holders.

2. All files are written in hypertext, with hyperlinks allowing users to navigate easily within and across databases according to their own informational needs. Hypertext differs from traditional linear text in that the user is free to follow associative pathways.

3. We are extremely grateful to the many teachers who have taken the trouble to provide students' compositions, and to the TELEC clerical and technical staff (especially Janice Cheung & Joseph Li) for their help in processing the text.

4. Genre labels (e.g. narrative, argument) are used instead of text type labels (e.g. diary entry, editorial) in order to reduce the possibility of confusion when assigning filenames, otherwise staff responsible for coding are faced with questions along the lines of: 'should this particular batch of scripts be classified as an editorial, or as an argumentative essay?' with the inevitable problems of inter-rater reliability that such choices generate.

5. In Hong Kong, schools are assigned a banding, with Band 1 schools attracting the strongest students academically, and Band 5 schools attracting the weakest. For a discussion of Hong Kong's banding system, see Vickers (1999).

6. Cobuild's 50 million word Bank of English is the major corpus we draw on. Further information is available at http://titania.cobuild.collins.co.uk/boe_info.html

7. For further information about studies into Hong Kong students' English language problems, see for example Bunton (1991), Bunton et al. (1992), Cheung (1986), Webster et al. (1987).

8. I wish to acknowledge the following colleagues, who have all contributed to *Students' problems* files: Graham Lock, Wu Kam-yin, Hugh Tyrwhitt-Drake and David Bunton. Special thanks are due to Hugh Tyrwhitt-Drake for his useful comments on an earlier draft of this paper, and to Sylviane Granger and Beverly Derewianka for help with specific questions. Naturally, I take full responsibility for the final version of this paper.

9. So far, we have approximately 15,000 words of Form 5–7 students' presentations and group discussion on a variety of sociological issues in Hong Kong. We are most grateful to Paul Paskiewicz for his contributions to the spoken component.

References

Allan, Q. (1999). Enhancing the language awareness of Hong Kong teachers through corpus data: the *TeleNex* experience. *Journal of Technology and Teacher Education, 7*(1), 57–74.

Berry, R. (1994). Using concordance printouts for language awareness training. In C. S. Li, D. Mahoney & J. Richards (Eds.), *Exploring Second Language Teacher Development* (pp. 195–208). Hong Kong: City University Press.

Bourne, J. (1998). Net-learning: strategies for on-campus and off-campus network-enabled learning. *Journal of Asynchronous Learning Networks, 2*(2), 70–89.

Brown, H. (1987). *Principles of Language Learning and Teaching.* Englewood Cliffs, NJ: Prentice-Hall.

Bunton, D. (1991). A comparison of English errors made by Hong Kong students and those made by non-native learners internationally. *Institute of Language in Education Journal, 2*, 9–22. Special Issue: *English Usage in Hong Kong.*

Bunton, D., Boyle, J., & Boyle, L. (1992). *Common Written and Spoken English Errors in Hong Kong.* Asia: Longman

Cheung, Y., & Lai, L. (1986). *A study of the English vocabulary of junior secondary textbooks in Hong Kong.* Hong Kong: Education Department.

Crewe, W. (1990). The illogic of logical connectives. *English Language Teaching Journal, 44*(4), 316–325.

Dagneaux, E., Denness, S., & Granger, S. (1998). Computer-aided error analysis. *System, 26*(2), 163–174.

Granger, S., & Tribble, C. (1998). Learner corpus data in the foreign language classroom: form-focused instruction and data-driven learning. In Granger, S. (Ed.), *Learner English on Computer* (pp. 199–209). London and New York: Addison Wesley Longman.

Johns, T. (1988). Whence and whither classroom concordancing? In T. Bongaerts, T. de Haan, S. Lobbe & H. Wekker (Eds.), *Computer Applications in Language Learning* (pp. 1–16). Dordrecht: Foris.

Lock, G., & Tsui, A. (1999). Customising linguistics: developing an electronic grammar database for teachers. *Language Awareness, 8*(0), 1–17.

Milton, J. (1998). Exploiting L1 and interlanguage corpora in the design of an electronic language learning and production environment. In S. Granger (Ed.), *Learner English on Computer* (pp. 186–198). London and New York: Addison Wesley Longman.

Milton, J., & Hyland, K. (1997). 'Qualification and certainty in L1 and L2 students' writing. *Journal of Second Language Writing, 6*(2), 183–205.

Pickard, V. (1994). Producing a concordanced-based self-access vocabulary package: Some problems and solutions. In L. Flowerdew & K. Tong (Eds.), *Entering Text* (pp. 215–226). Language Centre, The Hong Kong University of Science and Technology.

Sengupta, S., & Nicholson, S. (1996). On-line and on-going: teacher development through *TeleTeach. English Language Teaching Journal, 50*(4), 290–302.

Sinclair, J. (1986). Basic computer processing of long texts. In G. Leech & C. Candlin (Eds.), *Computers in English Language Teaching and Research* (pp. 185–203). London and New York: Longman.

Sinclair, J. (1991). *Corpus, Concordance, Collocation.* Oxford: Oxford University Press.

Stubbs, M. (1996). *Text and Corpus Analysis.* Oxford: Blackwell.

Tyrwhitt-Drake, H. (1999). Responding to grammar questions on the Internet: Providing correction through the corpus. *English Language Teaching Journal, 53*(4), 281–288.

Vickers, E. (1999). Response to the Education Commission's Consultation Document: The Aims of Education. *Hong Kong Human Rights Monitor.*

Webster, M., Ward, A., & Craig, K. (1987). Language errors due to first language interference (Cantonese) produced by Hong Kong students of English. *Institute of Language in Education Journal, 3*, 63–81.

Wu, K., & Tsui, A. (1997). Teachers' grammar on the electronic highway: Design criteria for TeleGram. *System, 25*(2), 169–183.

Pedagogy and local learner corpora

Working with learning-driven data

Barbara Seidlhofer
University of Vienna

Chapter overview

In this chapter, Seidlhofer extends the meaning of the term 'learner corpus research' in as much as the advanced learners providing the corpus data are also
the researchers working on this corpus, in an approach which Seidlhofer terms
'learning-driven data'. The relevance for language learning and language teaching thus arises directly from the fact that the learner corpus is not used to talk
about learners but to work with them, on a corpus to which they themselves
have contributed.

Building on Swain's (1985, 1995) Pushed Output Hypothesis, computer
tools are used for compiling and collaboratively analysing a written learner corpus consisting of short complete texts. The computer tools make it possible to
exploit the usual advantages of corpus linguistics, especially easy retrieval and
analysability of a large collection of relevant but basically anonymous texts,
while at the same time benefiting from the motivational asset of allowing students to work on texts which are personally meaningful to them and which they
feel they have a stake in. In short, this corpus analytic approach is methodolog-
ically innovative by enabling students to be both participants in and analysts of
their own language use.

Seidlhofer describes the success of the approach in motivating students to
adopt corpus analysis techniques for research in linguistics, notably language
description, and in advanced foreign language classes, for work on language
awareness as well as intertextual activities such as summarising and reacting to
texts.

1.   Introduction

Computer learner corpus research has witnessed a veritable explosion over the last few years, both quantitatively and qualitatively, and there is no doubt that findings of such research are already having a beneficial effect on foreign language teaching in some settings. As a teacher of both linguistics and ELT methodology, I am committed to the idea, obvious but often forgotten, that language learning and teaching is as much to do with learning and teaching as it is with language, and furthermore, that an appropriate pedagogy needs to be fine-tuned to specific learners and local conditions of relevance (cf. Holliday 1994; Kramsch & Sullivan 1996). In this spirit, I share Granger's criticism of global materials, the designers of which are "content with a very fuzzy, intuitive, non-corpus-based view of the needs of an archetypal learner" (Granger 1998b:7). To remedy this state of affairs, research on learner corpora can highlight what might be difficult for learners of specific L1s and so open up hitherto unavailable possibilities for tailor-made materials design and FLT methodology, as documented in a range of contributions to Granger (1998a).

Recent research in language description and language pedagogy thus seems to be converging on the insight that it is necessary to revise comfortable monolithic notions of both the target language and the 'archetypal' learner. Translated into classroom teaching, this has meant, amongst other things, that instead of spoon-feeding learners with rules and 'correct' examples for mere imitation, current thinking advocates learning by discovery, which encourages learners to bring their inductive abilities to bear on real data. Ideally, this might allow them to explore both L1 corpora and learner corpora in a process called data-driven learning (cf. Johns & King 1991). Since the explicit aim of the present volume is to bring together the concerns of computer learner corpora, second language acquisition and foreign language teaching, it seems appropriate to investigate a scenario in which the emancipation of pedagogy *vis à vis* linguistics is taken a little further. So instead of talking about *data-driven learning*, I propose to stand this expression on its head and explore the notion of *learning-driven data*.

2.   Corpus linguistics and language pedagogy

The relationship between large-scale, global L1 description and context-specific, localised L2 pedagogy is problematic and there is a need for clarification of and dialogue about claims and priorities as variously stated by researchers in the two fields. This is evidenced in a number of papers and exchanges such as Cook (1998) in response to Carter (1998), Prodromou (1996) in response to Carter and McCarthy (1995); Aston (1995), Owen (1996), Seidlhofer (1999); see also Bernardini (2000) for an excellent and wide-ranging discussion of the issues involved. The contributions by Sinclair and Widdowson to the 1991 Georgetown Round Table on 'Linguistics and Language Pedagogy' (Sinclair 1991a; Widdowson 1991) bring out the differences between the primary concerns of these two areas. While Sinclair's position (see also Sinclair 1991b) is that improved corpus-based descriptions of the language (in this case English) provide facts that necessarily constitute a basis for improved language teaching, Widdowson argues that the linguistic facts uncovered by corpus linguistics should not be transferred to language teaching before their relevance and appropriacy to the learning process have been subjected to empirical pedagogic enquiry.

It would seem that, rather than regarding this stage of the debate as an impasse, the most constructive way forward is to recognise and act upon the need for empirical classroom-based action research conducted by teachers who are aware of the potential as well as the limitations of corpus linguistics. And it is here, I would argue, that developments in learner corpus research are crucial because by definition, they start with the learners and so bring us an important step closer to understanding local conditions of relevance. In particular, my claim here would be that an analysis focusing on a situated, familiar learner corpus has an essential pedagogical advantage, especially if it includes whole texts produced by the learners working with it. Starting from what learners have said, not just what they might/should/must not say ensures the consideration of two – equally crucial – points of reference for learners: where they are, i.e. situated in their L2 learning contexts, and where they eventually (may) want to get to, i.e. close to the native-speaker language using capacity captured by L1 corpora. Foregrounding the learners' own criteria of relevance helps negotiate the route between the two, rather than simply displaying the rather remote target behaviour, which runs the danger of being perceived as overwhelming, unattainable or irrelevant.

This paper presents the account of a procedure I devised for approaching work with learner corpora from a pedagogic perspective, drawing on current ideas and debates in second language acquisition research and foreign language teaching. One might call the classroom experiment I describe 'getting the learners into learner corpora' – not just as perusers and purveyors of textual data, but as participants and analysts in the discourse process of drawing on the potential of corpus linguistics via their own texts and their own questions. The procedure I describe here can readily be adapted to different contexts and different levels of learners in both linguistics as well as straightforward foreign language classes.

3. Context: the course

The course which offered me an opportunity for getting my students acquainted with the notion of learner corpora is what we call a 'proseminar' at the English Department of Vienna University. This is a compulsory course which students attend in the first or (more usually) second year, and offers a variety of topics for students to choose from, such as grammar, semantics, sociolinguistics, pragmatics, etc. Whatever topic lecturers decide to offer, their brief for this type of course is to get participants acquainted with one area of linguistics in a more in-depth way than the introductory lecture does, and to combine this content work with fostering academic study skills (e.g. how to find literature on a topic, do empirical research or write an academic paper).

Given the fact that the vast majority of our approximately 3000 students are future teachers of English, it seemed desirable to make an effort to integrate into our teacher education programme an element aiming at some basic understanding of corpus linguistics. At the moment the curriculum is such that some students may incidentally find themselves working with corpora in linguistics in the second half of their studies, notably in historical linguistics. However, in the area of language learning and teaching, an area very central to our students' concerns and one in which they take courses throughout the entire duration of the programme, there is very little awareness amongst teachers and students in our department of the enormous impact of corpus linguistics on both language description and on the preparation of the very language teaching materials and reference tools they all use.

I therefore decided to offer a pro-seminar entitled 'Corpus linguistics and language pedagogy'. This enabled me to satisfy the core requirements, i.e. 'area of linguistics + study skills', while at the same time offering considerable scope for working on language awareness and language development – an aspect which seemed certain to be appreciated by the participants.

However, during the first run of this course, things did not go quite as well as I had hoped. For one thing, it became clear to me that – contrary to the commonly held belief that some degree of computer literacy is a matter of course for school-leavers nowadays – most of our undergraduates are genuinely technophobic. It turned out that many students did not even have access to a computer at home, let alone to any corpora or concordancing tools, which meant that I had to 'be their computer' and do searches and queries for them on my own PC. That first course focused mainly on raising students' awareness of the crucial role of corpus linguistics for language description, especially as a basis for the preparation of the dictionaries and grammars they themselves use in all their courses. After the introduction of some basic concepts and techniques, we used the English L1 corpora I had available (MicroConcord Corpus Collections A and B, see Scott & Johns (1993); BNC Sampler (1999)) and did a fair amount of practical work on concordance printouts provided by me (e.g. on collocation and colligation, semantic prosodies, relative frequencies, etc.). My students got quite good at this and also conducted successful small-scale research projects on topics they selected themselves, such as the role of concordancing in bible translation, the teaching of phrasal verbs and literary stylistics. Nevertheless, there was a strong sense of participants not really fully engaging with what they were doing, a lack of excitement and enthusiasm that I was unaccustomed to.

This prompted me to think hard about the process we had gone through and to look for a pedagogic approach which would genuinely draw students in from the very beginning. To achieve this, it seemed necessary to switch the main focus of our investigations away from L1 corpora and onto learner corpora, more specifically to our own learner corpus. This, I felt, would also enable us to connect familiar and unthreatening activities, such as reading or writing, with unfamiliar, apparently threatening ones, such as using computer tools.

For the second run of the pro-seminar in the following semester, I thus decided to make my students' own texts our primary objects of analysis. In what follows, I explain why this decision seems justified in the light of recent relevant research, and go on to show how these ideas were translated into practice.

4.   SLA: Output in language learning

It should be noted that my students are all advanced learners of English, and that the role of English is all-pervasive: it is medium of instruction, target language, object of analysis and the trainee teachers' future subject all at the same time. Whatever our students think of the relevance of literature and linguistics, the major content areas in the programme, they all agree that continuous language learning is of vital interest to them.

In the literature on second language learning, the role which learners' output plays in acquisition has been extensively discussed. In studies focusing on what has come to be called the Pushed Output Hypothesis, Swain (1985, 1995) argues that pushed output, i.e. sustained output which stretches the limits of learners' current linguistic capacity, can further their development significantly. Swain (1995) discusses three ways in which such output can help increase linguistic knowledge and contribute to accuracy:

a. it helps learners notice the gap between what they want to say and what they are linguistically able to say.
b. it enables learners to try out rules and, if the feedback they receive in reaction to their output warrants it, to modify their hypotheses.
c. it creates opportunities for metalinguistic reflection, which in turn allows learners to control and internalise language.

The first of these functions, noticing, refers to the fact that the linguistic problems learners encounter when producing target language utterances may prompt them to "notice what they do not know" and "make them aware of something they need to find out about their L2" (Swain 1995:129). This, of course, is particularly valuable in an advanced language course which aims at developing in students (and future teachers!) a high degree of language awareness, of declarative rather than merely procedural knowledge of the target language (cf. Schmidt 1990; Widdowson 1989). As to the second function, hypothesis-testing, it is obvious that "to test a hypothesis, learners need to *do* something, and one way of doing this is to say or write something" (Swain 1995:131). Finally, the third function, conscious reflection, is best served in "tasks which encourage reflection on language form while still being oriented to getting meaning across" (op.cit.:132).

All these observations gave support to my idea of getting my students to work with and on their own output. Swain's examples show how English-speaking teenage learners of French perform the processes of noticing, hypothesising and reflecting on such matters as verb forms and subject/object – verb concord, without any explicit help from their teacher. It therefore seemed reasonable to expect that my more mature students, who furthermore had a particular interest in the target language, would engage in similarly active linguistic analyses of their own texts.

It might be objected, of course, that by working on what is effectively "auto-input" (Schmidt & Frota 1986), learners rehearse their own errors, which, according to Ellis (1997:129), "may account for why some errors are so persistent and why learners often feel that their errors are not really errors". However, it has to be remembered that my students had chosen to study English at university because they took a special interest in it. I therefore felt I could count on their higher-than-average motivation and language awareness as well as on their ability to draw each other's attention to what they deemed incorrect usage, an expectation which was confirmed.

What is of particular relevance for the activities I outline below is Swain's (1995) claim that

> the importance to learning of output could be that output pushes learners to process language more deeply (with more mental effort) than does input. *With output, the learner is in control.* By focusing on output we may be focusing on ways in which learners can play more *active, responsible* roles in their learning (p. 126, emphasis added).

Swain also emphasises that

> output-based studies ... provide important evidence for the usefulness of collaborative tasks that lead learners to reflect on their own language production as they attempt to create meaning (p. 141).

It is precisely such collaborative tasks which promote the active, responsible roles of learners that I outline below, and for which the use of computer tools proved an invaluable asset. But in addition to arguments for a home-made learner corpus which emerge from SLA research, there are also ideas in the applied linguistics literature on foreign language teaching methodology which point in the same direction, and these I briefly outline below.

5.   FLT: Motivation, authenticity, appropriation

The two quotations from Swain (1995) above bring together the value of collaborative tasks and learners' reflection on their own output with the importance of learners playing active, responsible roles in their learning. If we now turn from SLA research to foreign language methodology, we find similar arguments under such headings as language awareness (e.g. Hawkins 1991), learner autonomy (cf. Dickinson 1995) and 'authenticity'. All these ideas are strongly linked in the literature with the desirable but elusive notion of motivation. Indeed, motivation seems certain to remain a perennial issue, the unattainable Holy Grail of foreign language teaching: despite the growing bulk of empirical research (eg. Crookes & Schmidt 1989; Dörnyei 2001; Oxford & Shearin 1994) there are no definitive answers, and it has become common practice in methodology textbooks to call research in this area "inconclusive" (e.g. Richard-Amato 1996:82). However, this very inconclusiveness points to a crucial insight: that there are no global solutions to motivational problems, no generally valid answers and truths. FL pedagogy, and presumably any pedagogy, has to be local, designed for specific learners and settings.[1] This means that any supposedly general principles have to be interpreted with reference to local settings, or otherwise they are doomed to remain meaningless.

A case in point here is the claim, put forward in most writing on communicative language teaching, that authentic texts should be used, i.e. texts which have not been designed specially for language teaching purposes, but which occur naturally in native speaker communication. But, as Widdowson has repeatedly argued (e.g. 1979: 12; 1990), authenticity in language teaching (and its very effectiveness for motivation) is not an inherent feature of texts but depends on authentication through learners. It thus cannot be an intrinsic quality of the texts used in classrooms, but of the discourse that learners can derive from those texts.

To finally make a connection with corpus linguistics here, authenticity means different things in language description and in language pedagogy. Compilers of L1 corpora are interested in collecting 'authentic' texts in the sense of 'attested': what native speakers have said. In language teaching, what is crucial is that learners should be capable of an authentic response to texts. This depends not so much on where texts originated but what learners can do with them in the way of performing appropriate activities which will engage their interest and stimulate the learning process. This is what is meant by authentication. In language pedagogy, then, "authenticity is not a matter of selection but of methodology" (Widdowson 1984: 240). For my pro-seminar with advanced learners, it seemed possible to draw on both the descriptive and the pedagogical sense of authenticity for motivation, provided that students had a secure jumping-off point in the form of texts they knew intimately because they had collectively written them themselves. These texts could, of course, subsequently be compared with texts that were authentic in the sense of attested, and accessible through the L1 corpora available to us.

This approach is also compatible with a widely-accepted concept of learning as a process of (re)construction and extension from what is familiar to what is new (cf. e.g. Wendt 1996). The business of FLT methodology is to help this process along, through an appropriate use of input texts, as well as learners' own output. Foreign language teachers are constantly coaxing their students into appropriating new words, into taking them up and accepting them as their own. In virtually all foreign language teaching activities the ultimate aim is to get learners to accept, adopt and use the foreign language vocabulary presented to them as input. It seems reasonable to assume then, that the most suitable activities for language learning would be overtly intertextual ones which invite learners to convert input into output (cf. Seidlhofer 2000).

Successful foreign language teaching can thus be seen as fostering appropriation, helping learners make the target language (or relevant parts of it) their own. This is consistent with the recently (re)discovered Vygotskian view of pedagogy, which advocates learning through dialogic interaction and collaborative co-construction. My proposal of using intertextual tasks as a starting point for working with students on their own output seems ideally suited for operationalising these pedagogic principles. Writing about the role of 'collective scaffolding' in second language learning, Donato (1994:39) emphasises the importance of "the construction of co-knowledge and how this co-construction process results in linguistic *change* among and within individuals during joint activity", to which Swain (1995:136) adds that "this process becomes particularly observable for language development when the task students are engaged in involves reflecting on their own language production".

6. Tasks and procedures

Against the background outlined above, I decided to compile our own manageable learner corpus, consisting of whole short texts written in response to two intertextual tasks. I distributed a one-page article from *Time* magazine (c. 1000 words) entitled 'The Dilemmas of Childlessness' at the end of the first session. I asked students to write, as homework, two 'intertexts': a short summary of the article, and another short piece I call 'account', which is meant to be a personal reaction to the article – developed from the text, but not directly derived from it.[2] The instructions for the summary were: "Please write a summary (in no more than 60 words) of the text, capturing as faithfully as you can the main points of the author's intended meaning", and those for the account: "Please give a brief account (in no more than 60 words) of what strikes you personally as of particular interest in the article. Give your account a title". Students were asked to hand in their writing on disk. Importantly, they were reassured that any discussion in class on what they had written would be done anonymously.

The next three ninety-minute sessions were spent familiarising students with the aims of the course and some very basic concepts and procedures in corpus linguistics, including design and purposes of learner corpora. We worked through a few examples in Tribble and Jones (1997) and analysed some KWIC concordances I had prepared beforehand, the highlight of which proved to be the replication of Stubbs' (1995: 254f.) findings on the semantic prosody of 'somewhat'.

When students had handed in their summary/account assignments on disk, I collated these into one file, with no changes made except that I deleted their names and numbered their summaries and accounts instead. At the next meeting, everybody received a photocopy of all these anonymised summaries and accounts (see Fig. 1).[3]

YOUR SUMMARIES:

sum1. The author claims that having children is not the absolute fulfilment for the modern women. By and large working times and economic realities oppose the upbringing of the infants, and the necessity to share the parenting is still denied by most men. So one can choose between living one's own life without a child, having one by chance or the possibility of borrowing children from relatives. {66 words}

sum2. High childless rates show that the decision of raising a child or not is negatively influenced by economic factors. Career, economic success and parentage are hardly to combine. So some people prefer rather to be an attentive relative than a parent. What remains is the question if the upbringing of a child is part of the human nature and if we will regret a childless life. {66 words}

sum3. Equal opportunities in their careers have resulted in a baby slack among childbearing women. As bringing up children interferes with the effort to make up for the males' advantage in competitive society, the decision on children is either deferred or never considered. Regret of having missed a singular experience is often played down and those reproached with neglect of duty blame the social structure. {64 words}

sum4. Although babies seem to be everywhere these days, even on TV, the birth rate is decreasing. Those who do not want children can be divided into the deliberate types, who chose between career or children, and the postponers, who let nature make a choice for them. Despite this trend many women regret not to have children when they grow older. {60 words}

sum5. Since the late '60s/ early '70s the baby's birth-rate has been declining, especially among college-educated women. Some women choose a childless life deliberately, others tend to postpone their decision until it is too late to have children anymore. Often their choice is influenced by their financial situation. Nevertheless, a rise of the birth-rate among higher-educated women has been noticed lately. {60 words}

sum6. During the last decades, the childless rate among educated working women in the U.S. has become higher than ever. Decisions of the deliberate types and the postponers not to choose "the burden of parenting" may nowadays be the career (maybe also feminism), economic realities, indecision or simply the choise of freedom. {51 words}

sum7. Men without babies are mostly well educated, live in urban areas, marry late and work not at home. The deliberate types had to care for younger brothers and sisters and the postponers leave their decision to relationships, professions and nature. Childlessness is not always intended but some can not change their situation. {52 words}

sum8. In the last years a lot of women decided agaist having children, among them mostly well educated, urban women. The cause for their childlessness is that they do not often get their husbands´ support with the child raising and cannot devote themselves entirely to their professional life. They often regret their decision, and see themselves as violators against the biological law. {61 words}

sum9. Despite the baby-mania in the cinemas, many women nowadays do not think that a child of their own would enrich their lives. Beside the wish for independence there are also fairly strong economic factors for childlessness. In any case regret is not unusual though the childless have found substitutes such as colleagues or nephews and nieces whom they can mother. {60 words}

sum10. The author divides women who have no children into two groups: those who decide intentionally to enjoy their lives without the "burden" that children involve and the others who refuse to make a decision at all. The main reasons not to have children for both groups are jobs, experiences with younger brothers and sisters or babies from friends and the financial situation. {62 words}

[etc.]

YOUR ACCOUNTS:

acc1. The new trend: DINKIE'S

What strikes me most is that women tend to become more and more egoistic these days. They occupy male jobs and want to spend their leisure time exclusively for themselves. The new life style is of the form "double income no kids". So in my point of view the increase of childless couples is an effect of the emancipation of women in the world of employment. {70 words}

acc2. The Biological Law

There are various factors which influence the decision of having a child or not. But mostly people are influenced by economical reason. So it is no question of biological law or women's fulfillment in giving birth to a child. Neither if she regrets it or not. It seems that childlessness is the result of an account of costs and the evaluation of a career. {65words}

acc3. Expectant women

The erasure of the clear-cut division line between breadwinning and the domestic virtues of house-keeping and child-raising has brought about seemingly equal rights to women. Contraception (not mentioned in the article) and economic necessity have made some women regard parenthood as a negligible value in life. Strangely enough it is business advertising and the entertainment industry that highlight the joy of having children. {63 words}

acc4. Childlessness – a curse or a blessing?

More and more women are against children nowadays because they consider them as a curse and decide on a free, independent life. They do not reject children personally but they do decline responsibility, giving up their career and spare-time, not to forget their husbands who think the same way. it seems that most people forget that children are a pleasure especially when parents grow old. {65words} acc5. **More women decide for children**

What stroke me most in the article was the news that young college-educated women tend to get their babies earlier nowadays. This surprised me because the present financial and working situation has probably changed for the worse and a life with children therefore means restriction. Yet, however a woman chooses, her decision should be accepted by everybody. {57 words}

acc6. **"I don't want to lose sleep!"**

It stroke me that some reasons and explanations for living a childless life are this odd. Truly, children may be a burdon, but how bad could it be to lose some sleep during a limited period of time. Besides, children may be hard work but isn't the delight you get worth it? The choise of a childless life should be a serious one. {63 words}

acc7. **Interesting points in the article**

It is interesting why women decide not to have a baby and so do not have descendants. In some cases childlessness is clear, for instance, if alcohol is involved. Many women regret their decision and therefore it has to be well thought over. The examples given in the article help to get an idea about what are the intentions for childlessness. {62 words}

acc8. **Lack of Information**

I found nothing striking in this article as its content was not new to me. It would have been useful to underline the author's arguements with some statistic material or other scientific facts. The reader does not really get informed about the 'Dilemma of Childlessness', mentioned in the headline. The article is neither informative nor interesting to read. {58 words}

acc9. **The World Is Growing Old**

What happens if those childless people grow old? Surely they will be no burden to their children but to society, as it has to look after them. Sooner or later the number of people at work will equal the one of pensioners. This means that every income will have to support one retired person, its receiver, and any possible offspring. {60 words}

acc10. **The monsters called children**

It is most interesting to note how children are presented in the article. The author emphasises only the less pleasurable sides of children. According to the article and what is already indicated by the picture, children are money-eating, pleasure-restricting monsters who get on your nerves. It seems that the future child is one you can hire. {56 words}

[etc.]

Figure 1. Sample handout: summaries and accounts as played back to students

It was gratifying to see what a keen interest students had in what everybody else had written. In particular, the motivating effect of their intimate knowledge of the input text and the tasks, coupled with the availability of a variety of different writings which had all been produced under identical conditions, became immediately apparent: students felt both competent and free to assume a stance which was simultaneously sympathetic and critical, and we spent a whole fairly unstructured session discussing their reactions to their writings. As homework, students were asked to consider which summary they found most faithful to the original and why, and which account they found most interesting and why. In addition, they were to make a note of all the questions that came to their mind while looking at their joint product, including some questions that might helpfully be tackled using computer tools. I should add here that we had of course talked about corpus size in previous sessions, and that the proseminar participants were aware of the fact that we could treat their summary and account protocols as part of a larger corpus of student writing (same input text, same tasks) collected by some of my colleagues[4] as well as by me for an earlier research project (Seidlhofer 1995).When students had handed in their questions, I collated these into one file, weeded out duplicates, and chose a mixed sample of as many as would fit onto one page, making sure that every student was represented. In the next session, I distributed photocopies to everybody. Students then formed pairs and trios to discuss a possible categorization of those questions that were amenable to exploration by computer tools, and came up with the following groups[5] (which, incidentally, turned out to be rather similar to those suggested by Meunier (1998)):

STATISTICS

a. How many words does an account / a summary have on average?
b. Is there a difference in sentence length between the original article and our summaries and accounts? And between summaries and accounts?

GRAMMAR/LEXICOGRAMMAR

a. Are there only main clauses used or are there also subordinate clauses?
b. What tenses do the writers mainly use?
c. Did we all use the same conjunctions?
d. Compare the adjectives used in the original with those in the summaries and accounts.
e. What adjectives/adverbs are used? Are they more positive or negative? Are there many adjectives used to reinforce the accounts? Which? Can you group them (meaning)?
f. Does the word order of the following phrases occur in British English?: *not so big a problem; that is much better than giving first birth*

LEXIS/FREQUENCY

a. Relation Summary – Account: are same words/expressions used?
    → 5 most frequent words in summaries
    → 5 most frequent words in accounts
b. How do two texts compare according to the frequency of words? How do whole genres compare? (frequency of types of words (adjectives, pronouns, ...))
c. Which particular words occur most often across texts? (intertextuality)
d. Word list: interpret the most frequent content words: what is the article about?

e.   Which pieces of information were considered important?

f.   Is *childless* the adjective most frequently used?

LEXIS/ CONCORDANCE, COLLOCATION

a.   What is the usage of the words *babies* and *children*? Analyse the different uses of the words *babies* and *children* by listing all occurrences and comparing different contexts.

b.   Does the word *family* also refer to couples without children in English corpora?

c.   Which summaries use the word *author*?

d.   How many people mention the subjective quality of the accounts in the first sentence (by stating *My* opinion, What *I* found, *I* consider, ...), how many did so later in their text, how many didn't mention it at all?

e.   Attestedness/correctness: do certain words/phrases occur in speech? (problem: many words exist, but are not recorded in a corpus!)

f.   Could teachers make a list of the most frequent 'error-collocations' and therefore be able to respond to individual mistakes? They could then use concordance exercises to practise certain things (collocations which occur frequently but not in the right word order or with wrong vocabulary and so on...)

g.   Are the following natural collocations in English?
     it would make my life complete *provided that I feel ready*
     I don't consider children *as* a burden
     a family nourishing husband
     they have children in far fewer numbers
     her opinion gets obvious
     the decision gets reinforced

h.   Do the headlines display accurately what the account is about?

i.   How does the title relate to the article?

LEXIS/ VARIATION, SOPHISTICATION

a.   Analyse lexical variation in texts: Are there many repetitions? Do students use their own words or do they adopt large chunks from the original text?

b.   Types and tokens: are individual expressions used repeatedly or did students find other words/terms?

c.   Did we use synonyms for words in the original articles?

d.   Did the writers of the summaries use their own words or did they use words from the original text?

e.   Which words are probably taken from the text (as they are not common vocabulary)? Which other vocabulary do advanced learners tend to use?

Figure 2. Students' questions about their summaries and accounts (extract)

Once we had these student-generated questions in front of us, a genuine interest in how computer tools would help in tackling them arose all by itself, as students asked: How do you find certain parts of speech? What statistics can you do with the computer? Can one compare texts? How do you find out about attestedness of certain expressions in a larger L1 corpus?

How do you search for all forms of a 'word'? Can one look for punctuation? How do you find out about frequencies? Keywords? Lexical variation? Couldn't you use some of these things for devising activities for teaching? Clearly, now that students had a sense of ownership of the texts we were working on, they concurrently developed an urgent desire for the tools that would allow them to capture, express and investigate their perceptions and responses: they came to feel a need for linguistic concepts, linguistic metalanguage, and computer tools. Obviously, we very soon also hit upon limitations, most notably the fact that our corpus was yet untagged and so forced us to look through word lists rather than simply searching, say, POS tags. Here again the advantage of a small, manageable and homogeneous corpus became apparent (cf. Aston 1995, 1997).

I can only give a very brief glimpse here of the kind of discussion we had once we got into actual analyses. Comparing keywords and negative keywords with WordSmith Tools[6] (Scott 1996) proved to be an amazingly powerful way of bringing out intertextual echoes between the different texts we were dealing with (see figure 3). The lexical investigation we performed highlighted the somewhat paradoxical status of 'plagiarism' in L2 writing ("summarise in your own words...") (Pennycook 1996; Seidlhofer 1996).

Since we all knew the same texts, it was easy to see what a high proportion of summary keywords (numbers 1–15) had been taken over verbatim from the input article (*deliberate types, postponers, educated*), while others reflected the application of the summarization macrorules of generalization and construction (cf. Kintsch & van Dijk 1978) based on particulars given in the original article (*some – others, groups, categories, rate*). In the accounts keywords (numbers 49–63) it was easy to discern intertextual echoes from the wording of the instructions ("what strikes you personally as of particular interest in the article"). The high occurrence of personal and possessive first person pronouns and of the words *opinion* and *think* surprised no-one – though Petch-Tyson (1998) indicates that writer visibility may well be worth pursuing in future. What did intrigue us was the relative frequency of *should* and *know*. So we ran a concordance of *should* in the accounts (Fig. 4).

This KWIC concordance gave rise to a consideration of the different functions of the modal (hypothetical vs advice-giving): how does *should* compare with *would* and *ought to*, and is the very marked predominance of the *ought to* meaning in the accounts an indicator of moral(istic) issues and societal norms and expectations? And what does it say about how the students had positioned themselves as writers in the different genres?

The concordance of *know* in the accounts can be seen in Fig. 5.

N	WORD	FREQ.	SUM.TXT %	FREQ.	ACC.TXT %	KEYNESS	P
1	CHILDLESS	109	1.23	39	0.38	46.0	0.000000
2	THEIR	176	1.98	94	0.91	39.5	0.000000
3	DELIBERATE	44	0.50	6	0.06	38.6	0.000000
4	TYPES	34	0.38	3	0.03	35.3	0.000000
5	POSTPONERS	36	0.41	5	0.05	31.3	0.000000
6	OTHERS	33	0.37	4	0.04	30.5	0.000000
7	REGRET	50	0.56	14	0.14	27.3	0.000000
8	EDUCATED	55	0.62	19	0.18	24.1	0.000001
9	REASONS	59	0.66	22	0.21	23.6	0.000001
10	LATE	35	0.39	8	0.08	22.6	0.000002
11	RATE	43	0.48	13	0.13	21.8	0.000003
12	SOME	59	0.66	26	0.25	18.6	0.000016
13	AMONG	23	0.26	4	0.04	17.8	0.000025
14	GROUPS	11	0.12	0		16.9	0.000038
15	CATEGORIES	15	0.17	1		16.9	0.000040
[...]							
49	PERSONALLY	0		13	0.13	16.2	0.000058
50	A	185	2.08	315	3.06	18.1	0.000020
51	IT	56	0.63	126	1.22	18.4	0.000018
52	STRIKES	0		15	0.15	18.7	0.000016
53	SHOULD	3	0.03	29	0.28	20.8	0.000005
54	OPINION	2	0.02	27	0.26	22.1	0.000003
55	KNOW	0		18	0.17	22.4	0.000002
56	THINK	6	0.07	42	0.41	25.4	0.000000
57	YOU	2	0.02	32	0.31	27.7	0.000000
58	INTERESTING	0		27	0.26	33.6	0.000000
59	WHAT	3	0.03	43	0.42	36.0	0.000000
60	THAT	82	0.92	212	2.06	42.5	0.000000
61	MY	0		46	0.45	57.3	0.000000
62	ME	0		57	0.55	71.0	0.000000
63	I	2	0.02	165	1.60	187.8	0.000000

Figure 3. Comparison of keywords in summaries and accounts

The discussion of *know* was even more open-ended than that of *should*: Are university students obsessed with 'knowing'? Or is there some evidence of L1 transfer from German here? If you wanted your writing to be as native-like and idiomatic as possible, would you replace *know* with a different verb in some of the instances?

1	only on their careers. Having children	should	be a wonderful experience. There
2	, however a woman chooses, her decision	should	be accepted by everybody.
3	r them when they are old. So everyone	should	decide by oneself for either havi
4	unhappiness. I think that everyone	should	find out what they consider most
5	women and giving birth to children. It	should	be stated more clearly that the b
6	lty of violating a biological law. Jobs	should	become more female-structured in
7	d by one's decision. But one's own life	should	be worth the effort.
8	herefore bringing up of children by men	should	be taken for granted.
9	suffer. This does not mean that mothers	should	not have a job, they simply shoul
10	I want to get children because nothing	should	ever be more important than famil
11	ife for every young woman. Moreover one	should	always bear in mind the economic
12	patible with each other, the parenthood	should	be divided fairly.
13	rtant aspect for a woman is whether she	should	sacrifice her life for her childr
14	hers should not have a job, they simply	should	not take their job too serious.
15	a very personal and intimate topic that	should	not be over-discussed by the medi
16	bies later regret their decisions. They	should	be proud of their ability of givi
17	first years and if it is possible this	should	be the mother. Therefore my opini
18	sually self-made. My opinion is that we	should	be glad that nowadays it is defin
19	his must be a wonderful experience. Why	should	a child prevent you from self-rea
20	My Way In my opinion, every woman	should	decide by herself if she would li
21	does not make sense. Moreover, no woman	should	feel bad about not wanting to hav
22	ery positive development, because women	should	at least get a chance for self-re
23	oes not necessarily mean that all women	should	regard this aspect as detrimental
24	to the duties of a mother? I think you	should	only conceive children when you a

Figure 4. Concordance of 'should' in students' accounts (extract)

1	hildren or not, but on the other hand I	know	that this is not always possible.
2	children ? All these women in the text	know	very well what they want and have
3	o finish my education. The only thing I	know	for sure is that I want to have chi
4	lessness ?" It would be interesting to	know	as to how far one can say that ther
5	hild and go to work. Every woman has to	know	what is most important for her. But
6	the right decision. It is impossible to	know	what my life is going to look like
7	ith me. This is mainly because I do not	know	if my job will be compatible with c
8	sions to fate or fortune or whatever. I	know	that it is easier just to wait than
9	elfish and pitiable. Doesn't this woman	know	that children could give you a lot
10	on her own individual life – you never	know	how much you will get in return.
11	"burden" of raising up a child. I don't	know	the reasons for this trend, maybe i
12	many problems with that. For example, I	know	two elderly women who hadn't had ch
13	sweet and pure. A lot of people do not	know	any better because they do not have
14	so women who want to realize themselves	know	that having children is only possib
15	things which can happen to you. Do you	know	the song "Everybody need's somebody
16	r themselves and need some luxury. They	know	that if they had children they woul
17	eelings of maternal love, although they	know	that having children cannot be a f

Figure 5. Concordance of 'know' in students' accounts (extract)

7. Summary and conclusion

In all of these activities and discussions, the main key to success was clearly the fact that we had a secure 'home base' through focusing on familiar, non-threatening texts, not decontextualised bits of language gleaned from 'remote' native corpora – which, in Scott's terms, enabled us to conduct "text-focused" rather than "language-focused" analyses on "language events" (Scott 2000). The linguistic investigation unfolded when both the texts and the questions students worked on had become clearly theirs: they did not pore over problems because their teacher asked them to, but because they themselves wanted to find out more. They discovered that close scrutiny of the language of a text in which they had a personal investment can be a fascinating process rather than a pedantic, tedious affair. For example, comparing the frequency of a word across two types of text is more meaningful if you are familiar with the way one of these types (the student summaries) came into being, and if the other text (the input text) is one that you have studied closely and summarised yourself. Also, the identification of key words takes on an extra dimension if you can find out which words were 'key' for you and your colleagues, and if you can see how these keywords give an indication as to what different texts are about. Another popular application that followed on naturally was the use of a big reference corpus for checking on the attestedness of phrases used in the student corpus, through which students also gained an understanding of the significance of corpus linguistics for the dictionaries and grammars they work with as learners and future teachers.

Of course this way of working will always include the consultation of L1 corpora and descriptions based upon them, but the crucial difference is that the practice described here does so while keeping sight of the realities of specific learners. Another agreeable side-effect of this teaching experiment has been that some of the language teachers who contributed to our learner corpus by setting their students the same summary and account tasks have become rather intrigued with the possibilities of corpus linguistics and classroom concordancing. These teachers also reported on the positive effect of having anonymised examples of their students' own writing to work on in class, in that this device put students in a kind of teacher role when querying and critiquing what their classmates had written without the danger of this being seen as a personal attack.

Plenty of scope for development and improvement remains for future courses. The biggest challenge will be to wean students from relying on me for the production of concordances, which should become easier as more terminals are made available. A next step might be to branch out into the use of other kinds of potentially relevant corpora. In particular, once our corpus has POS and error tagging, it will be interesting to try and replicate some of the published analyses on other, larger learner corpora, especially the International Corpus of Learner English (Granger 1998b). But after the success of the first study, I am confident that future projects will be approached in the same way, via our learning-driven data.

Notes

1. This observation, of course, harks back to the criticism of the assumption of "archetypal learners" at the beginning of this paper and underlines the value of descriptions and investigations of learner corpora on the basis of specific first languages.

2. I had already used these activities for a larger research project; for details see Seidlhofer (1995).

3. There was no modification of the students' language, so all student data, both in this paper and on the sheets distributed in class, retain all original interlanguage idiosyncrasies (of grammar, lexis, spelling, etc.). For the purposes of concordancing, this meant that I had to do some manual editing to ensure that, say, KWIC concordances would come up with all instances, even misspelt ones. For future analyses, I intend to use the Louvain Error Editor to tackle these problems.

4. I should like to thank my colleagues Astrid Fellner, Kurt Forstner, Angelika Hirsch, Gunther Kaltenböck, Barbara Olsson, Kurt Prillinger, Susi Reichl, Susanne Sweeney-Novak and Renatus Svoboda, who offered to set their students the same summary and account tasks in their classes and so helped me enlarge this corpus significantly. It is also worth mentioning that I prepared the same anonymised worksheets containing their students' summaries and accounts for my colleagues, and that they reported similarly vivid discussions from their classes – in contrast to my linguistics proseminar these were English language classes, which confirmed my assumption that the format described here can be successfully transferred to other teaching contexts.

5. For reasons of space, only selected examples of these questions are given here. The wording is that of my students.

6. WordSmith Tools, a "lexical analysis software for data-driven learning and research" (cf. Mike Scott's homepage: http://www.liv.ac.uk/~ms2928/) is a Windows program which produces concordances, word lists, and key word lists. A short description of what it can do is provided on the website of Oxford University Press, the publishers in charge of distribution: http://www.oup.com/elt/global/isbn/6890
As explained in the manual for WordSmith Tools, "KeyWords are those whose frequency is unusually high in comparison with some norm... "key" words are not the most frequent words ... but the words which are most unusually frequent in [a particular text]. Key words usually give a reasonably good clue to what the text is about. A word which is positively

key occurs more often than would be expected by chance in comparison with the reference corpus. A word which is negatively key occurs less often than would be expected by chance in comparison with the reference corpus. In a Key word list produced by Word-Smith Tools, words appear sorted according to how outstanding their frequencies of occurrence are. Those near the top are outstandingly frequent, whereas at the end of the list are any which are outstandingly infrequent (negative keywords), in a different colour. The Key Words display shows:

1. each key word
2. its frequency in the source text(s) which these key words are key in
3. the name of the source text file (or the word list file name if there's more than one) and %
4. its frequency in the reference corpus
5. the name of the reference corpus file (or the corpus word list file name if it was based on more than one text) and %
6. keyness (chi-square or log likelihood statistic)
7. p value (% danger of being wrong in claiming a relationship)

All the terms and procedures described in this note are explained very clearly in the Manual that comes with WordSmith Tools.

References

Aston, G. (1995). Corpora in language pedagogy: Matching theory and practice. In G. Cook & B. Seidlhofer (Eds.), *Principle and Practice in Applied Linguistics* (pp. 257–270). Oxford: Oxford University Press.

Aston, G. (1997). Enriching the learning environment: Corpora in ELT. In A. Wichmann, S. Fligelstone, T. McEnery & G. Knowles (Eds.), *Teaching and Language Corpora* (pp. 51–64). London: Longman.

Beaugrande, R. de, & Dressler, U. (1981). *Introduction to Text Linguistics*. London: Longman.

Bernardini, S. (2000). *Competence, Capacity, Corpora*. Bologna: CLUEB.

BNC Sampler (1999). Distributed by the Humanities Computing Unit of Oxford University, on behalf of the BNC Consortium. (http://info.ox.ac.uk/bnc).

Carter, R. (1998). Orders of reality: CANCODE, communication, and culture. *ELT Journal, 52*(1), 43–56.

Carter, R., & McCarthy, M. (1995). Spoken grammar: What is it and how can we teach it? *ELT Journal, 49*(3), 207–218.

Cook, G. (1998). The uses of reality: A reply to Ronald Carter. *ELT Journal, 52*(1), 57–63.

Crookes, G., & Schmidt, R. (1989). Motivation: Reopening the research agenda. *University of Hawaii Working Papers ESL, 8,* 217–256.

Dickinson, L. (1995). Autonomy and motivation: A literature review. *System, 23*(2), 165–1174.

Donato, R. (1994). Collective scaffolding in second language learning. In J. Lantolf & G. Appel (Eds.), *Vygotskian Approaches to Second Language Research* (pp. 33–56). Norwood, NJ: Ablex.

Dörnyei, Z. (2001). *Motivational Strategies in the Language Classroom*. Cambridge: Cambridge University Press.

Ellis, R. (1997). *SLA Research and Language Teaching*. Oxford: Oxford University Press.

Granger, S. (Ed.). (1998a). *Learner English on Computer*. London: Longman.

Granger, S. (Ed.). (1998b). The computer learner corpus: a versatile new source of data for SLA research. In S. Granger (Ed.), *Learner English on Computer* (pp. 3–18). London: Longman.

Hawkins, E. (1991). *Awareness of Language: An Introduction*. Revised edn. Cambridge: Cambridge University Press.

Holliday, A. (1994). *Appropriate Methodology and Social Context*. Cambridge: Cambridge University Press.

Johns, T., & King, P. (Eds.). (1991). *Classroom Concordancing. English Language Research Journal, 4* (New Series). Birmingham: University of Birmingham.

Kintsch, W., & Van Dijk, T. (1978). Towards a model of discourse comprehension and production. *Psychological Review, 85*, 363–394.

Kramsch, C., & Sullivan, P. (1996). Appropriate pedagogy. *ELT Journal, 50*(3), 199–212.

Meunier, F. (1998). Computer tools for the analysis of learner corpora. In S. Granger (Ed.), *Learner English on Computer* (pp. 19–37).

Owen, C. (1996). Do concordances require to be consulted? *ELT Journal, 50*(3), 219–224.

Oxford, R., & Shearin, J. (1994). Language learning motivation: expanding the theoretical framework. *Modern Language Journal, 78*, 12–25.

Pennycook, A. (1996). Borrowing others' words: text, ownership, memory, and plagiarism. *TESOL Quarterly, 30*(2), 201–230.

Petch-Tyson, S. (1998). Writer/reader visibility in EFL written discourse. In S. Granger (Ed.), *Learner English on Computer* (pp. 107–118).

Prodromou, L. (1996). Correspondence. *ELT Journal, 50*(4), 371–373.

Richard-Amato, P. (1996). *Making It Happen*. 2nd edn. New York: Addison-Wesley.

Schmidt, R. (1990). The role of consciousness in second language learning. *Applied Linguistics, 11*, 129–158.

Schmidt, R., & Frota, S. (1986). Developing basic conversational ability in a second language: A case study of an adult learner of Portuguese. In R. Day (Ed.), *Talking to Learn: Conversation in Second Language Acquisition* (pp. 237–326). Rowley, MA: Newbury House.

Scott, M. (1996). *Wordsmith Tools*. Oxford: Oxford University Press.

Scott, M. (2000). Focusing on the text and its key words. In L. Burnard & T. McEnery (Eds.), *Rethinking Language Pedagogy from a Corpus Perspective* (pp. 103–121). Frankfurt: Peter Lang.

Scott, M., & Johns, T. (1993). *MicroConcord*. Manual by S. Murison-Bowie. Oxford: Oxford University Press.

Seidlhofer, B. (1995). *Approaches to Summarization. Discourse Analysis and Language Education*. Tübingen: Narr.

Seidlhofer, B. (1996). L2 summarizing: in your 'own words' in a foreign language? Paper presented at *TESOL Convention*, March. Chicago.

Seidlhofer, B. (1999). Double standards: teacher education in the expanding circle. *World Englishes, 18*, 233–245.

Seidlhofer, B. (2000). Operationalizing intertextuality: using learner corpora for learning. In L. Burnard & T. McEnery (Eds.), *Rethinking Language Pedagogy from a Corpus Perspective* (pp. 207–223). Frankfurt: Peter Lang.

Sinclair, J. (1991a). Shared knowledge. In J. Alatis (Ed.), *Georgetown University Round Table in Language and Linguistics. Linguistics and Language Pedagogy: The State of the Art* (pp. 489–500). Washington DC: Georgetown University.

Sinclair, J. (1991b). *Corpus, Concordance, Collocation.* Oxford: Oxford University Press.

Stubbs, M. (1995). Corpus evidence for norms of lexical collocation. In G. Cook & B. Seidlhofer (Eds.), *Principle and Practice in Applied Linguistics* (pp. 245–256). Oxford: Oxford University Press.

Swain, M. (1985). Communicative competence: Some roles of comprehensible input and comprehensible output in its development. In S. Gass & S. Madden (Eds.), *Input in Second Language Acquisition* (pp. 235–253). Rowley, MA: Newbury House.

Swain, M. (1995). Three functions of output in second language learning. In G. Cook & B. Seidlhofer (Eds.), *Principle and Practice in Applied Linguistics* (pp. 125–144). Oxford: Oxford University Press.

Tribble, C., & Jones, G. (1997). *Concordances in the Classroom.* New edn. Houston, TX: Athelstan.

Wendt, M. (1996). *Konstruktivistische Fremdsprachendidaktik.* Tübingen: Narr.

Widdowson, H. G. (1979). *Explorations in Applied Linguistics.* Oxford: Oxford University Press.

Widdowson, H. G. (1984). *Explorations in Applied Linguistics 2.* Oxford: Oxford University Press.

Widdowson, H. G. (1989). Knowledge of language and ability for use. *Applied Linguistics, 10,* 128–137.

Widdowson, H. G. (1990). *Aspects of Language Teaching.* Oxford: Oxford University Press.

Widdowson, H. G. (1991). The description and prescription of language. In Alatis, J. (Ed.), *Georgetown University Round Table in Language and Linguistics. Linguistics and Language Pedagogy: The State of the Art* (pp. 11–24). Washington DC: Georgetown University.

Name index

Subject index